D0891737

Workers' Earnings
and Corporate Economic Structure

This is a volume in

STUDIES IN POPULATION

A complete list of titles in this series appears at the end of this volume.

Workers' Earnings and Corporate Economic Structure

Randy Hodson
Department of Sociology
University of Texas at Austin
Austin, Texas

1983

ACADEMIC PRESS
A SUBSIDIARY OF HARCOURT BRACE JOVANOVICH, PUBLISHERS
New York   London
Paris   San Diego   San Francisco   São Paulo   Sydney   Tokyo   Toronto

ACADEMIC PRESS, INC.
111 Fifth Avenue, New York, New York 10003

United Kingdom Edition published by
ACADEMIC PRESS, INC. (LONDON) LTD.
24/28 Oval Road, London NW1 7DX

Library of Congress Cataloging in Publication Data

Hodson, Randy.
  Workers' earnings and corporate economic structure.

  (Studies in population)
  Includes index.
  1. Wages--Wisconsin. 2. Labor and laboring classes
--Wisconsin. 3. Industrial organization (Economic
theory) 4. Industrial sociology. 5. Wisconsin--
Industries. I. Title. II. Series.
HD4976.W56H63 1983   331.2'9775   83-5996
ISBN 0-12-351780-X

PRINTED IN THE UNITED STATES OF AMERICA

83 84 85 86   9 8 7 6 5 4 3 2 1

Contents

List of Tables and Figures   ix

Preface   xiii

Acknowledgments   xvii

1. Industrial Structure and the American Worker   **1**

Introduction   1
Is There a Homogeneous Labor Market?   3
The Question of Economic "Dualism"   4
A Resource Perspective   5
Enterprise or Industry as the Unit of Analysis?   6
A Strategy of Analysis   7
What Can Be Expected from This Study?   8
Organization of the Volume   9
Notes   10

2. Theories of Economic Segmentation   **11**

Neoclassical Economics   11
Marxism   12
Institutional Economics   13
Labor Economics   14
The Sociology of Labor Markets   16

The Dual Economy Model   18
A Sympathetic Critique of the Dual Economy Model   29
Conclusions   36
Notes   38

3. A Resource Theory of Organizational Structure   40

A Revised History of Industrial Structure   41
A Resource Approach to the Study of Industrial Structure   46
Exploring Economic Structure and Labor Market Outcomes   51
What We Expect to Find   54
Conclusions   59
Notes   60

4. Industry and Enterprise Data and Measures   62

Introduction   62
Industry Data   65   16\6 category   84-5
Company Data   86
Individual-Level Variables Extracted from the Wisconsin Survey and the Current
    Population Survey   93
The Sample to Be Studied   96
Conclusions: The Task of Collecting Company and Industry Data   98
Notes   99

5. Distribution of Poverty, Union Membership, Class Positions, and Race and Gender Groups across Economic Sectors   102

Poverty   102
Union Membership   104
Class Positions   105
Race   107
Gender   109
Conclusions   109
Notes   110

6. Enterprise- and Industry-Level Models of Employees' Earnings   113

Introduction   113
A Sectoral Industry Model   114
A Continuous-Variable Industry Model   116
Application of Industry-Level Models to the Wisconsin Sample and the Restricted
    Current Population Survey Sample   127
A Sectoral Company Model   130
A Continuous-Variable Company Model   132

Comparison of Company- and Industry-Level Results   139
Conclusions   144
Notes   146

7. Economic Structure and the Individual Earnings Attainment Process   150

Introduction   150
Evaluation of the Industry-Level Model   152
Evaluation of the Company-Level Model   159
Social Background and Economic Structure as Determinants of Individual
   Earnings   162
Conclusions   165
Notes   167

8. Earnings Attainment across Economic Sectors, Classes, and Race and Gender Groups   169

Earnings Returns to Education within Economic Sectors   170
Class Inequality within Economic Sectors   177
Economic Structure for Whom?   178
Conclusions   184
Notes   186

9. Conclusions   188

Summary of Findings   188
The Study of Labor Force Outcomes and Corporate Structure   195
Policy Considerations   198

Appendix A. Industry Variables   200

Appendix B. Company Variables   209

Appendix C. The Operationalization of Class   212

Appendix D. Supplementary Tables   215

References   227

Index   237

List of Tables and Figures

Table 4.1. Industrial Structure Concepts and Variables

Table 4.2. Eigenvalues for First 25 Factors from Principal Components Analysis

Table 4.3. Change in the Error Sum of Squares and a Test Statistic for the 14–18-Cluster Solutions

Table 4.4. Classification of Industries into 16 Sectors

Table 4.5. Means of Some Key Industrial Characteristics by Sector

Table 4.6. Enterprise Structure Concepts and Variables

Table 4.7. Missing Company Data, 1975 Wisconsin Survey

Table 4.8. Definition of Corporate Economic Sectors

Table 4.9. Selection of Subsamples to Be Analyzed from Wisconsin Survey and CPS

Table 4.10. Means of Key Variables for Subsamples of ECLF Private Workers by Level of Reported Earnings, 1975 Wisconsin Survey

Table 5.1. Distribution of Persons across Union Membership and Poverty Status by Industrial and Company Sectors

Table 5.2. Distribution of Persons across Class Positions by Industrial and Company Sectors

Table 5.3. Percentage of Blacks across Occupational Categories by Industrial Sector

Table 5.4. Percentage of Females across Class Positions by Industrial and Company Sectors

Table 6.1.   Mean Earnings and Mean Log Earnings in 16 Industrial Sectors

Table 6.2.   Means, Standard Deviations, and Correlations with Log Individual Earnings of Industry Variables

Table 6.3.   Regression of Log Earnings on Industry Variable Models, Stage 1

Table 6.4.   Regression of Log Earnings on Industry Variable Models, Stage 2

Table 6.5.   Evaluation of Curvature in Basic Industry Model

Table 6.6.   Mean Log Earnings in Six Industrial Sectors

Table 6.7.   Regression of Log Earnings on Final Industry Model

Table 6.8.   Regression of Log Earnings on Corporate Economic Sectors

Table 6.9.   Means, Standard Deviations, and Correlations with Log Individual Earnings of Company Variables

Table 6.10.   Model Selection for Regression of Log Individual Earnings on Company Variables

Table 6.11.   Comparison of Industry- and Company-Level Sector Classifications and Correlations of Industry- and Company-Level Continuous Variables

Table 6.12.   Comparison of Industry- and Company-Level Sectoral and Continuous-Variable Regression Models of Individual Log Earnings

Table 7.1.   Regression of Log Earnings on Industry Model with Controls

Table 7.2.   Evaluation of Curvature in Industry Model with Full Controls

Table 7.3.   Contribution to Total Explained Variance R^2 by Sets of Variables in Industry- and Company-Level Log Earnings Models

Table 7.4.   Regression of Log Earnings on Company-Level Model with Controls

Table 7.5.   Regression of Log Earnings on Social Background Variables, Schooling Variables, Company Model, and Controls

Table 7.6.   Contribution to Total Explained Variance R^2 by Sets of Variables in Full Company-Level Log Earnings Model with Controls for Social Background and Schooling Variables

Table 8.1.   Regression of Log Earnings Model within Industrial Sectors

Table 8.2.   Regression of Log Earnings Model within Company Sectors

Table 8.3.   Regression of Log Earnings Model across the Cells of a Class-by-Sector Classification

Table 8.4.   Regression of Industrial Structure Log Earnings Model across Occupational Positions

Table 8.5.   Regression of Corporate Structure Log Earnings Model across Class Positions

Table 8.6.   Regression of Industrial Structure Log Earnings Model across Race and Gender Groups

Table 8.7.   Regression of Corporate Structure Log Earnings Model on Male and Female Subsamples

Table C.1.   Definition of Social Class Categories
Table D.1.   Distribution of Persons across Occupational Categories by Industrial Sector
Table D.2.   Intercorrelations of Industry Variables Used in Index Construction
Table D.3.   Correlation Matrix for Variables Tested in Selection of Industry Model
Table D.4.   Comparison of Three Functional Forms of Individual Earnings Regressed on Industry Model
Table D.5.   Intercorrelations of Company Variables Used in Index Construction
Table D.6.   Means of Key Company Variables by Company Size Index Present or Missing
Table D.7.   Correlation Matrix for Variables Tested in Selection of Company Model
Table D.8.   Comparison of Three Functional Forms of Individual Earnings Regressed on Company Model
Table D.9.   Comparison of Industry-Level Sectoral and Continuous-Variable Regression Models of Individual Log Earnings
Table D.10. Comparison of Industry-Level Log Earnings Model with Full Controls on Wisconsin and Restricted CPS Samples

Figure 4.1. Distance *d* between industries A and B on correlated dimensions *X* and *Y*.

Preface

The argument that social inequality arises from man's relationship to work has never been truer than in the modern industrial nations, where the vast majority of people earn their living as employees in large, complex work organizations. Labor force outcomes, such as earnings levels, are clearly patterned by the structure of the workplace. In the past, our understanding of social stratification has relied on the concepts of social class and social status. Although these concepts are essential for any understanding of social stratification, they leave unanalyzed many structural characteristics of the workplace that have a great influence on social inequality. The goal of the present study is to increase our understanding of the organization of the workplace as a step toward integrating that understanding with broader theories of social stratification.

We outline in this book an analytic approach that is based on an extensive review of the literature on economic segmentation and that allows systematic investigation of the role that workplace organization plays in determining social inequality. Our study focuses on the characteristics of the organization of capital rather than on different management styles or systems because we deem these characteristics more fundamental for understanding the actual processes operating at the workplace. In addition, our study focuses on earnings as a key labor force outcome and investigates this outcome at both the industry and company levels of economic organization. In many ways this plan of analysis is an exploratory one, oriented more toward providing insights than toward testing a particular theory. This strategy is seen as the one most likely to provide the kind of information and insight needed at the current stage of theoretical development in this field.

Arguing that economic structure provides potential resources for workers to use in their struggle to attain improved working conditions and job benefits, we develop a new approach to understanding the role of economic structure in determining employees' earnings. Corporate economic structure is created by owners as part of the drive for survival, growth, and profit, with labor control in mind as one requirement for the attainment of these goals. However, that structure, once created, may also provide a resource for workers to utilize in attaining their own goals. One way in which this may occur is that the structure may be inadequate for its goal of attaining labor control. Richard Edwards's (1979) discussion of the inadequacies of the foreman system for controlling expanded production is a good example of this situation. Alternatively, corporate structure may provide a worker resource because it was created with goals other than labor control in mind. Conglomerate structure, created with an eye to market factors, provides a possible example here. Finally, corporate economic structure may provide a worker resource because of secondary inadvertent consequences. The positive effect of capital intensity on earnings that we report in this study provides an example of a structure, implemented partially to attain technological control of workers, that inadvertently provides the workers with greater resources for attaining their own goals.

This view of corporate structure as providing possible resources for both workers and owners avoids the implication of a structural conspiracy by capitalists that emerges from much of the dual economy literature. It also encourages us to analyze the role of economic structure in relation to distinct actors at the workplace, because these structures may have radically different implications for different social groups and social classes.

As suggested previously, the research presented here is not organized in terms of the dual economy model of economic segmentation; however, it does include a lengthy review and critique of this approach. Although the dual economy model has served a useful heuristic function, we argue against its validity and continued use on the grounds that it lacks both theoretical clarity and empirical consistency. Major dimensions that are theoretically relevant to economic segmentation have been either ignored or *assumed* to align in a consistently dichotomous pattern. In addition, the dual economy model lacks a well-specified theoretical rationale for the existence of only two different sectors in the economy.

The empirical findings of this research indicate that organizational and technical factors at the workplace provide more important structural resources for employees than do market-based factors, such as profit rates. This is highlighted by the finding that market concentration has a negative impact on earnings after more proximate dimensions of industrial structure are controlled. Also, plant size is observed to have perhaps the largest influence of any workplace dimension analyzed. These findings suggest the need to develop a theory of the role of industrial structure in the workplace that focuses on sociological and organizational dimensions. We argue that the dual economy approach, and economic approaches in general, are more suited to analysis of commodity markets than to analysis of labor markets and working conditions. Such approaches cannot provide an adequate substitute for a more sociologically and organizationally oriented theory of the workplace.

This study seeks to achieve two broad goals. First, many of the findings, particularly those based on multivariate analysis of the dimensions of economic structure, are intended to provide insights useful for the development of new areas of research and analysis in the growing field of economic structure and labor market segmentation. Second, it is hoped that the critique of the dual economy model and construction of an alternative theoretical approach to the role of economic structure in determining labor force outcomes will contribute to the development of this field of study by helping to remove the fetters of an inadequate model.

We are optimistic that the analysis presented here will stimulate further development of theory and research on the organization of the workplace and the relationship of workplace organization to social stratification. Serious theoretical work specifying the key dimensions of workplace organization and the relationship of these dimensions to labor force outcomes is needed. Earnings is only one, albeit an important, outcome of the organization of the workplace. Other dimensions, such as underemployment, unemployment, and job satisfaction, also deserve investigation. In addition, there is a real need for theoretically selected case studies of key organizational environments. Such studies are essential for generating the kind of detailed understanding necessary for the development of sound sociological theory. It is hoped that some of the insights emerging from the present study will spur the development of such theory and research.

Acknowledgments

The debate in the academic literature on the role of economic structure at the workplace provides the intellectual backdrop against which the current research was formulated. The first and most important acknowledgment must therefore be to all the participants in that debate. Scholarly work is never carried on in isolation but always grows out of the work of others, whether by inspiration or by critique. In the present case an equally important source of inspiration was provided by the many people I have labored alongside at workplaces outside of the academic setting. These experiences, as well as more academic and intellectual ones, provided much of the motivation for this book and deserve to be recognized.

The original research on which this book is based was conducted during my dissertation work in the Department of Sociology at the University of Wisconsin at Madison. Accordingly, I owe the students and faculty at that university during the years from 1975 to 1980 special thanks for providing the stimulating and supportive intellectual environment in which I learned the trade of sociology. In particular, Bob Kaufman and Neil Fligstein collaborated with me on the collection and preliminary analysis of the industry data used in this study and on a paper about that analysis (Kaufman, Hodson, and Fligstein, 1981), parts of which appear in Chapter 4 of the current volume. In addition, Bob Kaufman and I collectively drafted a review and critique of the dual economy model (Hodson and Kaufman, 1982), parts of which appear in Chapters 2 and 3 of the present volume.

I would also like to thank Robert Hauser, who supervised my dissertation, as well as Erik Wright, Charles Halaby, Sheldon Danziger, and William Sewell, who read several drafts of the work and offered thoughtful and useful advice throughout the research project. In addition, William Sewell and Robert Hauser generously granted me access to data from the Wisconsin Longitudinal Study of Schooling and Status Attainment, which provide an important part of the empirical basis of this study.

The manuscript for the present volume was written at the University of Texas at Austin; I am indebted to colleagues at Austin for comments, advice, and support. In particular, I would like to thank Harley Browning, Omer Galle, Teresa Sullivan, Joe Feagin, Charles Bonjean, and Frank Bean for invaluable comments and suggestions. Finally, I would like to thank the reviewers and staff of Academic Press for the rigor with which they addressed the task of turning this research effort into a publishable manuscript.

Computational services were provided by the Center for the Study of Demography and Ecology under Population Research Grant 5P01–HD–05876 and by the Graduate School of the University of Wisconsin at Madison. I am indebted to the computing staff of the Demography and Ecology Center, and especially to Gordon Caldwell, for assistance in handling and analyzing the data collected for this project.

During the course of the research I received support from the Employment and Training Administration of the United States Department of Labor, Research and Development Grant 91–55–79–12, from a Wisconsin Alumni Research Foundation fellowship, and from the Wisconsin Longitudinal Study of Schooling and Status Attainment, National Institute of Mental Health Grant MH–06275. The findings and conclusions presented here, however, do not necessarily represent the official opinion of any of these funding agencies.

Information essential for the compilation of the company-level data was provided by the Wisconsin Department of Industry, Labor, and Human Relations and by Don Martineau of Dun and Bradstreet. This information provided an important supplement to the more limited publicly available sources of corporate data.

A special word of thanks is owed to Karen Price and Sharon Moon, who diligently and skillfully typed various drafts of the manuscript.

1

Industrial Structure and the American Worker

INTRODUCTION

Wages, working conditions, and other labor force consequences vary dramatically across industries and enterprises in the United States. Industrial workers in steel and automobile manufacture have achieved a level of earnings commensurate with that of many middle class positions. Workers in textiles and food processing, however, may be among the ranks of the working poor. The incidence of involuntary part-time employment is also strongly related to industrial location, being especially prevalent in retail and in related commercial industries. Employment opportunities for women are sharply limited to this commercial sector along with the financial, educational, and health sectors. Conglomerates, as a new organizational form of capital, have demonstrated the ability and willingness to move enterprises from one region of the country to another to take advantage of lower taxes and labor costs. Multinationals extend this ability to even the international movement of production facilities. Meanwhile, workers in small, locally based enterprises may face either limited horizons or rewarding personal opportunities, depending on the circumstances of their particular industry and enterprise.

The persistence of inequality among wage and salary employees in modern society is a central issue in theories of social stratification but an issue that has

1

been incompletely resolved. Recently, students of social stratification have begun exploring some of the structural characteristics of firms and industries to gain a better understanding of how social inequality arises (Beck, Horan, and Tolbert, 1978; Bibb and Form, 1977; Hodson, 1978; Kalleberg, Wallace, and Althauser, 1981).

In American sociology, previous explanations for the diversity of wage labor in modern society have most often been organized along the dimension of status. Duncan (1961) argues that socioeconomic status is the major summary dimension of social inequality. Treiman (1977) argues that prestige is the fundamental dimension in all stratification systems, past and present. Blau and Duncan (1967) and Featherman and Hauser (1978) argue that technical and social divisions between manual and nonmanual labor constitute a key element of social stratification.

Economic explanations for the diversity of wage labor have typically focused on inequalities in the characteristics of individuals, their "human capital" (Becker, 1964). Both this approach and the status-oriented approach in sociology stress the importance of educational differences in explaining inequality between individuals and between social groups.

Other explanations for the diversity of wage labor focus on the dimension of social class. Poulantzas (1975) argues that under monopoly capitalism a new salaried middle class has arisen, which both socially and politically is much like the old petit bourgeois middle class. Wright (1979) suggests that advanced capitalist class relations can be understood in terms of contradictory class locations between major social classes.

Although these answers are important, they still do not provide an adequate understanding of the fractionalizing of the class of employees in advanced capitalism. The majority of these theories specify the workplace as central in the creation and maintenance of social inequality; however, too little attention has been paid to the organization of the workplace itself.

Other disciplines have taken this imperative more seriously. Institutional economists and labor market sociologists have analyzed the organization of the workplace in great detail. Studies of unionization have contributed to our understanding of the institutional basis of worker power (Dunlop, 1944; Dunlop and Chamberlain, 1967; Johnson, 1975; Levinson, 1967). Studies of industrial structure focusing on economic scale, growth, and productivity have informed us about how the organizational characteristics of enterprises influence the workplace (Bain, 1964; Bright, 1958; Doeringer and Piore, 1971; Garbarino, 1950; Mileti, Gillespie, and Haas, 1977; Stolzenberg, 1978). Studies of market structure focusing on concentration, conglomerate structure, profitability, foreign involvement, and government regulation have specified how the constraints and possibilities defined by the organization of markets may influence employees' lives (Averitt, 1968; Barnet and Muller, 1974; Dalton and Ford, 1977; Galbraith, 1967; Weiss, 1966).

IS THERE A HOMOGENEOUS LABOR MARKET?

The leading question of this book is "Does the market for labor in the United States operate in a homogeneous fashion to match workers with different qualifications and statuses to specified levels of rewards? Or, is this process importantly structured by the organizational characteristics of capital?" In the effort to answer this question we shall be seeking to understand processes of economic determination that operate at a more aggregate level than the "returns to human capital" studied by neoclassical economists or the "family background" basis of status attainment studied by many sociologists. Our aim is to investigate the determination of labor rewards at the level of the organization of the productive enterprise itself.

Because our major analytic variable is industrial structure, this concept deserves careful definition. By industrial structure we mean the organizational characteristics of capital.[1] Concentration of assets, growth and profit rates, conglomerate organization, multinational structure, economic size, and capital intensity of production are some of the key characteristics of the organization of capital, or industrial structure, in our usage. Organizational characteristics such as the nature of supervision, the technology utilized, task organization, bureaucracy, and spans of control are not included within this definition of industrial structure, though they may be associated in systematic ways with different industrial structures. Organizational characteristics in the immediately preceding sense have been extensively utilized in the investigation of job satisfaction and worker motivation and commitment. From the current perspective these organizational characteristics are themselves seen as partially determined by the organization of capital. As such, although they may be associated with differences in earnings determination, the association is largely spurious in nature. That is, both organizational structure and workers' earnings may be seen as the product of industrial structure. Here we shall limit our attention to the study of industrial structure as defined previously and in particular to the manner in which industrial structure impacts earnings determination.

Other worker outcomes might have been selected for study instead. Analysis of job satisfaction, worker attitudes, authority structures, unemployment and underemployment, and racial discrimination would each produce interesting and potentially different conclusions about the role of industrial structure in determining workplace outcomes. We have selected the process of earnings determination because of its centrality and because it has served as a standard by which other influences on social stratification are evaluated. It should be stressed, however, that our focus will not be on explaining earnings determination per se as much as on evaluating the role of industrial structure at the workplace, with earnings determination selected as our standard of evaluation.

Additionally, we shall be interested in the extent to which industrial structure helps to explain unequal economic returns to education and the earnings effects of race and sex. We believe that this approach will provide a useful integration of research on the structural and the individual determinants of earnings. The cross-fertilization between industrial economics and sociology necessary to organize this research will offer a much-needed counterbalance to theories that stress only one set of factors.

Within the economic sectors defined by industrial structures there exist markets for many different kinds of labor. Thus, large multinationally based firms have managerial employees who by most definitions would fall within a broadly defined capitalist class, but they also employ many members of the traditional working class as well as employees located in "contradictory class locations" (Wright, 1979). Similarly, multinationals hire from labor markets for skilled university-trained engineers as well as from labor markets for unskilled Third World assembly workers. Part of our theoretical project is to investigate the connection between economic sectors and labor markets or class locations. We start our study with the assumption that labor markets and class locations are not directly reducible to economic sectors. In other words, there is no one-to-one correspondence or parallelism between economic sectors and job categories. Starting with this assumption will allow us to uncover, both theoretically and empirically, the connections that exist rather than constraining these relationships to a predetermined pattern of parallelism.

THE QUESTION OF ECONOMIC "DUALISM"

The "dual economy" model has been used as a major conceptual tool in the areas of economic structure and the differentiation of outcomes at the workplace. The model divides the economy into two sectors and argues that the characteristics of these sectors result in different labor markets and in different outcomes for labor.

Although the dual economy model has served a useful heuristic function, we shall question its validity and continued use on the grounds of both its theoretical clarity and empirical consistency. The dual economy model lacks a well-developed theoretical rationale for the existence of two and only two different sectors in the economy. Major dimensions that are theoretically relevant to economic segmentation have been either ignored or assumed to align in a consistently dichotomous pattern. The assumption, rather than empirical investigation, of relationships has contributed to a frequently observed circularity in the dual model. Labor force variables such as earnings and job stability are sometimes used as defining characteristics of economic sectors subsequently utilized for the analysis of these very job outcomes.

A RESOURCE PERSPECTIVE

In an attempt to move beyond the dual economy model, we shall survey existing theories of industrial structure for new ideas, concepts, and approaches. The theories surveyed will include institutional and neoclassical economics, the complex organizations literature, Marxist approaches to the structure of capital, and sociological approaches to labor market segmentation.

Based on this survey, we shall suggest a new perspective on the development of economic segmentation. Industrial structure arises from management strategies designed to promote profit and growth. However, that same structure may also provide employees with possible resources to use in their struggle for higher wages and improved working conditions.

Relying heavily on an organizational analysis of the relationships among size, technology, and modes of control in economic organizations, we shall argue that diverse strategies of corporate growth interact with the existing environment to produce a variety of dimensions and forms of industrial structure. Corporate structures are created by owners and their hired managers in response to the drive for survival, growth, and profit, with labor control in mind as one necessity for the attainment of those goals. However, that structure, once created, may also provide a resource for workers to utilize in attaining their own goals. One way in which this may occur is if the structure is inadequate to its goal of attaining labor control. Richard Edwards's (1979) discussion of the inadequacies of the foreman system for controlling expanded production is a good example of this situation. (Resistance to the harsh discipline typical of the "foreman's empire" provided an important impetus to union organizing drives at the turn of the century.) Alternatively, the structure may provide a worker resource because it was created with other goals in mind than labor control. Conglomerate structure, created with an eye to market factors, provides a possible example here. Corporate economic structures may also provide worker resources because of inadvertent secondary consequences. The positive effect of capital intensity on job satisfaction, argued by Blauner (1964), is a possible example of a structure that was implemented to attain technological control of production but inadvertently gives workers greater resources for attaining their own goals. The role of increased organizational size in creating opportunities for collective organization and action on the part of employees provides a final, and perhaps most compelling, example.

The dual economy model, while focusing attention on the organization of capital, conceptualizes the worker as basically a passive recipient of benefits accruing from the characteristics of the employing organization. For example, the dual model note that higher levels of concentration yield higher profit levels, and sees workers in monopoly sector firms as receiving a share of this expanded pie in the form of higher wages and improved benefits.

In contrast, the resource perspective suggested here focuses on the possibilities that different elements of industrial structure may provide for heightened worker power. Thus, certain dimensions of industrial structure, such as capital intensity and economic scale, may increase workers' abilities to secure wage gains. Other dimensions of industrial structure, such as conglomerate domination or multinational organization, may undermine workers' abilities to improve working conditions. In this perspective the worker is viewed as an active participant in the process of wage determination. Just as management creates organizational structure and then engages in wage bargaining based partially on the resources provided by that structure, so too do workers engage, either individually or collectively, in wage bargaining under conditions partially determined by the organizational and technical nature of the production system.

ENTERPRISE OR INDUSTRY AS THE UNIT OF ANALYSIS?

The resource perspective also highlights the importance of dealing seriously with the question of the appropriate unit of analysis in the study of industrial structure. That is, is industrial structure to be measured by industry averages of relevant characteristics of economic enterprises, or is only the enterprise level of analysis acceptable in the modern world of interindustry conglomerates? From a theoretical perspective, the question is whether the capital structure of an industry can provide a resource for workers or whether only the capital structure of the employing enterprise is relevant. As a working hypothesis we start with the proposition that no one level of analysis is the "correct" level in that it totally subsumes the potential effects of industrial structure at other levels of analysis. Certain characteristics may operate at the industry level but may be largely irrelevant as characteristics of particular employers. Other elements of industrial structure may provide worker resources only when these are actual characteristics of the employing organization. For some elements of industrial structure, similar effects may exist at both the industry and enterprise levels of measurement. An important goal of our analysis will be to evaluate which elements operate at which levels. Our efforts on this front should not only help resolve an ongoing methodological debate in the literature on this topic (see Baron and Bielby, 1980; Hodson, 1978; Stolzenberg, 1978) but should also shed light on the nature of the causation at work in the relationship between industrial structure and worker outcomes.

A STRATEGY OF ANALYSIS

In light of the preceding considerations, our plan for analysis relies on the use of both industry- and enterprise-level data. We collected industry data from government archives on a variety of dimensions of industrial structure across the entire range of industrial categories. It should be noted that we do not propose simply to utilize concentration ratios within manufacturing industries as the measure of industrial structure. We believe that many other factors are important for the determination of workers' wages beyond measures of monopoly market power, and that the study of the effects of industrial structure on the labor force should not be restricted to the manufacturing sector only. We link these industry data to persons in the March–May match 1973 Current Population Survey (CPS). This national sample was chosen because of its excellent earnings data and unionization measure. The linking of the industry measures to CPS data also allows us to utilize variables measuring individual, demographic, occupational, and human capital characteristics in our analysis.

We collected similar data at the enterprise level from business and trade sources for a 10,317-person sample of 1957 Wisconsin high school graduates (hereafter referred to as the Wisconsin data). In 1975, these respondents were surveyed and asked extensive job information (comparable to or exceeding in detail the CPS information), including earnings information as well as the name of their employers. (See Sewell and Hauser, 1975, for a fuller description of this data set.) To persons in the Wisconsin sample we attach both the industry-level and the enterprise-level measures of economic structure. Our duplication of the industry measures at a disaggregated enterprise level allows us to construct important methodological checks on the parameters calculated. In combination with industry-level data attached to the national CPS sample, this research design allows us to make informed arguments at a national level about the effects of economic segmentation on labor at both the industry and enterprise levels of analysis.

The principle contribution that this work seeks to make to the field of labor segmentation rests on the collection and analysis of these extensive data sets. In addition to utilizing both industry and enterprise levels of analysis, we also employ continuous as well as sectoral models of economic structure. The interpretation of these competing models at different levels of measurement provides important insights into the complex nature of economic segmentation. This strategy provides a wealth of potentially important information for use in both policy and academic applications. A similar contribution could not be made by relying on an approach restricted, for example, to dichotomous industrial categories within the manufacturing sector.

In analyzing this data base, we rely primarily on exploratory methods for deriving models of economic structure. This option was chosen because the resource approach outlined here is inadequately developed as a theory to a priori define fully specified models. The first step in this procedure is the derivation of continuous and sectoral models of economic segmentation. This is done by utilizing regression, factor analytic, and clustering techniques. The resulting models show the inadequacy of dualistic schemes for describing and comprehending the structure of the American economy.

The selected models will be used to investigate a variety of labor force issues. This analysis will be organized around the following questions:

1. How is corporate economic structure associated with the demographic characteristics of the labor force and with unionization, poverty status, and social class?
2. How is our understanding of the role of economic structure in earnings determination altered by the addition of controls for class, status, demographic, and human capital characteristics? (The analysis of this question will complete the argument that economic structure is an important independent determinant of earnings and will provide an important part of the context within which our theory of that structure can be integrated with theories of class and status.)
3. How are educational returns and class inequality patterned across corporate structures, and how are different classes and different racial and gender groups influenced by economic structure? (The section addressing this question will be crucial for exploring the different roles of corporate economic structure across class and status groups.)

WHAT CAN BE EXPECTED FROM THIS STUDY?

Several possible conclusions might result from our investigation. First, we might find that there is little or no relationship between industrial structure and workplace outcomes. In that case we would return to class and status as our primary tools in the analysis of social stratification. Alternatively, we might find that corporate structure is strongly related to workplace outcomes and that the configuration of that structure suggests a dichotomous conception of corporate sectors. In that case we might conclude that the dual economy is a suitable abstraction of that structure. We would then organize our analysis in a dual economy/dual labor market framework and conclude that corporate structure operates less as a resource for workers than as a successful strategy of manipulation by owners and managers. Finally, we might find that, whereas corporate economic structure is an important determinant of workplace outcomes, it is not analyzable in a dichotomous fashion and is not directly paralleled by racial and social divisions in the work force. In that case we would conclude that the various dimensions of that structure must each be analyzed separately as potential resources for workers.

We believe that this book has the possibility of contributing to the theory of economic structure and labor segmentation by its critique of the dual economy paradigm and by its outline of an alternative resource approach. Also, the state of the art of measurement of economic structure will be advanced by our utilization of multiple levels of analysis and by our specification of a variety of dimensions of economic structure. We shall be able to specify which aspects of economic structure (e.g., capital intensity, average company size, or market concentration) have what effects, if any, on specific workplace outcomes. This information should be of potential benefit to government policymakers, to union organizers, and to students of industry. Labor force training projects and job placement programs will gain information on the industrial and enterprise location of pockets of poverty. Union policymakers may benefit from new knowledge about which industrial structures allow for effective wage bargaining and which industrial structures create the conditions optimal for successful union organizing drives. Students of industry may come to understand better the causes of wage inequality and therefore to understand the workings of the system of social stratification in advanced capitalism.

ORGANIZATION OF THE VOLUME

The organization of our analysis will be as follows. Chapter 2 contains a review and critique of the dual economy model of industrial structure, and Chapter 3 outlines an alternative resource approach to the study of industrial structure and labor segmentation. In Chapter 4 we detail how data were collected and derive enterprise- and industry-level sectoral models of economic structure. In Chapter 5 we investigate the relationship between the sectoral models and poverty, class position, and racial and gender groups. We evaluate the ability of the sectoral models to explain workers' earnings and select continuous-variable models of the impact of economic structure on workers' earnings in Chapter 6. Chapter 7 contains an analysis of these models' performance in relation to individual and class determinants of earnings, and Chapter 8 contains an analysis of earnings determination within economic sectors and of the impact of economic structure across class, occupational, and status groups. In the final chapter we offer our concluding thoughts and reflections and integrate the insights derived from the study of industrial structure with themes from the broader field of social stratification.

NOTES TO CHAPTER 1

1. The social organization of labor in firms obviously has many aspects: hierarchy, bureaucracy, technical skill levels, prestige, on-the-job training, and internal labor markets, to name only a few of the most important. The theme that arises from recent work in stratification theory on the role of economic organizations in the creation of inequality is that the organization of capital must be seen as an underlying structure that influences the organization of labor and sets the terrain on which many of the other dynamics must operate (Baran and Sweezy, 1966; Mandel, 1975; O'Connor, 1973; Wright, 1979).

2

Theories of Economic Segmentation

The study of economic segmentation has drawn theoretical insights from a great variety of schools of research. In this chapter we shall review the most important of these traditions as they relate to the topic of economic segmentation, devoting special attention to the dual economy approach—an approach that has emerged in recent literature as a leading conceptualization of economic segmentation. The chapter will conclude with a critique of the dual economy model.

NEOCLASSICAL ECONOMICS

Insights from the neoclassical economists provide a starting point for the study of economic segmentation. Basically, the neoclassical view is that markets are undifferentiated arenas in which commodities (including labor) can be exchanged at a rate determined by their marginal utilities. However, market imperfections in the form of monopolistic restraints may distort this exchange, resulting in higher-priced commodities. Within this paradigm, trade unions are viewed as simply another form of market monopoly—a monopoly over the sale of labor power.

Neoclassical economists have also noted that large conglomerates, as an important emerging organizational form of capital, behave in basically the same way as monopolistic firms on questions of pricing, resource allocation, expansion of productive capacity, and so on (Scherer, 1970). Further, large corporate expenditures for advertising and product differentiation have been observed to produce market conditions similar to those within which monopolistic firms operate (Mueller, 1970).

The neoclassical paradigm sees market concentration as a multidimensional phenomenon that alters the workings of the otherwise homogenous marketplace. Product monopoly, conglomerate organization, and product differentiation all contribute to monopoly power. Trade unions are seen as an additional monopolistic factor that distorts the workings of the competitive market. Transient features, such as rates of growth, may also temporarily disrupt markets and produce nonequilibrium wages and prices.

MARXISM

An additional body of theory with direct bearing on industrial structure and working conditions is that developed by Marxist scholars. Superficially, their analysis is very similar to that of the neoclassical economists—monopoly power yields monopoly profits, some of which may be won by an organized working class (O'Connor, 1973). However, the Marxist concept of monopoly is not identical with the neoclassical economists' concept. The Marxist concept of monopoly rests on both the concentration (absolute size) and centralization (relative size) of capital (Sweezy, 1942). It is more nearly akin to the idea of share of the economy as a whole than to share of a particular product market. Additionally, monopoly structure typifies an entire stage of capitalist development from the turn of the century to the present; it is not simply an imperfection in an otherwise competitive market. This is the case even though a competitive sector remains in the era of monopoly capitalism and is continuously reproduced within that system (Poulantzas, 1975).

The monopoly stage of capitalism also ushers in a new era of world imperialism. The links between monopoly capitalism and world economic imperialism (Lenin, 1939), multinational corporations (Baran and Sweezy, 1966), and Third World dependence (Amin, 1976) are clearly drawn within the Marxist tradition.

Differences in the organic composition of capital (the ratio of dead labor or machinery to living labor power utilized in production) also become increasingly important in determining the rate of accumulation. Those companies with the highest organic composition of capital have an increased ability to realize and accumulate surplus value because workers in such enterprises receive a share of the product that dwindles in accord with the increasing use of machinery. "It is therefore the best-equipped enterprises, those with the highest organic composition of capital, that come out on top in capitalist competition" (Mandel, 1968:162). This differentiation in the utilization of productive capital is seen as a potentially powerful force in determining the conditions of labor because it occurs at the workplace—the site of the creation and appropriation of surplus value. In this account, market manifestations of economic activity, tallied in terms of profit and loss, are seen as only shadowy reflections of the real workings of the economy.

Industrial structure is also important in Marxist theory in that the monopoly sector is seen as the locus of the rise of the new middle class of educated experts and technicians. "The tremendous growth of constant capital engenders a *new hierarchy* in the enterprise, inserted between the old foreman and the general manager: technicians, engineers, chief engineers, production managers, planners, sales chiefs and publicity chiefs, market research staffs, heads of research laboratories, and so on. These are the *new middle class, . . .*" (Mandel, 1968:165). According to Wright and Perrone (1977), this new middle class occupies a contradictory location between the capitalist class and the working class, sharing certain interests with each. Thus, the emergence of monopoly capitalism and the differentiation of economic sectors is seen as having consequences not only for the conditions of labor but for the very structure of class relations.

Perhaps the most important Marxist insight for our topic is the idea that the effects of industrial structure on working conditions are relative to class positions. Thus, managers may benefit from a high profit level though workers do not, and the effects may be still different for professionals or for the new middle class (Poulantzas, 1975; Wright and Perrone, 1977).

The essential contributions of the Marxists to the problem of economic segmentation are the ideas of understanding monopoly as a stage of capitalism rather than as a market imperfection, the focus on share of the economy as opposed to share of the market, the specification of the composition of capital as a key aspect of industrial structure, the link between monopoly capitalism and international investment, and the relationship of industrial structure effects to class position.

INSTITUTIONAL ECONOMICS

Different levels of productivity across industries are the primary source of variation in wages and working conditions cited by institutional economists (Galbraith, 1967, 1973). High productivity allows cost savings and generates high profits, which may be passed on to consumers, captured by owners, or captured by labor (Garbarino, 1950). Plant size, operating through economies of scale, and technological innovation are seen as the most important foundations of productivity differentials (Bailey and Schwenk, 1980; Masters, 1969; Ross and Goldner, 1950).

Conglomerate organization and capital utilization are seen as additional factors that may influence productivity and, accordingly, wages and conditions. Conglomerate organization allows the transfer of resources among markets for the exploitation of advantage and the undercutting of competitors and labor. In this sense conglomerate organization has a potentially contradictory effect on workers' wages: workers may have the opportunity to gain a share of the profits of higher productivity but may also be placed in a situation where the employing company is able to undercut wages through outsourcing and other techniques. Capital-intensive production techniques, particularly in conjunction with public regulation as in the case of utilities, may also lead to a heightening of the economic power of the corporation and indirectly to a regularizing of employment for workers (Shepherd, 1979).[1]

The key theme of this school is that the relevant dimensions of industrial structure are defined by different abilities to raise productivity. Large size, operating through economies of scale, is the most commonly cited cause of higher productivity. Capital utilization and public regulation are also cited as possible causes of heightened corporate power and regularized employment conditions. In addition, this tradition highlights the importance of examining owners' and workers' abilities to win shares of the economic rewards of higher productivity respectively through conglomerate power and through trade unions.

LABOR ECONOMICS

Labor economics provides us with the most explicit conceptual links between industrial structure and workplace outcomes. These links are generally seen as operating through the agency of labor markets and trade unions. The outline of the argument is as follows. Employers have a downward-sloping demand curve for labor, which means that there is a trade-off between high wages (the price of labor) and high employment (the quantity demanded). However, under certain conditions the effects of this general truth may be mitigated by other factors. The existence of a product monopoly, which creates excess profits, or a labor monopoly, which can win higher wages while protecting job security, are two such factors (Rees, 1962).

Product Markets versus Labor Markets

This basic outline has been elaborated in several directions. For example, the degree of competition in local versus national markets has been thought to affect union ability to gain wage increases (Segal, 1964). The basic insight here is that unions dealing with competitive firms that operate only in local markets may be better off than unions dealing with firms in competitive national markets, *if* the unions can organize the entire labor force of the local area.

Levinson (1967) further develops the distinction between a firm's product market power within its selling area and a union's organizing power within the geographic area from which labor can be drawn into production. In a study of West Coast industries Levinson found that strong unions may flourish and win wage increases under competitive product market conditions if they can take advantage of spatial barriers to the entry of new firms into the physical area of production. For example, if a firm is to enter the business of unloading sea freight, it must locate on the dock and come to terms with the longshoremen's union.

Not only do competitive local markets offer the best opportunities for union activity under some conditions, but monopolistic market concentration may be seen as a potentially negative factor for union organization.

> Large oligopolistic employers have at their disposal substantial financial resources with which to resist union organizing efforts through such devices as the employment of spies and private police and the importation of strikebreakers; the funds available to smaller competitive employers for these purposes were usually much less. In addition, large financial reserves enabled the oligopolists to more easily absorb losses attendant upon a shutdown of operations caused by a lockout or a strike involving a demand for union recognition; . . . Hence, other things equal, the ability of a union to *organize* a new plant successfully was considerably greater if the employer were a small competitor rather than a large oligopolist.*

By analyzing the interaction between companies and their employees as one of continuing conflict, the outcome of which is partially determined by the resources available to each, Levinson arrives at the argument that monopolistic market concentration may actually result in a hostile environment for the growth of unionization and the improvement of working conditions.

Concentration and Unionization

The interaction of commodity market power and union power has also been investigated through statistical analysis as well as on a case study basis. Although both high levels of unionization and high levels of market concentration produce higher wages, the combination of concentration and unionization is observed to depress wages (Dalton and Ford, 1977; Hendricks, 1975; Weiss, 1966). In particular, "a high level of concentration was seen to have a negative effect when the degree of unionization was low" (Hendricks, 1975: 416).

The explanation generally offered is that, whereas both unions and market concentration may statistically produce higher wages, we must think of these two

---

*Reprinted with permission from Harold M. Levinson, Unionism, concentration, and wage changes: toward a unified theory. *Industrial and Labor Relations Review*, Vol. 20, No. 2 (1967), p. 203. © 1983 by Cornell University. All rights reserved.

forces as struggling over the same limited pie. When each is powerful the size of the pie does not necessarily expand to accommodate both the owner's expectation of monopoly profits and the union's expectation of higher wages.[2]

Taken as a whole, these studies indicate that market concentration cannot be seen as unilaterally producing improved working conditions. Rather, concentration appears to operate as a double-edged sword, providing an expanded base of revenues, from which wage increases may be secured, as well as providing heightened corporate power, which may be used to undermine worker power.

We should also note that, in spite of the organizing focus of these studies on commodity and labor market concentration, other dimensions of industrial structure have repeatedly emerged as important determinants of wages. Hendricks (1975) finds that the most consistently significant variables in predicting higher wages are size of firm and level of capitalization. Masters (1969) similarly finds that size is more important for wage determination than is concentration. The explanation offered is that organizational size, especially plant size, allows tremendous organizing economies of scale for unions, which in turn are responsible for securing improved wages.

The key suggestions we can extract from labor economics are (1) the idea that union power as a monopoly on the sale of labor may be affected both by ability to control the spatial area of production and by interaction with concentration in the product market, (2) the idea that industrial concentration may not represent an unmixed blessing for workers, and (3) the importance of firm size and capitalization in determining wages.

THE SOCIOLOGY OF LABOR MARKETS

Sociologists approach the topic of economic segmentation from the joint perspectives of organizational analysis, social stratification, and occupational analysis. Labor markets are defined by the interaction of these factors "as arenas in which workers exchange their labor power in return for wages, status, and other job rewards. The concept, therefore, refers broadly to the institutions and practices that govern the purchase, sale, and pricing of labor services" (Kalleberg and Sorensen, 1979:315). This perspective has encouraged sociologists not to examine only industrial or organizational characteristics in relation to worker outcomes but also to give equal attention to social and individual characteristics as determinants of labor market outcomes. Sociologists have made their unique contribution to the analysis of economic segmentation through a focus on segmentation along the dimensions of class, occupation, race, and sex, and also through expanding the range of job-related outcomes that come within the purview of segmentation analysis.

Segments and Shelters

Undertaking a comprehensive empirical study of labor force and labor market characteristics, Freedman (1976) discovers that labor market characteristics define from 14 to 16 "shelters" and that labor force characteristics define a similar number of differentiated worker "segments." The most important defining characteristic of industrial shelters is the provision of year-round full-time employment. Corporate size and unionization are additional important factors, but somewhat surprisingly, the existence of internal labor markets and market concentration do not differentiate industrial shelters in relation to workers' earnings. Worker segments, representing different patterns of earnings, are most importantly defined by the age of workers. Race as a declining factor and education as a rising factor are additional characteristics important for defining worker segments.

Freedman notes that industrial and occupational categories are grouped in roughly similar fashion, whether approached from the stand-point of industrial characteristics (used to define shelters) or worker characteristics (used to define segments). In other words, the occupational and industrial shelters with the lowest wages are roughly similar to the worker segments with the lowest wages. Although these findings are by no means definitive, they do indicate the importance of examining labor force characteristics as well as organizational characteristics when attempting to understand the nature of labor market segmentation. This analysis also highlights the benefits attainable by attempting to examine a reasonably comprehensive list of organizational and worker characteristics rather than focusing on only one or two dimensions, as economists have done in the case of market concentration and unionization.

The Economic Payoff for Education

One of the chief areas of interest for sociologists has been the manner in which industrial structure mediates basic societal processes such as economic returns to education. In a recent work investigating the differentiation of earnings returns to education, Stolzenberg (1978) finds a nicely patterned set of effects with returns to education increasing monotonically across plant size categories. He cites the literature on complex organizations as a source of interpretation for these findings. He argues that greater documentation, standardization, and bureaucracy (all proxied by the size dimension) lead to a greater reliance on the type of abilities taught in school. The higher earnings returns to education in large shops result from the greater reliance on educational training in these shops. Although Stolzenberg's findings are interesting in and of themselves, what is perhaps more interesting is his attempt to interpret them within the framework of complex organizations theory. In the next chapter we shall return to this field as a source of potential insight for the development of a new approach to understanding economic segmentation.

Going Beyond Earnings

Sociologists have also become interested in the effects of industrial structure on racial discrimination in hiring (Daymont and Kaufman, 1979; Kaufman, 1981), on career lines (Spilerman and Miller, 1976; Stolzenberg, 1978), on patterns of mobility (Hauser and Hodson, 1977; Hogan, 1975), and on unemployment (Schervish, 1981). Schervish's findings are particularly important in light of the economic depression that began in the early 1970s and the resulting high levels of unemployment. Schervish finds that economic sectors are both a key explanatory variable in the analysis of unemployment rates and that economic sectors account for a large portion of the racial difference in unemployment rates.

The unique contribution of sociologists lies in their ability to look beyond the narrow issues of wages and earnings and to focus on the social processes that both implement and mediate the effects of industrial structure on workplace outcomes. Sociological analysis suggests that we need to look at the broader effects of industrial structure (its impact on economic returns to age and education, mobility, racial discrimination, and so on) and to look also to individual characteristics as important determinants of labor markets and labor market outcomes.

THE DUAL ECONOMY MODEL

Based on a synthesis of some of the themes previously reviewed, the dual economy model posits the existence of two segregated economies in the United States. This model has been widely used both as a heuristic device and as a theoretical construct and has helped to focus attention on structural inequalities arising from a differentiated industrial structure. In the following sections we shall review this approach in detail and offer a sympathetic critique of its major theoretical assertions.

Overview and Background

Cain (1976) identifies the motivation for the dual approach as having arisen from social policy issues of the 1960s. One goal was to understand the persistence of poverty and the continuation of large racial and gender inequalities in the face of a rapid expansion of education and training programs. Also of concern was the perceived deterioration of the work ethic and rising levels of job dissatisfaction among both factory and nonfactory workers.

Conceptual issues revolving around the role of monopolies and the use of educational and training certificates as pure screening devices were also important in motivating the development of the dual approach. Theoretically, the dual economy approach was grounded on a critique of the assumption of labor market homogeneity prevalent in neoclassical economics and in the human capital theory of economic rewards to labor.

The basic assertion of the dual economy theory is that capitalist development in the twentieth century has resulted in the existence of two private economies with differentiated working conditions and labor markets. Different authors have used different terms to describe these sectors. The two private capital sectors have been called monopoly and competitive sectors (O'Connor, 1973),[3] core and periphery sectors (Averitt, 1968), planning and market economies (Galbraith, 1967), and concentrated and unconcentrated industries (Bluestone, 1970). Each conception implies basically the same sets of features for the two sectors.

This dual economic structure interacts with existing demographic and human capital characteristics of the labor force to accentuate inequality. High-paying primary sector jobs are offered as employment to educated and experienced white males, and low-paying secondary sector jobs employ the young and inexperienced, women, blacks, and other discriminated-against groups (Gordon, 1972; Thurow, 1975). This process of interaction increases social inequalities and creates separate, closed labor markets that constrain certain categories of workers to inferior job positions (Rosenberg, 1975). The resulting fragmented labor market is seen as an important cause of the persistence of poverty in the United States.

A primary motive behind the fragmentation of jobs into primary and secondary sectors lies in the capitalists' desire to fragment workers into antagonistic and competing subclasses. Such fragmentation diffuses class struggle, which would otherwise be centered on the conflict between the working class as a whole and the capitalist class (Reich, Gordon, and Edwards, 1973).

Research within the dual economy tradition has also investigated the possibility of different economic returns to education across economic sectors. Osterman (1975) grouped occupations into upper-tier primary, lower-tier primary, and secondary sectors. He then showed that earnings returns to education vary across these sectors. Workers in the upper-tier primary sector enjoy the highest returns to education, whereas workers in the secondary sector receive virtually no returns to education. These findings suggest that economic sectors are not only important in determining earnings but are also key for the explanation of different *processes* of earnings attainment.

In the effort to understand economic and labor market segmentation it is necessary to give serious attention to insights emergent from the dual economy model. Unfortunately, a well-defined theoretical model of the dual economy does not exist in the literature. Instead, most researchers interested in the notion of a dual economy have invoked a set of loosely defined and interconnected concepts. A major prerequisite for our task, then, is to delineate the underlying model of the dual economy. As long as the dual approach remains a collection of ideas rather than a concrete model, it is difficult to assess how useful the approach has been or to attempt to develop or move beyond it in any systematic fashion.

In our attempt to reconstruct the model underlying the dual approach it will be useful to recognize four basic elements: a dual economy, which represents the organizational structure of capital; a dual labor market, which represents the organization of labor within capital structures; a set of outcomes for workers that results from their participation in these labor markets; and a related social division of labor in terms of racial, ethnic, and gender groups. In the following discussion we shall first note how each of these elements has been defined and then discuss the relationships between elements as they have been specified in the dual economy literature.

The Dual Economy

The core sector (however named) refers to firms with large numbers of employees, high capitalization, large profits, and large yearly sales.

> Production is typically large scale and markets are normally national or international in scope—for example, capital goods such as steel, copper, aluminum, and electrical equipment; consumer goods such as automobiles, appliances, soap products, and various food products; transportation industries such as railroads, airlines, and branches of shipping (O'Connor, 1973:15–16).

Most important, such firms control their markets and operate as price-setters because of the oligopolistic or monopolistic nature of their markets. These firms tend also to employ advanced technologies and to have high productivity and high rates of unionization.

The periphery sector is characterized by low levels of capitalization, small size, regional or local marketing, and single-product lines. These firms operate in highly competitive markets. Further, they employ little advanced technology, tend to be labor intensive, and have low rates of productivity, profit, and unionization.

> In the competitive sector the physical capital-to-labor ratio and output per worker, or productivity, are low, and growth of production depends less on physical capital investment and technical progress than on growth of employment. Production is typically small scale, and markets are normally local or regional in scope. Familiar examples include restaurants, drug and grocery stores, service stations, and other branches of trade; garages, appliance repair shops, and other services; clothing and accessories, commercial displays, and other manufacturing industries (O'Connor, 1973:13).

Unlike the shielded and protected monopoly sector, the market for goods produced by firms in this sector is open to entry by new firms. Profits and retained earnings are low, and long-term financing from external sources is difficult to secure. Additionally, the firms of the competitive sector are "price takers" in the factor market for capital goods produced in the monopoly sector. This results in their direct exploitation by firms in the monopoly sector, just as monopoly-sector firms also exploit final consumers.

Origins of the Dual Economy

When theorists have attempted to specify the origins of the dual economy they have relied heavily on Marx's conception of the capitalist dynamic of concentration and centralization (see Edwards, 1979; O'Connor, 1973; Reich, Gordon, and Edwards, 1973).[4] According to this dynamic, the owners of capital accumulate capital primarily through the extraction of surplus value from labor and secondarily through competition among themselves. Thus, over time, capital becomes increasingly "concentrated," with ever-larger amounts controlled by individual capitalists. There are also periodic economic crises brought about by the overproduction and underconsumption of commodities. During these crises, many businesses fail and are bought out at devalued rates by other capitalists. This leads to the "centralization" of capital into the hands of progressively fewer and fewer capitalists.

Exploitation of the Periphery by the Core

A central theme in the dual economy literature is the relationship of exploitation between the core and the periphery sectors. Averitt (1968) specifies three possible types of relationship between core firms and periphery firms. Periphery firms may be direct "satellites" of center firms. Alternatively, they may be what Averitt calls the "loyal opposition," that is, small competitive enterprises operating in industries dominated by oligopolistic firms. Finally, the periphery sector is partially composed of "free agents." These are autonomous firms operating in peripheral industrial sectors of the economy.

In each of these situations the peripheral firms are at a disadvantage. Galbraith verbalizes the resulting relationship between what he calls the "planning" and "market" economies in the following way:

> The market system buys at prices which are extensively subject to the power of the planning system. And an important part of its products and services are sold at prices which it does not control but which may be subject to the market power of the planning system. . . . The terms of trade between the two systems will have an insouciant tendency to favor the system that controls its prices and costs and therewith the prices and costs of the other system as well (Galbraith, 1973:50).*

*Taken from "Economics and the Public Purpose" by John Kenneth Galbraith. Copyright 1973 by John Kenneth Galbraith. Reprinted by permission of Houghton Mifflin Company.

As a result, the planning or monopoly sector achieves higher productivity through constantly higher capitalization and through direct price exploitation. O'Connor (1973) specifies this relationship as constituting a "law of uneven development." As capital is invested in profitable areas, this investment transforms production in those areas toward even higher productivity and profitability, which further increase investment and uneven development.

The Role of the State

O'Connor (1973) highlights the role of the state in increasing segmentation between the monopoly and competitive sectors of capital through taxation and investment policy. The structure of corporate income taxes, depreciation and depletion allowances, investment tax credits, and specific industry loopholes benefits monopoly capital over competitive capital. The allocation of state investment into defense, automobile-related industries, energy, and so on also favors monopoly capital.

The relationship between the state and such corporations as Lockheed and General Dynamics provides an example of the manner in which production costs in the monopoly sector are socialized. Because these firms are important defense contractors, a large part of their working capital is supplied by the government as progress payments, and a large part of the plant and equipment they utilize is directly owned by the government. In fact, as the case of Lockheed illustrates, the company may be financially rescued by the government if necessary.

This government support provides a kind of security undreamed of by competitive firms. The unequal distribution of state subsidies and investments reinforces a secular dichotomization of financial size, capital intensity, concentration, and profits.

Two qualitatively distinct sectors arise as a result of these dynamics. The core sector includes those firms in which capital has become increasingly concentrated and centralized, and the periphery sector consists of the remaining small competitive firms. Core firms continue to grow, not only by buying out businesses within their product line, but also through horizontal and vertical integration. Galbraith (1967) argues that the utilization of technology and long-range planning are also fundamental for distinguishing between the two sectors, whereas O'Connor (1973) argues that government support for monopoly factors is crucial. These factors affect the ability of firms to survive economic crises, to be more successful in competition, and thus to make the transition from periphery to core status.

Dual Labor Markets

The dual model progresses from distinguishing between organizational forms of capital to distinguishing between organizational forms of labor by linking dual economic sectors to dual labor markets. It is argued that corresponding to the core and periphery sectors, respectively, are two separate labor markets: a primary labor market and a secondary labor market. Perhaps the most critical distinction that has been drawn between these two labor markets is the extent to which employment is stable and secure.[5] As a result of the alignment of economic sectors and labor markets, there is a stable and well-paid labor force in the monopoly sector—the aristocracy of labor—whereas the competitive sector offers only marginal employment. O'Connor describes competitive sector employment in the following terms:

> *Unstable and irregular product markets and unstable and irregular labor markets go together in competitive industries.* Employment in the competitive sector tends to be relatively low paid and casual, temporary, or seasonal. Workers who want and are unable to find full-time, year-round, well-paid work in the monopolistic or state sectors will accept employment in the competitive sector on almost any terms (O'Connor, 1973:14; emphasis added).

Conversely, the monopoly sector ensures the stability of its labor force by paying higher wages and tying the workers' lives directly to the company via company insurance and retirement plans, company credit, company-sponsored education, and so on.

Internal versus External Labor Markets

The distinction between the two labor markets based on stability has often been conceptualized in terms of internal versus external labor markets (Doeringer and Piore, 1971).

Workers participate in different job markets depending on their current employment. If they are already in an internal labor market, they compete for jobs at the next rung of the ladder. If they are in an unstructured market, their only connection to a job and an employer is the sale of their labor power at the going market price. Workers in the latter category and the irregular jobs they hold comprise the external, or unstructured, labor market. Points of contact exist between internal labor markets and unstructured labor markets. These points of contact, called "ports of entry," are generally at the bottom of the job ladder. However, Kerr (1954) and Bluestone (1971) argue that there are strong barriers to mobility between internal and external labor markets and suggest that strongly segmented labor markets are historically on the rise.

Wages and job conditions in the external labor market are determined by market forces and can, therefore, be explained by neoclassical economic theory. Given a continuing economic situation with less than full employment, the low wages and poor working conditions of these jobs pose no problems of explanation for conventional economics. However, the pricing and allocation of labor in internal labor markets is governed by administrative rules and procedures. Doeringer and Piore (1971) argue that the skill specificity of jobs, the prevalence of on-the-job training, and the predominance of "customary law" in internal labor markets are important explanations for the inability of neoclassical economics to explain wages in this sector. They note that the wage structure in internal labor markets stands in direct contradiction to "human capital" models of individual earnings attainment.

Because of their large size, high technology, and long-range planning horizons, core firms have internal labor markets consisting of sets of positions within the firm, linked together in skill hierarchies. Access to these jobs is restricted to those already within the internal labor market or to specified entry ports. Periphery firms, on the other hand, operate wholly through the external labor market, in which there are no barriers to movement into or out of positions.

Origins of the Dual Labor Markets

Explanations for the origins of dual labor markets corresponding to the two economic sectors have relied on the different abilities of firms in the sectors to maximize profits through the organization of works.[6] There are two distinct but related arguments in the literature about how the drive toward profit maximization produces differentiated labor markets. The first argument focuses on technology and skill specificity, and the second focuses on the issues of labor control and class consciousness. According to the first argument, job skills in the core sector are specific to the firm (or perhaps to the industry), and jobs are arranged in sequences such that current job skills are the foundation for later job skills. This specificity and sequencing of job skills arises because of the utilization of advanced technologies and integrated production processes in core firms. Given the extent of skill specificity, the most cost-efficient method of procuring workers with the requisite skills is via on-the-job or in-plant training. One of the problems with this arrangement (from the firm's viewpoint) is that it increases the costs of labor turnover because workers are no longer close substitutes for one another: a new worker has to be trained in order to substitute for a "lost" worker. The rational, profit-maximizing solution for core firms is to promote less turnover by providing job security and other incentives (higher wages, fringe benefits, better working conditions, etc.). Periphery firms, on the other hand, employ an older mode of production and organization of labor and do not need to adapt their labor policies to this new organization of work. (See Doeringer and Piore, 1971, Edwards, 1979, Piore, 1969, and Vietorisz and Harrison, 1970, for elaboration of this argument.)

The second argument differs from the first in that it examines reasons beyond short-run cost efficiency for the creation of a differentiated labor market structure. The problem of labor control is seen as providing a central dynamic in the creation of differentiated labor markets. Edwards (1979) points out that historically there have been different basic forms of labor control employed by business. Simple, or direct, control relying on personal supervision represents the oldest form and still characterizes the periphery sector today. This form of labor control especially as typified by the ''foreman's empire,'' results in harsh and arbitrary working conditions. Wages are kept low because profitability depends on the owner's ability to extract surplus labor directly from the workers.

Changes occurred in the requirements for labor control with the emergence of monopoly capitalism in the United States in the 1890–1920 period (Reich *et al.*, 1973). During this period, production was shifted to large plants employing large bodies of labor, who worked under oppressive and homogeneous conditions. This situation gave rise to the possibility of class consciousness and united working class action against the capitalist class. To counter this possibility and in response to rising discontent, the owners and managers of these large factories introduced new forms of labor control.

These new forms of labor control, primarily technical control, typified by the assembly line, and bureaucratic control, typified by an orientation to rules, still dominate in the core sector today. Beyond their obvious functions of coordinating work and delegating authority, both technical and bureaucratic control structures promote the fragmentation of the working class by heightening the division of labor and by introducing artificial distinctions of pay and rank. Similarly, core firms introduced credentialism within an expanded managerial hierarchy to diffuse further the working class and avert the possibility of collective action. This fragmentation contributes to long-run profit maximization in the core by undermining the development of organizations that are oriented toward increasing the relative wages of workers.

The role of organized labor in tying wages to productivity increases and in creating job security systems is also an important ingredient in the association of high wages and stable employment with the core sector. In the final analysis, however, it is the role of monopoly pricing that sets the stage and allows these other forces to operate on wages. The power of core-sector firms to set monopoly prices allows the cost of wage increases to be passed on to the consumer. Monopoly profits also provide more money for investment in on-the-job training and for the creation of internal labor markets, thus reinforcing the binding of a certain fraction of labor to better-paying jobs in the core sector.

These labor market conditions help to produce the stable planning horizons required in the monopoly sector to ensure that large capital investments do not go underutilized. The provision of stable employment opportunities in the monopoly sector produces an enduring differentiation of conditions between workers in this sector and those in the unstable and exploited competitive sector.

Worker Outcomes

The third element in the dual approach consists of three sets of outcomes for labor. First, there is the extent or likelihood of mobility between sectors. Second, there are the conditions of labor in terms of various tangible and intangible rewards. Third, there is the consciousness of workers, that is, their awareness of collective conditions and interests.

Mobility

Associated with dual labor markets are a number of institutional rules and practices concerning hiring, the attachment of workers to positions, promotions, transfers, and so on. One of the key elements in the operation of dual labor markets is the existence of barriers to mobility between labor markets. These barriers arise partially as a result of the creation of internal labor markets that shelter incumbents from competition with workers in the external labor market. As noted earlier, for each internal labor market there are one or more entry ports, which are the only positions that can be entered directly from the external labor market. It is at these entry ports that employers exercise control over mobility between labor markets, and it is here that the selection of workers with desired characteristics takes place (Doeringer and Piore, 1971; Kerr, 1954). Barriers to mobility between labor markets also arise as a result of different availabilities of on-the-job training, job information, and job security, and because of geographic location and other institutional factors (Bluestone, 1970). On the local level, the mix of core and periphery firms present in the community determines the kinds of jobs available to workers (Baron and Hymer, 1968; Freedman, 1976; Wachtel, 1970).

Writers such as Thurow (1975) and Doeringer and Piore (1971) have argued that we can think of entry into the primary labor market as being governed by a queue. Workers are ordered in the entry queue according to their trainability; that is, according to the cost of training them as permanent employees. As a number of authors have pointed out (e.g., Bluestone, 1970; Gordon, 1971), this can lead to a vicious circle for workers who begin in the secondary labor market, which imposes unstable work histories on workers that primary labor market employers use as "evidence" of their undesirability. Such workers cannot gain entrance to the primary labor market because their unstable work histories are seen as evidence that they would not be good steady workers.

The persistence of poverty can be partially explained by the blockage of mobility between the primary and secondary labor markets (Bluestone, 1970; Gordon, 1971; Rosenberg, 1975). Once workers enter the secondary market, they acquire unstable work histories and face obstacles to entering the primary labor market. Moreover, workers in the primary labor market have a degree of security that protects them from downward mobility. Even when core employers need to reduce the size of their labor force, they typically lay off employees rather than terminate them to protect the firm's investment in the employees' training (O'Connor, 1973; Schervish, 1983).

Economic Rewards and Working Conditions

In addition to providing an explanation for the persistence of poverty, the dual economy model also suggests that the general conditions of labor should be differentiated across sectors of the economy. Jobs in the primary sector are seen as "good" jobs with high rewards and jobs in the secondary sector as "bad" jobs with low rewards (Vietorisz and Harrison, 1970). Wages and fringe benefits are kept above the competitive rate in the core to diffuse discontent and to keep worker turnover low (Reich *et al.*, 1972). Bibb and Form (1977), classifying industries into primary and secondary sectors on the basis of descriptive accounts in Averitt's "The Dual Economy" and Galbraith's "The New Industrial State," demonstrate that industrial structure is a strong determinant of individual earnings, even when demographic and human capital variables are held constant. On the criterion of explained variance, industrial structure easily surpasses human capital determinants of earnings such as education, specific vocational training, and job tenure.

Several studies have also indicated that there are higher earnings returns to education in the core sector (Beck, Horan, and Tolbert, 1978; Osterman, 1975; Tolbert, Horan, and Beck, 1980). The hypothesis of differential returns can be derived from themes in the dual model along two lines of argument. First, higher returns act as an incentive to keep turnover low in the core. Second, the greater size and bureaucratization of the core firms lead to a greater reliance on the type of skills taught in school; accordingly, education is more valuable to core employers than to periphery employers (Stolzenberg, 1978). The hypothesis of differential educational returns is important within the dual model because it adds to the critique of neoclassical labor theory, which assumes a single homogenous labor market operating under uniform principles.

Work in the two sectors also differs in the nature of worker discipline. Discipline in the primary labor market is rule-oriented because of the more formal structuring of work and the greater bureaucratization of the core firms' supervisory structure. Discipline in the secondary sector is typically harsher and more arbitrary because of the more direct and personal forms of labor control utilized (Edwards, 1979).

Worker Consciousness

The effect of a dual economic structure on worker consciousness is to create fragmentation and thus to inhibit collective organization. Between the two sectors there is competition and jealousy because of the superior conditions and opportunities of the core workers. This manifests itself in "fraction" politics, with conflict arising between different groups of workers over different immediate interests in the work and political arenas (Edwards, 1979; Friedman and

Friedman, 1979; O'Connor, 1973; Reich *et al.*, 1973). Moreover, there is additional fragmentation of worker consciousness within the core sector, owing to the artificial hierarchy of status and authority that is imposed by the bureaucratic system of control (Edwards, 1979; Stone, 1974).

The Social Division of Labor

The final element of the dual model concerns the social division of labor based on racial, ethnic, and gender divisions in the labor force. Much of the motivation for the dual approach was provided by the persistent poverty of urban blacks, by persistent racial wage differences, and later by a focus on gender wage differences (Bibb and Form, 1977; Bluestone, 1970; Bluestone, Murphy and Stevenson, 1973; Gordon, 1971). The basic argument is that the observed racial and gender differences are largely spurious; that is, a large component of these differences is caused by the structure of labor markets.

There are a number of different arguments that have been used to explain the initial sorting of minorities into the periphery. One is that the jobs geographically available to ghetto minorities are almost exclusively within the periphery. In addition, the dual model borrows from the neoclassical economics paradigm the idea of direct employer discrimination as an explanation for the sorting of minorities across economic sectors. Many employers have a "taste" for discrimination, but only core employers can indulge these tastes because of the latitude allowed by their excess monopoly profits (Becker, 1957; Shepherd, 1970). It has also been suggested that core employers may use race as an inexpensive screen to separate workers who are easy (inexpensive) to train from those who are difficult (expensive) to train. Because minorities differ from nonminorities *on the average* in terms of various characteristics that employers find desirable (human capital, stability, etc.), minority status can be used as a relatively inexpensive screen for these characteristics (Beck *et al.*, 1978; Doeringer and Piore, 1971; Thurow, 1975). A number of radical theorists have also argued that discrimination between social divisions is promoted by the capitalist class as a means of consciously fostering disunity and fragmenting class consciousness (Bonacich, 1976; Gordon, 1972; Reich, 1971; Szymanski, 1976).

The idea of a vicious circle is again invoked to explain the persistence of this social division of labor. According to this hypothesis, the initial employment of blacks and other minorities-in the periphery gives them an unstable work history, which core employers use as evidence that they are not good workers; hence, they are blocked from subsequently moving into the core (Bluestone, 1970; Doeringer and Piore, 1971; Gordon, 1972).

In summary, the dual economy model attempts to address the full range of issues in social stratification. It has something to say about how the differentiation of positions and rewards in contemporary society has developed. The process by which individuals are sorted into these positions is a central concern, as is workers' consciousness about their positions. The model also addresses important issues concerning the development and maintenance of inequality among social groups.

A SYMPATHETIC CRITIQUE OF THE DUAL ECONOMY MODEL

In a recent appraisal of measures of the dual economy, Zucker and Rosenstein (1981:880) noted that different researchers within the dual economy approach have reported strikingly different findings. They concluded that "the need for further development of the underlying theoretical models is clear." The message is obvious: serious empirical inconsistencies have rendered existing models of the dual economy unusable. Empirical inconsistencies aside, there has also been a growing trend in the segmentation literature to question some of the theoretical propositions of the dual model (Baron and Bielby, 1980; Bridges, 1980; Hodson and Kaufman, 1981; Kalleberg, Wallace, and Althauser, 1981; Kaufman, Hodson, and Fligstein, 1981; Wallace and Kalleberg, 1981).

Perhaps the most damning criticism of the dual economy approach is that a full theoretical model has never been elaborated. As a result, research utilizing this approach has remained ambiguous about the exact theoretical model being specified. Key components of the model (core sector, primary jobs, etc.) have been unclearly defined, and the links between these concepts and other components of the model have not been clearly laid out. Because there is no consistent theoretical model, connections are left at the level of images rather than specific arguments. "[The] theories are sketchy, vague, and diverse if not internally conflicting. Description, narratives, and taxonomies crowd out model development" (Cain, 1976, as quoted in Zucker and Rosenstein, 1981:872). The theoretical problem presented by this lack of specificity is that research utilizing the dual approach has not been constrained and disciplined by interaction with a formal model.

Another general criticism of the dual approach is that it is primarily descriptive rather than theoretical in nature (Kalleberg and Sorensen, 1979; Kaufman et al., 1981; Wachter, 1974). A description of the economy as dual in structure (based mainly on the existence of different amounts of market power) is combined with a description of the labor market as dual in structure (based mainly on the existence of jobs with different levels of stability and different rates of pay). The knowledge that blacks and women as subordinate social groups are employed in inferior jobs is then added, and a parallelism between powerful and weak sectors of the economy, good and bad jobs, and dominant and subordinate social groups is then postulated.

This criticism calls into question the specification of two and only two sectors. An important social relationship (such as that between the buyers and the sellers of labor, that is, the capitalist class and the working class) may be the basis for a dichotomous theory, but the dual economy is grounded on no such relationship between the primary and secondary sectors. The theory is primarily descriptive and on that basis the number of sectors, or for that matter the use of sectoral over continuous measures, must remain open to empirical evidence or to further theoretical specification.

To answer the question, "Why, then, dualism?" we need to consider an epistemological critique of the concept of a dual economy based on analyzing its nature and purpose *as a concept*. One question we might ask about a sociological concept is, "Does it refer to something that is supposedly extant in the social consciousness?" This has never been systematically argued as a basis for the use of the dual economy model, so we can conclude that this is not a rationale for its use. If the dual economy is not something that exists in the social consciousness or at least is not defended on that grounds, then its use must be justified as an analytic construct developed by social scientists. Considering the construct in this way, we can see that it was developed primarily as a vehicle for the critique of an earlier theory; it has had little autonomous development outside of that critique. The dual model has two major motivations. First, it is meant to contain a critique of the neoclassical and status attainment schools of research, which are based on the assumption of a free competitive market. Second, it is meant to motivate and mold social policy. The dual model is less a theory in its own right than a convenient heuristic device to contain this theoretical and policy critique. However much one may agree with this critique it is essential to note that the dual model has been unable to provide a systematic new theory of economic segmentation to replace the neoclassical and status attainment theories, and this inability is a primary cause of the current theoretical stagnation in the field of labor market segmentation.

In the following sections we present a systematic critique of the dual approach. Although we conclude that there are several important contributions to be retained from the dual model, including the insight that the structure of capital affects labor market outcomes, we argue that many of its assertions are invalid and that overall it is inadequate for sustaining theoretical and empirical development. Let us consider each major component of the dual model in turn to detail these criticisms.

A Dual Economy?

Starting with the notion of the dual economy, it is noteworthy that only one reason has been offered as to why a two-sector approach is the appropriate tool for understanding the reality of economic segmentation.[7] The basic argument, developed most clearly by O'Connor (1973), is that the monopoly sector exploits the competitive sector. However, this argument, which we believe is sound in and of itself, was developed primarily for use in an analysis of fiscal politics and is most relevant in that area. It is somewhat tangential to the larger concerns of the dual approach, which focus on the linkage between economic structure and labor market structure. Outside of this single argument the two sectors are generally defined by a contrasting of characteristics rather than by a theoretically based relationship, and scant evidence is offered that the characteristics are actually arrayed in any way approximated by a dual economy.[8]

This two-sector model is particularly troublesome when one recalls the great variety of themes it summarizes, each of which seems to have been resolved as a dualistic contrast. Reviewing the literature surveyed, we can list the following characteristics alternatively used to distinguish the two sectors in the dual economy model: concentration in commodity markets, profits, size, productivity, growth, unionization, irregular product markets, capital intensity, advanced technology, advertising expenditures, intercorporate conglomerate domination (satellite status), market scope (local, regional, or national), multinationalism, state subsidy support, and influence over the state. It is difficult to believe that each of these themes can be realistically summarized by a dichotomous contrast. Indeed, we might go further and question as well the choice between categorical and continuous measures of economic structure.[9] This choice seems to have been made at some point in the history of the dual approach, but it has never been vigorously argued or defended. In sum, the dichotomous solution to the question of economic segmentation seems arbitrary and undefensible on any but heuristic grounds.[10]

The strongest critique of the dual economy component of the model focuses on the issue of the consistent alignment of the various dimensions of economic structure. This is a key assumption of the dual approach because important inconsistencies in the alignment of these dimensions would demand a radically different conceptualization. The argument from the dual approach is that the various dimensions cluster together with a sufficiently high correlation to be conceptualized in terms of a single factor or dimension of economic structure.[11]

For example, concentration is typically seen as leading to large size because of the accelerated accumulation possible under conditions of monopoly profits. Similarly, the dual approach assumes that size tends to produce concentration because of the ability of large corporations to undermine competition.

It is the linking of monopolization and growth in firm size that generates the dramatic transforming effect of centralization. As centralization occurred within the basic industries, it tended to produce monopoly. As it occurred within the context of an expanding national (and international) economy, it tended to produce firms of enormous size. The combination of monopolization and growth proved to be highly profitable. And as the core firms reaped enormous profits, they experienced inexorable pressures to spill over into new markets—

through vertical integration, diversification, and multinationalism. The end results of this process of centralization have been, for the largest firms, an enduring state of high profitability and a low risk of failure (Edwards, 1979: 73–74).*

It seems plausible that concentrated firms have a tendency to grow, but the argument that large firms have an inevitable tendency to become concentrated cannot be accepted at face value. Stabilized, competitive market conditions exist in many industries dominated by relatively large firms. Structural steel products (Weiss, 1971), limited price variety and department stores (Bloom, Fletcher, and Perry, 1972), and insurance (Thieblot and Fletcher, 1970) provide some of the most important examples of this kind of large-firm competitive market structure.

Recent empirical research provides little support for this assumed alignment of dimensions (Hodson and Kaufman, 1981; Kalleberg *et al.*, 1981; Kaufman *et al.*, 1981; Wallace and Kalleberg, 1981). Indeed, if we examine the correlations between major dimensions of industrial structure as presented in the work of Tolbert *et al.* (1980) or Wallace and Kalleberg (1981), we see that the correlations range from fairly high positive correlations to insignificant and even negative correlations.[12]

Another weakness in the dual economy account is the lack of a sound theoretical argument about how the sectors came into being. Marx's theory of the increasing concentration and centralization of capital is the most frequently relied-upon groundwork. But we believe that this theory is neither sufficient nor well selected for this task. In Marx's work, this theory serves as one component of the laws of capitalist development. These laws apply to the historic development of capitalism; they are clearly at too high a level of abstraction to afford guidance for the study of labor conditions across economic sectors.

To this highly abstract theory, Reich *et al.* (1973) add the argument that labor market segmentation arises in response to a conscious capitalist class action. This action is motivated by the desire to fragment possible working class consciousness emerging from the growth of the large factory system with large bodies of workers laboring under homogenous and oppressive working conditions. It is difficult to accept such a narrowly focused instrumentalist argument as an adequate explanation for a phenomenon as pervasive as labor market segmentation. Inability to provide an adequate explanation for the historical rise of two differentiated economic sectors that does not ultimately rest on a unacceptably conspiratorial theory of social structure represents one of the principal failings of the dual model.

Some researchers have claimed empirical support for the existence of a closely aligned dual industrial structure, but serious questions can be raised about the validity of their findings. Oster (1979) asserts that he has confirmed the existence of a dual economy structure. However, his demonstration is based on a reversal of standard hypothesis-testing norms. Using the dual structure as the null hypothesis, he incorrectly places the burden of proof on the evidence that forces us to reject a dual structure, whereas the burden of proof should be on the evidence that forces us to accept the dual structure as a valid description. Similarly, Tolbert *et al.* (1980), in spite of claims to the contrary, offer no evidence in support of the dual economy. Their approach is simply to define two groups of industries and then to maintain that their ability to define two sectors constitutes evidence for the existence of a dual economy.

In addition to assuming high correlations among the various dimensions of industrial structure in the face of evidence to the contrary, the dual model has also assumed that the various dimensions have parallel effects on workplace outcomes. The assumption is that all the dimensions, if aligned in the correct manner, lead to uniform effects on a variety of dimensions from wages (O'Connor, 1973) to stability (Rosenberg, 1980) to returns to schooling (Osterman, 1975) to discrimination (Reich, 1971). No argument is offered for this assertion other than that all the dimensions tap some aspect of corporate power that somehow produces positive results for labor in general and negative results for minorities and women. No support has been offered for this assumption and, indeed, it is largely untestable within the dual model. That is, once a set of characteristics has been forced into a single dimension, it is impossible to test for the possibility of different, or even contradictory, effects of these dimensions. Counter-evidence is rapidly accumulating in the form of oppositely signed coefficients for different dimensions of industrial structure in analyses of a variety of labor force outcomes (Bridges, 1980; Comanor, 1973; Hodson, 1981; Kalleberg *et al.*, 1981; Kaufman and Daymont, 1981).

Researchers within the dual economy approach have been reluctant to pursue this idea, though a more thorough analysis of industrial structure would have led them to it almost inevitably. Early work by Weiss (1966) and later Hendricks (1975) indicates that concentration, a principal dimension of the dual model, may have negative effects on workers' earnings in contrast to the effects of other "core-type" dimensions. Similarly, even a cursory review of labor history would indicate that the largest firms and the most concentrated industries have often been the most difficult to unionize, again in direct contrast to the dual supposition of parallel structures. The strong resistance to unions in steel, auto, rubber, and other key industries until the unionizing drives of the Great Depression should give us pause before wholeheartedly accepting the hypothesis of dual parallelisms. Even today, some of the largest conglomerates in leading industries, such as IBM in electronics and DuPont in chemicals, remain bastions of antiunionism.

Finally, measures of the dual economy have often been dangerously circular. Industrial characteristics are combined with labor force characteristics and with outcome variables, and a summary measure of the dual economy is extracted (Oster, 1979; Tolbert *et al.*, 1980). Such operationalizations are unusable for scientific investigation of the relationships between these various aspects of economic structure and labor market segmentation because they combine causal and outcome variables in the measure of the major explanatory concept. More concretely, it is simply not valid to use percentage black, earnings levels, and measures of job stability both as dependent variables and as indicators of the major independent variable.[13]

When relationships are assumed rather than tested, it becomes all too easy to group units of analysis on the basis of whatever industrial dimension is thought to be most closely related to the dependent variable of interest. The entire "dual economy theory" is then invoked as an explanation for that relationship. This style of analysis in the dual economy literature has contributed to a frequent confusion of the concepts of a "dual economy" and "dual labor markets." Where explanatory and dependent variables are not clearly separated, research becomes little more than an exercise in description, no matter what its theoretical pretensions.

And Dual Labor Markets Too?

Turning now to a consideration of the concept of dual labor markets and the linkage between these and the dual economy, we again see that there is no theoretical explanation of why two sectors are used to depict the reality of labor market segmentation. Yet almost the entire dual economy tradition has assumed two separate and internally homogeneous labor markets corresponding to the core and peripheral economic sectors. This supposed correspondence represents a serious oversimplification of reality. For example, in the author's hometown there is a large plant engaged in the manufacture of technologically advanced products for an international market. The plant is part of a major multinational firm and is run in accordance with highly bureaucratic procedures. Yet the bulk of the jobs at the plant offer starting salaries at minimum wage. In addition, job ladders at the plant are extremely short, and employment is comprised largely of women and minority group members. This labor market structure is just the opposite of that predicted by the dual model for a "core-type" firm.

The theoretical association of good jobs with core firms rests either on the argument that core firms utilize technology requiring firm-specific skills or on the argument that core firms use their resources to reward their workers to lessen labor discontent. Neither argument appears well-grounded. Braverman (1974) convincingly argues that the inherent dynamic of monopoly capitalism is toward the deskilling of jobs, not the creation of more skilled positions. Further, there are strong indications that core firms use their resources to undermine working conditions by such actions as plant closings and capital flight at least as readily as they use these resources to reward workers (Barnet and Muller, 1974; Bluestone and Harrison, 1982).[14] The existing empirical evidence concerning labor markets within economic sectors strongly suggests that the core and periphery sectors are anything but homogeneous in labor market characteristics (Hodson, 1978; Kaufman, 1981; Schervish, 1983; Wallace and Kalleberg, 1981). In summary, the assumption of a direct parallelism between dual economic sectors and dual labor markets appears to be an abstraction unsupported by either sound theoretical argument or valid empirical evidence.

Basically, the dual model has failed to retain economic sectors and labor markets as distinct concepts. Instead, labor markets have been reduced to a reflection of economic sectors. Although economic sectors may be an important determinant of labor markets, the two components of the dual model demand distinct conceptualization.

The Question of Worker Outcomes

Turning now to the relationship between the dual economy and various labor force outcome variables, it is evident that if we cannot assume a single labor market for each economic sector, then the relationship between sectors and outcomes cannot be correctly specified by examining mean differences in outcomes across economic sectors. Indeed, aside from the outcome variables of earnings and the provision of full-time employment, the connection between the dual economy and worker outcomes receives only very inconsistent support (Wallace and Kalleberg, 1981; Zucker and Rosenstein, 1981). The investigation of patterns of restricted mobility across sectors has received much attention within the dual approach, but this area in particular has produced meager and highly inconclusive findings (see Leigh, 1976; Rosenberg, 1975).

Sociologists have focused on differential earnings returns to schooling as a key research agenda for the dual economy approach, but this investigation has also produced highly inconclusive findings (Hauser, 1980; Zucker and Rosenstein, 1981). The motivation for this investigation was based on a desire to substantiate empirically the critique of the neoclassical assumption of labor market homogeneity (Cain, 1976; Osterman, 1975). However, it has become apparent that this research question was incorporated from the status attainment and human capital literature and applied to a new investigation in an almost totally undigested fashion. Internal motivation for the study from within the dual model itself has never been elaborated (see Granovetter, 1979; Stolzenberg, 1978).

Within the dual approach the generally stated expectations concerning educational returns are that (1) returns will be lower within the secondary sector because of the irregular nature of jobs and (2) returns will be higher within the core sector because of the linking of job ladders and earnings to educational credentials. However, the opposite expectations could just as legitimately be derived from arguments extant in the dual literature. Because the core is sheltered from competitive pressures, returns to human capital elements (such as education) should be depressed. The tying of wages to seniority rather than to human capital characteristics via union job security arrangements should further exacerbate this tendency. Similarly, because the competitive sector is where the market rules in an unrestricted fashion, this is where economic returns should be most closely linked to human capital characteristics. Given our criticisms concerning the ambiguity of the link between the dual economy and dual labor markets, it is hardly surprising that research on sectoral differences in economic returns to education has produced highly inconclusive findings.

The Issue of Race and Gender Groups

Once we relinquish the assumption of direct parallelism between dual economic sectors and dual labor markets, we must also begin to rethink the nature of the proposed mediation of racial and gender inequality by economic and labor market structure. Support for the differential distribution of minority groups across dual economy sectors has been either weak or absent (Beck *et al.*, 1978; Hodson, 1978; Tolbert *et al.*, 1980). Some studies have, in fact, shown that blacks and women may be more likely to be in the core sector or in industries with core characteristics (Bridges, 1980; Kaufman and Daymont, 1981).

These weak findings, in our opinion, again result from the incorrectly assumed parallelism between the dual economy and the dual labor market. A large number of core jobs are unskilled and offer low rewards. Applying Marshall's (1974) idea of social distance between positions rather than physical distance between persons as the metric of discrimination, the prevalence of women and blacks in poor jobs in the core sector becomes perfectly understandable. This understanding, however, would be prohibited if we remained within the dual framework.

CONCLUSIONS

In summary, we do not believe that the dual economy model offers a sufficient conceptual guide for the study of the differentiation of working conditions and labor market segmentation. It should be questioned, not simply because it lacks sufficient detail, but because it is based on assumed correlations and on assumed consistent patterns of effects. An alternative scheme more accurately reflecting reality might have 5 or 20 categories. The level of detail is not the issue. The primary criticism of the dual model is that it rests on a faulty abstraction of industrial structure in the United States.

These criticisms also shed doubt on research findings within the dual economy tradition. If the concept of dual economy bears little relation to economic reality, then findings using this concept also have an ambiguous interpretation. Any scheme for dividing the economy into industrial sectors identified with good and bad jobs is likely to produce some statistically significant empirical results. But if any dichotomous scheme can produce such results, then we have learned little about the real structure of economic segmentation and are not likely to learn more by remaining within such an approach.

Although the dual economy/dual labor market approach has provided an important critique of the assumption of labor market homogeneity prevalent in neoclassical economics and in the status attainment field, it does not appear capable of providing a well-specified alternative theory. The criticisms detailed here allow us to understand why research utilizing the dual approach has produced so many contradictory findings and why there has been so little systematic theory building based on cumulative research and scholarship in this area.

Nevertheless, certain components of the dual economy model are useful and provide essential insights that must be retained. A critique of the neoclassical model of free competitive market determination of wages is conclusively established by the dual approach and must be incorporated in any new theory of economic segmentation. An investigation of stratification in the work force that proposes that we go beyond the concepts of social class and social status by directly analyzing the organization of the workplace is also a major contribution.

What is to be avoided in the formulation of a new theory is the concept of a dual economy/dual labor market with assumed parallel structure at each level. The relationship between the various levels of analysis (economic structure, labor markets, labor outcomes, and the social division of labor) must be investigated both theoretically and empirically, not assumed to align in a parallel "good/bad" fashion. Similarly, in analyzing the various dimensions within each level of analysis, we must retain more intellectual flexibility. Some of these dimensions may be best considered as relations (e.g., the relationship of exploitation between monopoly and competitive capital) and other dimensions as continuous scales (e.g., size of establishments), and still others as multiple categories (e.g., market scope).

The contribution of the dual approach is to demonstrate that the neoclassical model of earnings attainment is faulty. But this does not provide a sufficient basis for a new theory. Several additional components are also needed.

1. The originating question needs to be precisely specified. The dual economy approach has often seemed to be caught within a menagerie of competing questions. Why is there so little working class unity? Why does poverty persist in a rich country? How does the matching of categories of jobs and social groups occur? How do differentiated outcomes for labor arise? In this book we shall focus our attention mainly on the last question, leaving the others for later analysis and, we hope, arriving at a more adequately formulated answer to our one leading question.

2. New concepts for measuring industrial structure are needed to replace the concepts of the dual economy and dual labor markets.

3. Clear and specific arguments are needed to specify the mechanisms through which industrial structure is translated into outcomes for workers.

In the next chapter we shall outline a "resource perspective" on industrial structure and workplace outcomes that will serve as the theoretical basis for our empirical study. This perspective will retain insights from the dual approach, while avoiding its overly restrictive assumptions of parallel structure and duality, and will attempt to integrate insights that the dual model has overlooked.

NOTES TO CHAPTER 2

1. In an important empirical study in this field, Rees and Shultz (1970) found that establishment variables (size, location, industry, and unionization) were more important for determining the wages of blue-collar workers than were individual characteristics (education and experience). The reverse was found to be true for white-collar workers.

2. In a related study, Feinberg (1979:16) found that market concentration produces increased instability of employment during periods of economic downturn because of fixed pricing structures. "It appears as if highly concentrated industries are successful in shifting some of the risk they face without compensation onto their employees."

3. O'Connor (1973) considered the state sector a third important arena of economic production in advanced monopoly capitalism. The state sector is defined as all workers employed by the government as well as workers in state-contracted production. Wages and working conditions in this sector are tied to those in the monopoly sector. In this book we shall concern ourselves exclusively with the private capitalist economy; accordingly, analysis of the state as a productive sector and labor market will lie outside our focus of attention. For an empirical study employing O'Connor's model of a distinct state sector, see Hodson (1978).

4. Averitt (1968) specified long-run falling costs for certain firms as an important explanation for the development of distinct center and periphery sectors. However, this formulation has received little attention in subsequent developments of the dual approach.

5. A number of researchers have also used labor outcomes (such as low wages, limited mobility, and the prevalence of underemployment) to distinguish between the two labor markets (see Oster, 1979, Rosenberg, 1980, and Tolbert *et al.*, 1980; on this point see also Cain, 1976, and Wachter, 1974). Although we shall return to this point later, it should be noted that defining labor markets in terms of differences in outcomes is different from arguing that there should be different outcomes across labor markets. Arguing that there should be different outcomes across labor markets is a valid theoretical hypothesis; using such outcomes to define labor markets is merely tautological. (See Hodson and Kaufman, 1981, on this point.)

6. A number of writers have argued for the existence of dual labor markets without relying on dual economic sectors as the explanation. The argument is that dual labor markets have come into existence because they are of mutual benefit to the firm and the worker (Freedman, 1976; Kalleberg and Sorensen, 1979; Thurow, 1975). These writers have pointed to factors such as skill specificity and nontransferability, collective organization of workers, interdependence of work tasks, licensing of practitioners, and civil service regulations as causes of dual labor markets. Similarly, the idea of internal labor markets has been utilized by researchers outside the dual economy approach. Doeringer and Piore (1971) point to the existence of craft internal labor markets (e.g., labor markets for construction workers and longshoremen) that crosscut enterprise and sectoral boundaries (see also Althauser and Kalleberg, 1981).

7. Even models of the dual economy that have utilized more than two sectors have treated these additional sectors as residual categories (Hodson, 1978; Schervish, 1983). The analytic construct has consistently been that of a two-sector economy.

8. One possible response to this criticism is that the dual economy is better conceived of as a trend or tendency. Thus, at any one time exactly two sectors might not be observed. Instead, we might observe a periphery sector, a core sector, and a set of firms or industries in transition from periphery to core organization. Evaluation of this possible counterargument must await a detailed longitudinal analysis of industrial structure, and it will not be considered further at this time.

9. For example, increasing concentration and centralization of capital as a dynamic of capitalism can be theoretically specified as producing a continuum of firms with differential market power as easily as it can be specified as creating a dichotomous industrial structure.

10. The duality of these structures has been reified by many researchers operating within the dual approach (Beck *et al.*, 1978; Bibb and Form, 1977; Oster, 1979; Rosenberg, 1980; Tolbert *et al.*, 1980). Even if valid, a point that is in much dispute here, the concept of a dual economy is best seen as an analytic construct, not as an empirical measure. That is, a dual mold cannot be forced on empirical reality without any allowance for transitory, anomalous, or residual categories. The reification of what are rightfully analytic constructs, even when the analytic constructs are valid ones, leads to a stifling of theoretical development and an inability to generate new knowledge.

11. Our criticism on this point focuses on the number of dimensions needed to describe economic segmentation theoretically and leaves aside the issue of how many sectors might be defined along even a single dimension. (On this point see Hodson and Kaufman, 1981.)

12. A strategy that might salvage part of the dual approach from this critique would be to specify two principal sectors, with subsectors defined along secondary dimensions of industrial structure. This strategy will not be adopted here because we believe it would place an inadequately supported prior conceptual constraint on our analysis.

13. For more detailed discussion of this issue, see Wallace and Kalleberg (1981) and Hodson and Kaufman (1981). See Horan, Tolbert, and Beck (1981) for a counterargument.

14. It should be noted that the dual economy interpretation of labor markets in which core firms use high wages as a mechanism of labor control is at odds with the more coercive ways in which large corporations use their resources in other spheres of production and accumulation.

3

A Resource Theory of Organizational Structure

We have seen that the dual economy theory has specified many important characteristics of industrial structure that influence the system of social stratification. However, the theory, by coalescing these elements into a model of questionable validity, has greatly limited their potential usefulness. In general, the various elements of industrial structure cannot be assumed to converge into a unitary dimension, nor do these elements necessarily have uniform effects on workplace outcomes.

As we shall see in this chapter, the dual model falters because it is grounded on an inadequate reconstruction of the history of industrial structure. Labor control is only one of the goals of the capitalist class that has an impact on industrial organization. Capitalists also pursue goals in relation to the state and, most importantly, in relation to other capitalists. A variety of structures emerge as various strategies are developed and implemented in the pursuit of these goals.

The history of working class struggles, particularly as that history is embodied in the trade union movement, has also been misread in the dual approach. Union-organizing victories are not simply a reflection of the emergence of monopoly-controlled mass production industries at the turn of the century. Working class struggles have their own dynamics, which are not reducible to reflections of the organizational characteristics of capital. Emerging forms of corporate organization may provide a rich soil for union organizing or they may seriously retard these efforts. In either case, the pattern of worker struggle has a significant degree of autonomy from the organizational structure of capital. Modern trade unions cannot be understood as simply the organizational form of labor that emerged to win a share of the monopoly profits of core industrial sectors by helping to provide a stable and reliable work force.

A REVISED HISTORY OF INDUSTRIAL STRUCTURE

A review of the organizational history of capitalist enterprises reveals that many different structures have emerged that provide strategic solutions to a variety of problems posed by the development of capitalism. Because of its focus on the internal structure of organizations, the literature of complex organizations will be particularly useful in the attempt to construct a new historically grounded theory of industrial structure. (See Azumi and Hage, 1972; Blau and Schoenherr, 1971; Chandler, 1962; Hage and Aiken, 1970; Hickson *et al.,* 1969; and Woodward, 1965, for representative studies.) Although we were able to extract many interesting ideas from the economics literature reviewed in the previous chapter, most of it utilized concepts focusing on commodity markets and pricing arrangements (even when the commodity priced was labor). It is hoped that the internal analysis of the firm offered by the complex organizations literature will provide precisely the leaven necessary for the development of a new theory of labor market segmentation.

The Drive for Profit

Both Marxist and non-Marxist students of the historical development of capitalist enterprises have emphasized the causal role of profit-seeking behavior (Braverman, 1974; Chandler, 1962). The growth of firms is generated by profit seeking, operating through technological advances and the drive toward social control. Whereas the motivation for growth arises from the drive for profit, the strategy for growth and its resulting structures arise from the interaction of technology, social control mechanisms, and environmental constraints.

Beginning in the post-Civil War United States, new organizational structures were developed to reap the profits made possible by the introduction of new technologies and by the shift to national markets. This heightened opportunity for profits was affected by two imperatives labeled the profits/technology imperative and the profits/control imperative (Chandler, 1962).

Profit/Technology Imperative

The adoption of more complex technologies involving a greater utilization of machinery opened up new profit-making opportunities. The effect of technology on the division of labor was twofold. First, it tended to break down tasks into component parts and thus deskill portions of the labor force. Second, it tended to create sets of industries that relied on highly skilled and specialized labor. The overall result was a greatly heightened division of labor.

Profit/Control Imperative

To use complex technologies and increase the scale of production, it became necessary to develop more elaborate internal social control mechanisms. This involved creating layers of supervisory personnel. The results of this dynamic included the so-called "Managerial Revolution," the advent of Taylorism, and the emergence of the human relations school of industrial management. It also became necessary to develop complex planning and control structures to deal with the firm's external environment. Immense administrative structures were required to coordinate purchasing and investment decisions, to deal with government regulation, to accommodate the trade union movement, and, in general, to maintain the overall level of profitability.[1]

Three Stages of Development

The development of these dynamics resulted in at least three identifiable stages of United States industrial organization. In the 1865–1870 period, enterprises with a greatly expanded scale of production emerged in the United States, based in machinery manufacture and chemicals (Chandler, 1969, 1977). Economic centralization during the depression of the 1870s and 1880s contributed to the greatly expanded scale of these enterprises. These monopolies did not develop from the existing primary industrial sectors of textiles and steel. Instead, they were made possible by the emergence of a national transportation network and the existence of vigorous national markets for their goods. Later, technological leadership in the 1870–1895 period maintained and reinforced the monopoly position of these industries.

Mergers to restrict competition and to coordinate the utilization of technology, the implementation of purchasing and administrative techniques, and the distribution of commodities were the rule in the 1900–1920 period. The central dynamics of this period were the rationalization of production and the drive for reduction in unit costs. As a result of these dynamics, this period saw the rise of mass production industries. This period also saw the transition in leading sectors to "modern management" practices, wherein administrative coordination proved itself to be more profitable than market coordination. The rationalization of production at this time also motivated the first great drive toward vertical integration (both backward and forward). Control of suppliers and sellers proved to be an essential component of the transition from market determination to administrative determination.

In the 1920s, diversification strategies came to the fore in the struggle for new markets. These strategies, and the resulting conglomerate industrial structure, were reinforced by the Great Depression, which closed off many markets and forced companies to search for new markets to engage their idle resources. These developments, in conjunction with antitrust regulation, are the source of the curtailment for the last 50 years of industry-specific concentration, whereas economywide concentration has continued to climb at a rapid rate.

The diversification strategy continues to dominate the U.S. industrial structure. In the post-World War II period this strategy has been important in the rise of the great multinational corporations based on U.S. control of foreign markets. This strategy has also led to the development of multiproduct lines based on control of specific technologies and to the development of multidivision production units.

Structural Diversification

This historical argument has suggested that to heighten profit and secure organizational survival the firm must face two variables that are controllable in the long run—technology and organizational structure—and one less-controllable variable—the environment. As the firm expands, new control devices and structures will be developed. The uncertainty of the environment and the search for higher profits through growth will push the organization toward a strategy that will guarantee one or more of the following: its markets (by increasing to national or international scope or by increasing product lines), its supplies (by vertical integration), or its productivity (by developing new technologies and modes of labor control). The strategy that any given firm or industry attempts to employ depends on the product it produces, the technology it utilizes, its internal organization, and its external constraints.

If an organization is to be successful in increasing its scale of activity, it must continue to develop new strategies and structures that will guarantee control of the labor force (Edwards, 1979), promote the development and implementation of new technology (Chandler, 1962), and maximize control of the external environment (Galbraith, 1973; O'Connor, 1973). The issue of organizational survival in an insecure environment, along with the profit motive, helps to explain how technology and control mechanisms interact to produce larger and larger firms in *some* industries. In other industries, the nature of the product or the available technologies will have determined the presence or absence of multinational links, capital-intensive production, high levels of unionization, and so on. From this perspective, the development of economic segmentation is seen as the result of working out organizational imperatives over a long period.

Steel, Food Processing, and Other Examples

Some examples will perhaps clarify the argument we are constructing. Steel companies have, on the whole, grown larger over time but have not diversified their product lines. On the other hand, many electronics firms and other high-technology corporations (e.g., United Technologies and North American Rockwell) have made a conscious strategy of diversification into new areas. A dual economy approach would place both high-technology growth companies and stagnant steel companies in one sector, the monopoly sector. But such an allocation does not capture what is important and unique about these industrial locations. Consider also the contrast between the food processing industries and large utilities, both of which might be placed in the core sector under a dualistic scheme. Food processing industries are heavily involved in foreign markets but are relatively labor intensive. Utilities, on the other hand, have minimal foreign involvement but are extremely capital intensive.

Although the specifics of this historic development are interesting, what should be particularly striking is the great diversity of the emergent industrial structures. Different organizational imperatives and environments produce different styles of management, modes of control, and corporate structures. In their drives to control labor, influence the government, and dominate other enterprises, corporations have developed and implemented a variety of strategies. These developments have resulted in an industrial structure typified by diversity along a great number of dimensions. Not only are there a variety of dimensions of industrial structure, but important differences may exist between firms that employ the same strategy but are at different levels of development.

Many dimensions of corporate structure that have possible direct relevance for labor force outcomes are discussed by Chandler (1977). Size is by far the most prominent of these because of its link to the rationalization of production and to the development of hierarchy at the workplace, but also included are multiplant versus single-plant structure, conglomeration or horizontal integration, vertical integration, capital intensity, and the development and utilization of new technology. An additional factor stressed by Chandler is the emergence of a new class of managers in the large modern corporation.

To review and systematize the argument, let us consider the following points. Corporate structure is developed with the goal of maximizing profit. Control of labor is an important strategy in moving toward this goal but not the only one. Other strategies may be purely market-oriented in nature, or they may be oriented toward increasing productivity through technological innovation. There is no rigid parallel arrangement of the various aspects of organizational structure; in fact, many of these dimensions are best seen as representing alternative strategies. This is certainly the case with vertical and horizontal integration, and it may be the case as well with the utilization of high-technology production systems versus the expansion of employment. Thus, we have a theoretical basis for arguing that many of the dimensions of corporate structure will not in fact group together, both because they represent alternative strategies and because each historic period and the problems and possibilities it presents leaves its own peculiar stamp on the industrial structure that emerges at that time.

The perspective we have just presented would suggest that there has been structural differentiation along enterprise and industry lines on the basis of different strategies utilized in the pursuit of profit. But this differentiation does not imply that only two sectors should emerge. Given the multiplicity of growth strategies, a great variety of differentiated structures and sectors should emerge. This differentiation implies both quantitative and qualitative distinctions as the various fractions of capital take on different organizational forms.

The Role of Unions

Trade unions have had a tremendous impact on working conditions in advanced industrial nations. In their struggle to improve conditions unions have taken advantage of whatever social resources were at their disposal, including those offered by specific organizational forms of capital. However, their history cannot be understood as simply a reflection of the history of the organization of capital.

In the 1880–1920 period, which saw the emergence of monopoly capital, trade union activity was dominated by a number of competing groups, each with a different agenda and vision of the future, and none of which was grounded in the emerging monopoly sector. The Knights of Labor had its greatest strength among the immigrant groups seeking integration on an equal basis into American society. The International Workers of the World possessed a revolutionary vision of the future and was strongest in the extractive industries of the developing Western frontier and in textiles in the East. The American Federation of Labor (AFL), founded in 1886, was an umbrella organization for craft unions, which were strongest in the small shops where skilled craft work still predominated (Commons, 1951; Perlman, 1932).

The 1920–1940 period saw the development of the mass production industries. It also saw the rapid growth of the AFL and the eventual splintering of the AFL with the Congress on Industrial Organization (CIO) over the issue of how to organize the new mass production industries. Capitalizing on the waves of sit-down strikes in the mid-1930s, the CIO made leaping organizational gains in these industries, but in the end the mass production industries were organized under a hybrid form of craft and industrial unionism by both the AFL and the CIO, which eventually rejoined forces in the 1950s (Boyer and Morais, 1955; Brecher, 1972).

The post-World War II period saw the emergence of the Cold War against the Soviet Union and successful red-baiting drives against American trade unions. This period culminated in the political purges of the McCarthy era and the passage of the infamous Taft–Hartley amendments to the National Labor Relations Act, which reinstated the injunction and allowed states to outlaw the union shop. A period of union stagnation followed. This period also saw the development of conglomerates spreading across industrial sectors as the newest organizational form of capital. Because of the general social climate, unions were unable to deal effectively with this new organizational form of capital or to turn it to their advantage as they had done earlier with the development of mass production techniques (Brecher, 1972).

The period since the 1960s has seen the spread of the conglomerate, the development of the multinational organization of capital, and a continued union inability to devise adequate strategies to deal with these organizational forms (Brecher, 1972; Litwack, 1962). Indeed, this period has witnessed union retrenchment in all areas except the public and service sectors, in which capital is anchored to given locales by the nature of the product or service and plants and resources cannot be shuffled around the nation or the globe.

During certain historic periods the trade union movement has gained great advantage from new organizational forms of capital. During other periods, the trade union movement and the organization of capital have developed in highly autonomous directions. In the most recent period, trade unions have been stymied by the organization of conglomerates and multinationals and have suffered a period of retrenchment. Only during the 1930s was there a convergence between the organization of capital and the organization of labor in the emerging mass production industries. Even this convergence, however, was dependent on the general social setting of the Great Depression, with its massive general strikes, its high level of solidarity between the active labor force and the unemployed, and the historic compromise between labor and capital that resulted in the New Deal.

The argument we are developing here is that it is misleading to think of the history of the workplace as simply the history of different strategies developed by management to control labor. This is only one part of the story. The history of the workplace is also the history of the development of organizational strategies by capital that have nothing to do with labor control but are primarily oriented toward competition with other capitalists or toward relations with the state. Further, it is the history of an autonomous labor movement, which also developed strategies and structures that were sometimes aided and sometimes impeded by the organizational strategies of capital.

A RESOURCE APPROACH TO THE STUDY OF INDUSTRIAL STRUCTURE

Our reading of the organizational history of capital and labor indicates the possibility that corporate structure may provide a resource to workers for use in the battle over working conditions. This is because some of these structures were developed with goals other than labor control in mind but also because of the inadvertant and unexpected consequences of the development of certain types of corporate structure. The capacities for worker power created by automation and capital-intensive production is a possible example of the former case, and the organizing economies of scale provided to labor unions by large corporate size is a possible example of the latter case. Internal and technical factors, such as size and capital intensity of production, which are more proximate to the workplace, are suggested by this theory to be of more consequence for working conditions than are more distant factors, such as profit rates. However, it is obvious that such market factors as growth rates and profit rates will also have a potential impact on workplace outcomes.

One of the most important themes emerging from this new perspective is the conceptualization of structure in terms of resources and vulnerabilities for the actors at the workplace provided by the various dimensions of economic and labor market organization. This type of resource approach is already widely utilized in the sociology of occupations and labor markets.[2] The project at hand is to apply it systematically to the study of the impact of capital organization at the workplace.

Our theoretical perspective, which indicates that the structural organization of capital may serve as a resource for workers as well as a vehicle for the attainment of management strategies of control and profit maximization, has a variety of intellectual roots. Blauner (1964) and Blau and Meyer (1971) both exhibit this perspective in their discussions of automated technology. Edwards indicates it repeatedly, if only implicitly, in "Contested Terrain" by showing how the contradictions of each historic solution to the problem of capitalist control at the workplace become the impetus to a new round of struggle. Even bureaucratic control offers some possibility for increased worker power as the workings of the firm become more transparent, more public, and, therefore, more open to participation. Similar implications can be drawn from research in institutional and labor economics that analyzes the interaction of corporate structures and union power (see Levinson, 1967). This interpretation is also utilized by Schervish (1983) in an analysis of the organizational determinants of types and rates of unemployment.

In implementing this approach it is important to specify carefully the key actors and the mechanisms available to them to attain their goals. Thus, when we are seeking to understand the firm's role, we must study corporate decision making and behavior. Such a study must focus on the rationalization of production, the creation of specific corporate structures such as internal labor markets, and so on.

To understand workers and their role in determining workplace outcomes, we must look not only at the interconnected tasks and internal labor markets of rationalized production systems that may allow workers greater possibilities for power but also at the factors that facilitate the exercise of power. Unionization or the threat of unionization, either of which is a powerful tool for the attainment of improved working conditions, is an important example of these organizational factors. The point to be stressed here is that, when analyzing the labor force as an actor, we need to pay particular attention to how the organizational features of the workplace may promote or retard the exercise of collective power. Firms may prosper or fail based on market forces, but their work forces fare better or worse based on the structure of the workplace as an important resource in their struggle for benefits.[3]

Within the dual economy framework, capital structure was seen only as a resource for the capitalist class. Large size and monopoly market position allowed capitalists in core firms to manipulate workers as a means of reducing turnover costs and diffusing discontent. The insight that economic structure is created and manipulated by the capitalist class is valuable, but it tells only one side of the story. Economic structures are created through interaction with labor, and the structures have effects that are limited and defined by the collective and individual actions of labor. The resource approach allows us to overcome the conspiracy aspect of the dual economy interpretation of the effects of industrial structure. Categories of workers are not simply matched with categories of jobs in a totally manipulative fashion so that social divisions parallel workplace divisions and the working class is divided against itself. Corporate structures, motivated by the drive for profit, may inadvertently provide workers with substantial resources for use in their own struggle for control.

Three Examples

Discussion of some of the key dimensions of economic structure will help to illustrate the utility of the resource approach. It has been argued that a firm's monopoly market position results in improved conditions for workers because the firm utilizes its discretionary resources to "buy off" workers as a form of social control. This interpretation seriously underplays the role of workers as active subjects in this interchange. The effects of concentration can also be interpreted as indicating that workers are able successfully to demand a larger share of the profits from the owners of monopoly firms. Under this interpretation, higher wages are not given as a mechanism of social control but are conceded in response to demands from workers because costs can be passed on to customers.

A second example is provided by the role of capital intensity in the determination of working conditions. Increases in capital intensity are initially implemented by management to increase productivity through increased capital utilization and to control the labor force through technical means of control. However, capital intensity as a mechanism for increased technical control of labor has a substantial potential for backfiring. Under capital-intensive conditions, workers become responsible for the care and maintenance of expensive production equipment. Workers may be able to secure improved conditions through the implicit threat of misuse, sabotage, or outright destruction of this machinery. This is perhaps part of what is suggested, but left implicit, by Blauner's (1964) idea of greater "responsibility" emerging from automated production.[4]

The crucial role of company size in the workplace epitomizes how industrial structure may operate as a resource for workers as well as for owners and managers. Large firms have the resources to manipulate the environment in which they operate to maximize profits. They can manipulate consumers, coerce other companies, construct economic realities that governments must take into account in policy development, and reputedly pay above market wages to ensure a compliant work force.

Examining organizational size as a possible worker resource, we would ask how the corporate organization of large firms can serve as a resource in the struggle for improved working conditions. Part of the answer is that workers in large firms have greater possibilities for communication and organization than do workers dispersed in a multitude of small shops. Specification of this as a crucial mechanism in determining wages is not a new insight; Marx made this same argument in 1867. The labor struggles of the 1930s in this country provide a clear example of the way in which size can be used as a worker resource. Conditions in the large mass production industries were some of the worst in the nation prior to the organizing drives of John L. Lewis and the CIO. The power of the large companies was unchecked by worker organization; regular speedups and extremely harsh conditions were the result. The development of the sit-down strike provided a mechanism for the unskilled workers in these industries to take advantage of the organizational possibilities offered by large-scale enterprises. Once workers had a mechanism for tapping into the power offered by large-scale operations, wages rose rapidly and overall conditions improved dramatically (Brecher, 1972; Brooks, 1960).

Other dimensions of industrial structure can also be analyzed as providing possible resources for capital and labor. Conglomerate organization is an increasingly important feature of modern industrial structure that obviously provides substantial resources for capital. For example, internal pricing arrangements allow the judicious realization of profits in carefully selected locations, facilitating predatory pricing practices and tax avoidance. From the standpoint of labor, conglomerate organization may offer the possibility of gaining toeholds in new industries by following the parent company into new production activities. On a craft, rather than enterprise, basis, the successful organization of loading-dock and lower white-collar workers by the Teamsters exemplifies this possibility.

Multinationals, an increasingly important organizational form in the latest stage of capitalist development, offer tremendous advantages to capital but relatively few to labor. The ability of multinationals to shop in the global market for labor and to engage in the multiple sourcing of production components allows tremendous latitude for undermining local and national wage standards (Bluestone and Harrison, 1980; Mandel, 1975). These features parallel and amplify the advantages available to domestic conglomerates. However, multinational organization creates vulnerabilities for labor without providing any compensating resources. These realities pose a major problem for organized labor today, a problem for which an adequate solution has not been devised.[5]

The Worker as Active Subject

As a starting point for a theoretical model to replace dualism, we have elaborated on the resource perspective as a new approach to understanding the role of capital structure at the workplace. This approach argues that different dimensions of capital structure can be considered both as resources for owners and managers and as potential resources for workers. Under this approach, labor markets are conceptualized, not as direct reflections of capital structure, but in terms of different structures of worker resources and vulnerabilities provided by the combination of firm, industry, and job characteristics. The resource approach implies that we need to refocus our attention on workers as well as on firms as active participants in determining workplace outcomes.

The resource perspective also demands a multidimensional approach to industrial segmentation; an approach that is strongly in accord both with criticisms of the dual approach and with emergent research in this area. Also, the resource approach does not lead us to the expectation that powerful corporate sectors will be aligned in a totally parallel fashion with good working conditions.

In conclusion, we feel that the resource approach is more sociological in orientation than the dual economy/dual labor market approach is. The dual approach relies primarily on economic interpretations of the forces at play. Key factors are mediated by market mechanisms and corporate profitability. Worker outcomes, from higher wages to discrimination against minority workers, are seen as the result of systems of control mediated primarily by market considerations. The dual model presents only one part of what takes place on the job site. It ignores important social relations and issues of power. In our revised resource approach the key concepts that have motivated the study of stratification are allowed to come to the fore. Issues of power and social relations on the job rather than cost/benefit analysis, become the primary focus. Our argument is not that the economic interpretations are incorrect. Rather, we are arguing that they present only one aspect of the determining factors of economic and labor market segmentation, and more sociological concerns cannot be ignored, least of all by sociologists themselves.

EXPLORING ECONOMIC STRUCTURE AND LABOR MARKET OUTCOMES

The ideas presented previously indicate that we should investigate a greater variety of dimensions of economic segmentation than the single dimension allowed by the dual economy model. However, these ideas do not allow for complete a priori specification of a new model of industrial structure. For this reason, we shall proceed in a largely exploratory fashion in our study of economic structure and labor segmentation. In this endeavor we shall develop and utilize a variety of both categorical and continuous measures of industrial structure, and we shall employ data from the company as well as the industry level of analysis.

Industrial Structure and Workers' Earnings

The theoretical arguments developed previously specify two different aspects of industrial structure as potentially important for the determination of workplace outcomes: market factors and internal organizational factors. Market factors, although external to the actual workplace, are important for corporate survival and growth. These include profit rate, autonomy, concentration, regulation, growth, and foreign involvement. Workplace factors can be further divided into either technical or organizational elements. The key technical factor that can be measured across productive units is capital intensity. The key internal organizational factors are size, productivity, and unionization.[6]

Multiple indicators of these concepts will provide the empirical basis for our investigation. Workers' earnings will provide the major dependent variable to be analyzed. Individual-level earnings is selected as our focus because of its centrality to prior research and to the everyday concerns of the labor force.

The Social Mediation of the Impact of Industrial Structure on Earnings

To understand the impact of economic structure on workplace outcomes we must realize that these effects take place through social relationships that are highly variable across different groups. Two primary sets of social factors will concern us here. First, class and unionization variables tap important forms of social organization that can be expected to mediate the impact of industrial structure on workers' earnings. Second, demographic and human capital variables constitute a set of individual characteristics whose effects can be expected to be mediated by industrial structure. Labor demand, or the provision of full-time employment, is also expected to be an important mechanism through which the effects of industrial structure are felt at the workplace.

The role of industrial structure in determining workplace outcomes may be very different depending on one's class location (Rees and Shultz, 1970). For managers, the important feature of enterprises may be their large bureaucratically structured hierarchies. Within this large and steeply graded hierarchy, new managers are evaluated on the basis of educational credentials and performance; if they reach the upper levels of the managerial hierarchy, they have access to very large pools of resources. Given these conditions, we can expect large earnings returns to education and ability for managers in large firms. For members of the working class, employment in this sector may mean that they face a very different set of conditions. The work setting may be more alienating and allow for less control on their part than under less-centralized systems of production. For workers, the existence of large pools of corporate resources may mean only that management has the ability to undercut employment security by runaway shops or the ability to deskill work activity through technological automation.

Unionization can also be expected to mediate the impact of industrial structure on working conditions, at least for the working class (Levinson, 1967). A powerful union may be able to take advantage of centralized production conditions and the possibilities for organization opened by large numbers of workers laboring on the same shop floor under harsh and alienating working conditions. Organized workers may be able to defend themselves aptly against the power of large pools of managerial resources and even win a share of those resources for themselves in terms of higher wages or better working conditions.

The role of individual characteristics in determining workplace outcomes can be expected to be importantly affected by industrial characteristics. For instance, high earnings for whites may be conditional on their privileged access to employment in sectors with large institutional resources. Similarly, human capital is realized at the workplace only as allowed by enterprise economies of scale, productive efficiency, hiring and evaluation practices, and so on, all of which vary by industrial sector. In investigating this process of social mediation we shall pay particular attention to the role of gender. Although this is a theoretically underdeveloped area of analysis, recent empirical work indicates that industrial structure may be one of the most important determinants of women's unequal role in the workplace (Bridges, 1980; Hodson and England, 1982).

Finally, an important part of the impact of industrial structure on earnings is expected to be mediated by the hours of work provided. The volume of demand for labor time and its regularity are key theoretical components of the hypothesized role of industrial structure. The provision of part-time and seasonal work versus full-time year-round work is expected to account for a substantial portion of the impact of industrial structure on earnings.

The Unit of Analysis—Industry or Corporation?

The remaining issue to be resolved in our attempt to build a new model of industrial structure and earnings concerns the appropriate unit of analysis for that study. Most theorists within the dual economy approach consider the firm to be the ideal unit of analysis.

> It is economic size, not industrial location, that defines firms in the center economy. (Averitt, 1968:66)

> All of these points are intended to suggest that it may be growing relatively more important to study variations in employment and income variables among and within groups based on corporate size and power—controlling for industrial product and price variations—rather than studying industrial variations and controlling for establishment size and market concentration. It may be, that is, that variations within industries (as conventionally defined) have begun to equal inter-industry variations in their importance for explaining the behavior of employers and the incomes of workers. The differences between giant corporations and single-unit establishments may effectively outweigh differences among industries. (Gordon, 1972:126)

The basic rationale here is that firms, not industries, are the important economic actors. As such, firms make and implement the key decisions influencing economic and labor segmentation.

Most economic data collected, however, are aggregated to the industry level. For this reason, many researchers argue that industry is an adequate proxy for economic segmentation originating at the level of the firm. The argument generally includes three points. First, firms in specific industrial locations generally share many characteristics. Second, even firms that are deviant on some dimensions often resemble the industry profile on characteristics such as technology, profits, wages, and job stability. Third, trade union struggle and federal legislation have had primarily industrywide effects, rather than firm-specific effects.[7]

A central problem with these arguments is that firms and industries are not necessarily interchangeable units of analysis. Researchers have been too willing to argue in favor of industries as the unit of analysis on the basis of data availability or to engage in specious arguments about which is the "better" unit of analysis. From a theoretical perspective, the question is whether the capital structure of an industry can provide a resource for workers or whether only the capital structure of the employing enterprise is relevant. Posed as an either/or proposition, the question is unanswerable. Different processes may well occur at each level. There are, in fact, three levels of analysis among which we would like to maintain conceptual distinctions. The *shop floor* is where relations of production occur. *Companies* are where organizational imperatives operate. Finally, market relations are dominant in *industries*. Of course, all these levels are influenced by some common forces, for example, technology and union struggle. However, we have no reason to assume that an entirely consistent set of processes operates at all levels. Arguments about which level is best overlook the different forces that may be operating at different levels.

In selecting shops, firms, or industries as the unit of analysis, one should attempt to link concepts to the appropriate unit of measurement. Some concepts, such as organizational size, are most appropriately measured at the firm level.

Other concepts, such as technology, may apply to an industrywide environment: all firms operating in the industry must attempt to match the "state-of-the-art" technology in that industry. Arguments about which is the best level of analysis should be replaced by arguments about which concepts are truly operational at which levels.

To conclude, the methodological debate over the level of measurement of industrial structure has often been biased by the availability of data and has been less than rigorous in its arguments. An important part of our project will be to investigate the effects of the various dimensions of industrial structure at as many levels of measurement as possible. It is hoped that our efforts will allow the methodological debate on the appropriate unit of analysis to generate new theoretical insights unconstrained by the limitations of investigations restricted to one level of measurement.

WHAT WE EXPECT TO FIND

In this section we shall attempt to summarize the theoretical discussion in the previous chapters in the form of a set of expectations about the empirical results of the study. Although many of these will be stated in the form of hypotheses, this style is chosen mainly for clarity of presentation. Because we shall be relying heavily on exploratory statistical techniques to drive our models of industrial structure, it is impossible at this time to develop a complete set of hypotheses about the findings. The expectations stated here are intended more to guide the presentation of results than to represent a formal test of theory.

Industrial Structure as a Predictor of Earnings

Corporate structure is expected to be a significant predictor of earnings. This follows from the argument that corporate structure provides important resources for both capitalists and employees in the struggle over the conditions of work.

When controls are introduced for the other major determinants of workers' earnings, industrial structure is still expected to exert a powerful influence on earnings. This expectation is derived from prior theoretical work that specifies industrial structure as a direct determinant of earnings, not just as a sorting mechanism for workers with different attributes (see Bluestone, 1970). The theoretical argument here is that earnings are determined not only by individual characteristics and by the matching of these into corporate structures but also in an independent fashion by corporate organization as a structural resource. This expectation is also suggested by a large body of prior research on labor segmentation (Beck, Horan, and Tolbert, 1978; Bibb and Form, 1977; Hodson, 1978; Stolzenberg, 1978; Tolbert, Horan, and Beck, 1980).

The Dimensions of Industrial Structure

A second set of expectations deals with the separate roles of the various dimensions of corporate structure. The leading hypothesis is that the internal organization of production is more important in determining earnings than are the technical factors that in turn are more important than the market factors. The rationale for the hypothesized ordering is the proximity of each aspect of corporate structure of the workplace, the site where wage determination occurs. If, instead of studying employees' earnings, we were studying firms' growth patterns, we would probably specify market factors as the most important dimension. The findings relating to this hypothesis will provide an important, though incomplete, test of competing theories about the role of corporate structure in determining earnings. We reviewed a variety of theoretical approaches that offer interpretations of this relationship: neoclassical economics, labor economics, institutional economics, Marxism, the sociology of work, and organizational theory. All of these theoretical traditions, except neoclassical economics, stress the importance of internal organizational factors of production. Technical factors are stressed by organizational theory and, in an approach/avoidance fashion, by Marxism. Market factors are stressed by economic approaches to labor market segmentation. Obviously, because of the impossibility of attaching broad theoretical traditions directly to only one set of factors, this test cannot be definitive. However, evaluation of the relative importance of the different factors should allow us to make an informed judgment about the validity of the various theoretical approaches to industrial structure and workplace outcomes. Our expectations about the roles of specific dimensions are detailed next.

Internal Production Factors

ORGANIZATIONAL SIZE   Organizational size is expected to have a positive impact on wages for two reasons. First, the rationalization of production and the need for long-range planning horizons in large enterprises demands that the factors of production be provided in an orderly fashion. For this reason the owners of large enterprises may provide increased wage payments to ensure a stable and compliant work force. Size is also important in determining the viability of union-organizing drives and other forms of workers' collective action. Under both these arguments, one important component of higher earnings in large firms will result from the provision of year-round full-time employment. This expectation, in one form or another, can be derived from all the theoretical schools reviewed except perhaps neoclassical economics.

PRODUCTIVITY   Productivity is expected to have a positive impact on wages because of the increased size of the pie over which owners and employers struggle. This interpretation is supported most strongly by institutional economics.

UNIONIZATION   Unionization is expected to have a positive impact on wages because of the collective power it provides workers. This interpretation is supported by all the theoretical schools reviewed.

Technical Factors of Production

CAPITAL INTENSITY   Capital intensity is expected to have a positive impact on wages because of the increased complexity of work resulting in an increased reliance on firm-specific skills and full-time workers, because wage increases can more easily be made when labor represents a relatively small portion of the costs of production, and because the use of expensive capital equipment gives workers who are responsible for it an increased base of power. This expectation is supported by institutional economics, by the sociology of work, and, to some extent, by Marxist writings.

Market Factors

GOVERNMENT REGULATION   Government regulation is expected by the institutional and labor economics traditions to have a positive impact on wages because of the guaranteed profits and working conditions associated with regulation. However, regulation might be expected by neoclassical economics to have a negative impact on wages because of the reduced productivity and inefficiency supposedly associated with government regulation.

CONCENTRATION   Concentration is expected by neoclassical and institutional economics to have a positive impact on wages and earnings because of the increased size of the pie out of which benefits are secured. However, counterarguments from labor economics, and from some researchers within the institutional school, lead to the expectation that concentration will have a negative impact on workers' wages because of monopolistic restriction of output and employment, and because of the tremendous increase in corporate power associated with concentration.

GROWTH   Growth is expected by neoclassical, institutional, and labor economics to have a positive impact on wages because of the increased demand for labor and the resulting inflation in the competitive price of labor.

PROFIT   Profit is expected by the various schools of economics to have a positive impact on wages because of the increased size of the pie out of which benefits can be won.

CORPORATE AUTONOMY   Corporate autonomy is expected by institutional economics to have a positive impact on wages because of the exploitation of more competitive firms by ones with greater monopolistic power. The costs of this exploitation is expected to be partially absorbed by employees in the exploited firms.

FOREIGN INVOLVEMENT   Foreign involvement is expected by institutional economics, and perhaps also by Marxist scholars, to have a positive impact on workers' wages. Some of the economic profits of imperialism, initially captured by U.S.-based multinationals, may be repatriated to the domestic work forces of these firms to ensure support for imperialism and a massive military budget. It is also possible, however, to derive from many of these same writings the counterexpectation that multinationals may use their positions to undercut domestic wages, though it is not clear that this effect would be specific to the labor force of the multinational itself.

Industrial Structure and Labor Markets

The third set of expectations deals with the association of corporate structure and labor markets per se. Prior literature has specified size as a central dimension of industrial structure, and this dimension will serve as a basis against which the various hypotheses in this section can be organized. (On the central role of size in industrial organization see Aldrich, 1972; Blau and Meyer, 1971; Freeman, 1973; Kimberly, 1976; Marsh and Mannari, 1981; Mileti, Gillespie, and Haas, 1977; Mohr, 1971; Porter and Lawler, 1965.) By specifying size as a central dimension of industrial structure in this section we do not wish to retreat from our position that industrial structure is a multidimensional phenomenon. In this section, as in others, alternative dimensions will also be examined for potentially interesting interpretations and insights.

Large corporate size is expected to be associated with high rates of unionization, both because of organizing economics of scale and because of the importance of specific historical events in union-organizing history, such as the key organizing victories in the 1930s in mass production industries. Large size is also expected to be associated with a predominance of workers from dominant social groups (i.e., white male workers). Majority workers are expected to have privileged access to these superior positions. Small corporate size is expected to be associated with a prevalence of poverty-level wages because of the extreme lack of organizational resources in such workplaces.

Large enterprises are also expected to employ disproportionate numbers of managers, professionals, and other white-collar workers. The exception follows from Poulantzas's argument in "Classes in Contemporary Capitalism" that the monopoly sector is the home of the new middle class of salaried employees and from Braverman's (1974) and Edwards's (1979) arguments that the organization of tasks into bureaucratically organized white-collar jobs is an important form of labor control increasingly utilized in large firms. As a counterexpectation, organizational theory argues that the administrative ratio is lower in large firms, suggesting a smaller proportion of such salaried employees (Blau and Meyer, 1971).

Industrial Structure as a Mediator of Other Determinants of Earnings

RACE, GENDER, AND EDUCATION   The effects of race, gender, and education are expected to be substantially reduced when corporate structure is introduced as a control. This expectation arises from the argument that race, gender, and educational level have an effect on workers' earnings partially through sorting workers into sectors with different pay and employment opportunities. Under this argument the organization of production is seen as playing a key role in determining outcomes that are observed at the level of the individual.

FAMILY BACKGROUND   Family background and corporate structure, however, are expected to have largely independent effects on earnings. Organizations are expected to be relatively "blind" to the social background of persons (those characteristics derived from their family of origin) aside from the dimensions of race, gender, and education. The social and psychological mechanisms through which such factors influence earnings are not expected to be strongly affected by corporate structure.[8] (For a counterargument see Beck *et al.*, 1978)

SOCIAL CLASS   The income differential between the classes is expected to be wider in the large-enterprise sector because of the importance of income inequality as a mechanism of social control in these corporations (see Wright, 1979).

EDUCATION AND EXPERIENCE   Greater earnings returns to education and experience are expected in large corporations owing to the rationalization of production in such enterprises and the need to reward characteristics deemed important for the correct functioning of standardized rules and procedures.[9]

The final expectation about economic structure and workers' earnings again involves the relationship between class and economic structure. Wright and Perrone (1977) find that managers have much higher earnings returns from education than do workers. This finding, in conjunction with our own expectation that the highest returns from education occur in the large enterprise sector, leads to the expectation that *the very highest educational returns will go to managers in large firms*.

Industrial Structure and Social Groups

Corporate structure is expected to have a greater role in determining the earnings of manual workers than in determining the earnings of managerial workers (see Rees and Shultz, 1970). This expectation follows from our interpretation of corporate structure as a resource to be utilized in the determination of benefits. Manual workers are expected to rely on and to be vulnerable to corporate structures to a greater extent than are white-collar and managerial workers, whose earnings will be more strongly determined by the individual human capital characteristics, such as education, that they bring to the workplace. (*Owners'* profits are no doubt also strongly affected by corporate structure, but this is not the primary object of analysis here.)

The earnings of women and blacks should also be more strongly determined by corporate structure than those, respectively, of men and whites. Again, the reasoning is that these workers have less ability to secure human capital resources and to utilize these resources to secure benefits at the workplace. Because of social discrimination against women and blacks involving the attainment and utilization of personal resources, their earnings can be expected to be more strongly determined by the organizational resources they find at the workplace.

The evaluation of these five groups of hypotheses should not only give us a good overview of the general impact of corporate structure on earnings but should also provide the detailed analysis necessary for a more fruitful understanding of the manner in which that impact occurs. We hope our findings and their interpretation within a resource framework will contribute toward the development of a more sophisticated theory of social stratification that links organizational theory to earlier understandings of social class and the role of individual characteristics.

CONCLUSIONS

In previous chapters we argued that the division of the U.S. economy into central and peripheral sectors does not constitute an adequate representation of the structure of that economy and that the single dynamic of increasing concentration and centralization does not offer a sufficient theoretical basis for comprehending economic segmentation. Rather, it is only one of several dynamics, based on the interaction of profit seeking, technology, control structures, environment, union struggle, and government intervention, that act to produce economic segmentation. We also questioned the assumption that these multiple dimensions align in a consistent pattern with high and low values grouping together and having similar effects.

In this chapter we developed additional concepts, primarily from the complex organizations literature and attempted to organize these within a truly multidimensional framework. The various separable dimensions of industrial structure were seen as representing resources and vulnerabilities for workers in their struggle to attain higher wages and better working conditions. We also outlined some organizing expectations about the impact of economic structure on earnings. In the next chapter we shall discuss the corporate- and industry-level data sets collected for this research project and present some new methods for organizing these data for the study of workplace outcomes. In subsequent chapters, as guided by these expectations and models, we shall attempt to map the differences in working conditions among economic sectors and across the dimensions of industrial structure.

NOTES TO CHAPTER 3

1. With the development of capitalist enterprises into larger and more complex units of production, the concept of a ''free market'' became increasingly irrelevant. The pricing and allocation of resources, labor, and commodities came increasingly to be determined by administrative factors and conscious design. These developments eventually lead to a situation where the external market, as well as the organizational and technical factors of production, was consciously manipulated by the ''visible hand'' of administrative decision making.

2. The dimensions of capital structure are obviously not the only important factors in determining the nature of labor market segmentation. The dimensions of skill, routinization, licensing of workers, and functional task specialization all create different occupational and labor market structures (Freedman, 1976; Kalleberg, Wallace, and Althauser, 1981; Kaufman, 1981; Schervish, 1981, 1983). These kinds of occupational factors have often been conceptualized in the sociology of work literature in terms of the resources they provide workers vis-a-vis employers (Caplow, 1954; Hall, 1975; Montagna, 1977; Ritzer, 1977). The dimensions of occupational structure and economic segmentation are related but not coterminous; the two sets of factors affect each other as well as influencing outcomes in the labor market.

3. This point is similar to Giddens's (1973) argument that paratechnical relations are the key to understanding class fractions in the modern working class.

4. A compelling example of this possibility is provided by the pivotal role of the Iranian oilfield workers in the anti-imperialist revolution of 1978 to 1979. The threat of sabotage, and sometimes the actual sabotage and destruction, of extremely expensive capital equipment by Iranian oilfield workers was crucial in destabilizing the Shah of Iran's regime, both domestically and internationally. This role could have been occupied by no other sector of the labor force because only the oilfield workers were in a structural position that allowed them to disrupt the economy to this extent (see Holliday, 1978; Nore and Turner, 1980; Sweezy and Magdoff, 1979).

5. Although multinational organization and large organizational size are clearly associated, the different pattern of resources and vulnerabilities provided by each clearly testifies to the need to deal analytically with these factors as separate dimensions of industrial structure.

6. It would be possible to develop a model of how the various dimensions of corporate structure interact to determine each other. In such a model size would clearly have a leading role. However, such a model would be largely tangential to the project at hand and will not be elaborated.

7. Spilerman (1977:579) has even argued that industries offer a better unit of analysis than firms because all firms in an industry are "likely to have comparable technologies and organizational forms and are subject to identical fluctuations in demand for their products."

8. The role of family background in determining the subsequent position of individuals in the stratification system has been extensively studied within the status-attainment approach. In the form cast by Blau and Duncan (1967), the attainment model posits the dependence of individuals' educational attainments on their parents' occupational status and education. Individuals' occupational statuses depend on their parents' occupational status and education and on their own educational attainment. Individuals' earnings are dependent on all prior variables in the model. This basic form has been elaborated into what has come to be known as the Wisconsin model by Sewell and his associates (see Sewell and Hauser, 1975, and the works cited therein.) This elaborated model introduces measured intelligence, educational and occupational aspirations, educational and occupational encouragement from peers, parents, and teachers, and other factors into the basic model. (See also Leibowitz, 1977, for a survey of the literature in this field.)

9. As noted earlier, it is possible to derive an opposite expectation about the earnings returns to education in large enterprises from the theoretical literature on the topic. Working from the argument that the neoclassical human capital model of wage attainment works better under competitive than under monopolistic conditions, we would expect higher returns to education and experience in the more competitive sectors. We feel that this quandary again results from the unanalyzed nature of the divergent dimensions of industrial structure as summarized under the concept of a dual economy. It is hoped that an analysis that is sensitive to the role of competing dimensions will help to resolve this ambiguity. In any event, although the role of differential educational returns has been argued by some to be central to the study of industrial structure and workplace outcomes, in the current analysis attention has been shifted from this area and focused instead on understanding the role of the separable dimensions of industrial structure.

4

Industry and Enterprise Data and Measures

INTRODUCTION

The present study consists of two major components. In the first component, we shall use industry-level data and a national sample to analyze the impact of industrial structure on workers in the United States. Industry data were collected from a number of primary sources. The industry data set developed and utilized for this study is to the best of our knowledge the most extensive and up-to-date data set of its kind. This industry data will be linked to persons in the March–May match 1973 Current Population Survey (CPS). This sample was chosen because it contains detailed data on employment, hours worked, earnings, and unionization. And, of the CPS data available, it is the nearest in time to the second survey utilized in this study—the 1975 Wisconsin survey. We shall select for study private sector employees in the Experienced Civilian Labor Force[1] (ECLF). There are 20,643 respondents in the ECLF subsample of the CPS.

The second component of the proposed study relies on the use of enterprise-level data. These data were collected from various published and unpublished sources for the employers of the respondents to the 1975 Wisconsin study, which also includes extensive labor force participation information. This project constituted our major data collection task.

The Wisconsin data set includes all the variables contained in the CPS, plus name of employer and data on social background, school performance, intelligence, and many other factors. This data set does not, however, constitute a representative national sample. The 1975 Wisconsin survey was conducted on a subsample of Wisconsin high school graduates initially interviewed in their senior year, 1957. In that year the entire cohort was surveyed. In 1964 and again in 1975, follow-up studies on a one-third random sample of the cohort were conducted under the direction of William Sewell and Robert Hauser. The 1975 follow-up study of 10,317 individuals achieved an unusually high response rate of 89%. Of the respondents, 56% are private sector employees in the ECLF. Our initial sample size is, therefore, 5140. In the 1975 survey extensive data were collected on educational and occupational attainments, labor force participation and earnings, plus several other areas of family and work life more tangential to the present study. In addition, name of employer was recorded for those respondents who had worked in the past 5 years. Except for name of employer, these data were coded, cleaned, and compiled in a machine-readable form before the current project was begun. To this data set we shall add both the enterprise-level and the industry-level information collected.

The Wisconsin sample is basically composed of men and women in their late 30s living in the north central United States. It has relatively few blacks and no young or old people. It is, therefore, an unsuitable sample for an in-depth study of secondary workers. However, we believe that it is suitable for a more broadly conceived study of the impact of industrial structure on workplace outcomes. (See Sewell and Hauser, 1975, for tests establishing that this sample is representative of a similarly constrained national sample.) The Wisconsin data have provided the empirical base for important contributions to the field of status attainment research in sociology (see Sewell and Hauser, 1975, and the works cited therein). The wealth of detail that this data set provides on social background and on work and educational careers offers a unique opportunity to incorporate sophisticated measures of the social forces and mechanisms that are related to the impact of industrial structure on workplace outcomes. For these reasons a large part of our analysis will focus on this data set.

It is perhaps easiest to think of our research design as a two-factor experimental design with four cells, one of which is missing. One factor is composed of the two samples—a national CPS sample and a Wisconsin sample. The second factor is composed of two levels of measurement—industry-level data and firm-level data. The four cells are then (1) a national sample with industry-level data; (2) a national sample with firm-level data (the missing cell); (3) a Wisconsin sample with industry-level data; and (4) a Wisconsin sample with firm-level data. A comparison of selected analyses run on the CPS sample and on the Wisconsin sample will allow us to evaluate the adequacy of the Wisconsin data for making inferences about the effects of corporate structure at the national level. In addition, for purposes of comparison, we shall run selected analyses on a CPS subsample composed of high school graduates in their late 30s. Thus, although we do not have a national sample with firm-level industrial structure data, we believe that this research design will allow us to make reasonable inferences about the impact of firm-level measures of industrial structure on employee earnings at a national level. This research design also allows us to evaluate the argument that the growth of large cross-industry conglomerates and extreme intra-industry variance in economic characteristics renders industry-level measures of economic structure invalid. The demonstration of similar effects for industry-level and enterprise-level measures of the same industrial structure concepts would indicate that industry remains a viable unit of analysis.

The enterprise- and industry-level data collected will be used to construct both continuous and categorical measures of industrial structure. Used as continuous measures, the data directly tap key components of industrial structure—size, concentration, foreign involvement, and so on. This use avoids many of the problems associated with the "industrial sector" approach, for example, the placement of qualitatively different industries in the same sector, the question of how many industrial sectors to construct, and the inability to discern exactly what characteristic of the different sectors produces observed outcomes.

The data will also be used to sort enterprises and industries into economic sectors. Sectors are conceptually preferable to gradational measures under certain conditions. Many differences between enterprises are primarily qualitative in nature rather than operating along a continuum. For example, monopoly power implies qualitatively different effects at different levels. A company in a monopoly position may be able to set prices and restrain output at will, whereas an oligopolistic company may only be able to extract a small premium contingent on the cooperation of other large firms in the same industry. Similarly, a certain level of foreign involvement implies the ability to shift production to any spot in the world, an option not available below some specific level. Various dimensions of industrial structure may also interact in ways that do not produce continuous outcomes. For example, an industry that has a high degree of concentration and foreign involvement is qualitatively different from an industry that has a high degree of concentration but a low degree of foreign involvement. The different combinations of characteristics imply options that may not be adequately indicated by continuous measures.

Both the continuous and the categorical approaches to the measurement of industrial structure have strengths and weaknesses. In sketching as full a picture as possible of the impact of industrial structure on working conditions we shall utilize the data we have collected in the form of both continuous and categorical measures. Proceeding in this way, we hope that key findings can be verified under different operationalizations. In this way we shall learn more, both about the impact of industrial structure and about how to conceptualize and measure it, than we would have learned by arbitrarily choosing one type of measurement design.

Now that the basic research design has been presented, we can proceed to the details of data collection and to a specification of the variables that we collected. First, we shall discuss the industry-level data collected. This discussion will include sections specifying the data collected and detailing the manipulation of these data into analysis variables. Second, we shall discuss the company-level data collected. This discussion will include sections on the coding of company names and data, the exact company variables collected, the problem of missing data, and the transformation of the data into analysis variables. Third, we shall identify the individual-level variables extracted from the CPS and from the Wisconsin survey, at which time we shall also specify the exact subsamples to be studied. Finally, we shall offer our thoughts and reflections on the task of collecting industry- and enterprise-level data from archival sources.

INDUSTRY DATA

The first step in handling the industry-level data was to transform the data from various sources into a consistent set of industry codes. The 1970 Census Industry Classification was chosen for this purpose because we anticipated using the data in conjunction with individual-level data sets that employ the Census Industry Classification.

Data selected from the ''Census of Population'' were initially reported in the Census Industry Classification; data from the other sources were reported in unique classification schemes adapted to each collecting agency's particular needs. All of these schemes were based either on the Census Industry Classification or on the Standard Industry Classification (SIC). Two sources allowed us to recode these competing schemes into the Census Industry Classification. First, the ''Public Use Samples of Basic Recodes for the 1970 Census'' (1972) reports the 1967 SIC equivalents of the 1970 Census Industry Classification. Second, the ''Standard Industrial Classification Manual'' (1972) describes the four-digit components of the 1967 and 1972 SIC coding schemes and records changes between these two classifications. By utilizing these two sources we were able to recode each coding scheme in a reasonably straightforward and satisfactory manner. Where problems arose because of changes in the allocation of detail components of industry categories across coding schemes, we relied on matching the names of categories or made a decision based on our examination of the industry descriptions in the ''SIC Manual''.

After we created the ''dictionaries'' necessary to transform each coding scheme into the Census Industry Classification, we machine-processed the data

TABLE 4.1

Industrial Structure Concepts and Variables

Factor	Concept	Variable	Source	Year to which data apply
Internal	Size	Employment per company	Enterprise, 1977	1972
		Sales per company	Enterprise, 1977	1972
		Assets per company	IRS, 1977	1972
		Net income per company	IRS, 1977	1972
		Value added per company	Input/Output, 1974; Enterprise, 1972	1967
		Percentage of companies that are corporations	Enterprise, 1977	1972
		Establishments per company	Enterprise, 1977	1972
	Productivity	Value added per employee	Input/Output, 1974; Enterprise, 1972	1967
		Value added as percentage of total output	Input/Output, 1974	1967
		Net national product per employee	NIPA, 1976	1972
	Unionization	Percentage of all workers covered by collective bargaining agreements	Freeman and Medoff, 1978	1970
Technical	Capital intensity/labor intensity	Assets per employee	IRS, 1977; Enterprise, 1977	1972
		Payroll as a percentage of sales	IRS, 1977; Enterprise, 1977	1972
		Constant capital as a percentage of assets	IRS, 1977	1972
		Constant capital as a percentage of constant capital and variable capital	Input/Output, 1974	1967
			IRS, 1977; Enterprise, 1977	1972
		Percentage of employment that is part time	NIPA, 1976; Enterprise, 1977	1972

Market			
Government regulation 5	Federal government purchases as a percentage of total output	Scherer, 1970	1970
	Federal government purchases per firm	Input/Output, 1974	1967
	State and local government purchases as a percentage of total output	Input/Output, 1974; Enterprise, 1972	1967
Concentration 6	State and local government purchases per firm	Input/Output, 1974	1967
	Eight-firm employment concentration	Input/Output, 1974; Enterprise, 1972	1967
	Eight-firm sales concentration	Enterprise, 1977	1972
	Eight-firm assets concentration	Enterprise, 1977	1972
	Percentage of industry sales in companies with over $250 million sales	IRS, 1977	1972
	Percentage of industry assets in companies with over $250 million assets	Enterprise, 1977	1972
		IRS, 1977	1972
Growth 5	Advertising per company	IRS, 1977	1972
	Ratio of 1972 to 1967 employment	Enterprise, 1972, 1977	1967, 1972
	Ratio of 1972 to 1967 sales	Enterprise, 1972, 1977	1967, 1972
	Ratio of 1970 to 1960 employment	Census, 1962, 1972	1960, 1970
	New capital expenditures per company	Enterprise, 1977	1972
	Ratio of 1972 to 1967 employment per firm	Erterprise, 1972, 1977	1967, 1972
Profit 3	Net income per sales	IRS, 1977	1972
	Net income per assets	IRS, 1977	1972
	Ratio of net income to constant capital plus variable capital	Input/Output, 1974; IRS, 1977	1967, 1972
Corporate autonomy 1	Percentage of industry work force employed by companies operating primarily in that industry	Enterprise, 1977	1972
Foreign involvement 4	Foreign dividends per company	IRS, 1977	1972
	Foreign tax credits per company	IRS, 1977	1972
	Exports per company	Input/Output, 1974; Enterprise, 1972	1967
	Exports as a percentage of total output	Input/Output, 1974	1967

sets into a single file. If the data from a given data set were grouped in too aggregate a fashion to match perfectly with the Census Industry Classification, we gave each industry in the census group the value of the aggregate group. For example, if we had data from some source on mining but not on the subcategories of mining, then each subcategory of mining was given the value of mining as a whole. Obviously, the data would be unusable if left in this raw form. However, all our final-analysis variables were computed by taking the ratio of one number to another, for example, sales per company, assets per employee. Accordingly, this allocation procedure allowed us to make maximum use of whatever level of detail was available in each data set without forcing us to use arbitrary weighting schemes for the distribution of values within a category for which we had only aggregate data.[2]

Some of the primary sources did not provide information on all the industries covered by the Census Industry Classification. Variables missing on industries because of noncoverage of the industry in a source were treated as missing throughout the analysis.[3] This problem is relatively minor, affecting only 10–15% of the observations. In addition, many of the industries affected were either "Not specified" categories, for example, "Manufacturing, not specified," or were public administration industries. Very few people are allocated to the "Not specified" categories in labor force surveys, so relatively few observations were lost to missing data when we matched the industry data to individual-level surveys. Similarly, many of the industrial structure concepts did not apply to government industries, and these industries were excluded as a group from our analysis.

The empirical measures used to tap the industrial structure concepts developed in Chapter 3 are listed in Table 4.1, along with the sources from which the data were taken for each variable. In some cases more than one empirical measure was used to tap a given concept. Details on the operationalization of these measures are reported in Appendix A. The sources from which the data were extracted are also listed in the References, and a discussion of these sources can be found in the work of Hodson (1980).

A New Sectoral Classification

The variables described in Table 4.1 will be used directly in Chapter 6 to develop a continuous-variable model of industrial structure and employee earnings. The problem remains, however, of how best to utilize the multiple characteristics of industrial structure to define industrial sectors. The key question here is: "How does one define the overall similarity of a pair of industries based on multiple nonindependent measures of similarity between the two industries?" The issues involved will become clearer as we look at a simple two-dimensional picture of industries A and B plotted on variables X and Y (Figure 1). What we

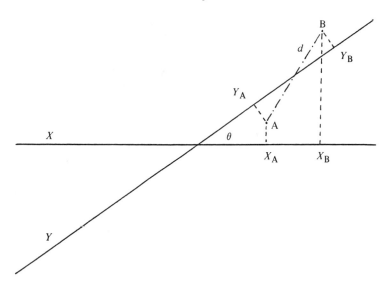

Figure 4.1.   Distance d between industries A and B on correlated dimensions X and Y.

really wish to measure is the distance d between A and B as an indicator of the closeness or similarity of A and B. Because X and Y are nonorthogonal (correlated), we cannot define d^2 as $(X_A - X_B)^2 + (Y_A - Y_B)^2$. If we know the correlation between X and Y, which corresponds to $\cos \theta$ in Figure 1, then

$$d^2 = (X_A - X_B)^2 + [(Y_A - Y_B) - (X_A - X_B) \cos \theta]^2 \csc^2 \theta.$$

But the calculation of distance in nonorthogonal space for three or more dimensions quickly becomes complex. On the other hand, the calculation of distance in an n-dimensional orthogonal space is quite simple.

This suggests that if we could transform our industrial characteristics into a set of orthogonal characteristics, then it would be easy to calculate the similarity of any pair of industries. Such an orthogonalization of our original 40 industrial characteristics can be readily accomplished using a principal components factor analysis. The principal components procedure differs from other types of factor analysis in that the extracted factors are exact mathematical transformations of the original variables and in that no inferences are drawn concerning the structure of common versus unique variance among the variables. Using the orthogonal factors extracted from our 40 variables, it is easy to calculate the distance between any pair of industries for any number of factors:

$$d^2 = \sum_{i=1}^{k} (F_{Ai} - F_{Bi})^2,$$

where F_{Ai} and F_{Bi} are the scores on factor i for industries A and B. These interindustry distances can then be used as indicators of dissimilarity in a hierarchical clustering analysis to produce industrial sectors. The combination of a factor analysis to orthogonalize the original variable space with a cluster analysis to systematically group the industries provides an elegant solution to the problem of multiple indicators, which should prove useful in other similar research situations.

The key issue in performing the principal components analysis concerns the number of factors that should be used for the computation of distances. If we were to use all of the 40 possible factors we would exactly replicate the original variable space. But it is likely that beyond some point the factors would only be picking up error variance (e.g., variance as a result of measurement error or of differences in the level of aggregation) and therefore not all 40 factors should be used. Although it is hard to determine at what point this would be true, it is instructive to compare the difference between an 11-factor solution and a 25-factor solution. In Table 4.2 we present the eigenvalues and the cumulative percentage of variance explained for the first 25 factors from our principal components factor analysis.[4] The 11-factor solution accounts for 83% of the total variance of the original variables. However, this solution differentially accounts for the variance of variables from different concept groups. In particular, this solution best replicates the variances in the size concept group and most poorly replicates the variances in the concentration concept group.[5] If we were to use the 11-factor solution, we would be reproducing the differences between industries in terms of size and concentration with differential accuracy. On the other hand, the 25-factor solution accounts for 99% of the total variance, and it accounts for a minimum of 95% of the variance of any one variable. Using the 25-factor solution, then, we almost exactly replicate the original variable space with good reproduction of variables from all concept groups.

We chose to use the 25-factor solution because it had uniformly high accuracy for the different concept groups. For each industry we computed factor scores for each of the 25 factors. Factor scores were not computed for any industry in which half or more of the variables were missing.[6] Factor scores could not be computed for only 11 of 213 industries: the 4 public administration industries and 7 of the "not-specified" manufacturing industries.[7]

Based on these factor scores we computed the interindustry distances and used these distances for input to a hierarchical clustering procedure.[8] The clustering method that we utilized is known as Ward's method (1963), as implemented in the Clustan package (Wishart, 1968). This method of clustering is based on minimizing a total error sum of squares, which is defined as the sum of the within-cluster error sum of squares. For each cluster the within-cluster error sum of squares is the sum of the squared distances of each cluster element from the centroid of the cluster. At the beginning of the clustering procedure each industry

TABLE 4.2

**Eigenvalues for First 25 Factors from Principal
Components Analysis**

Factor	Eigenvalue	Cumulative % of variance
1	15.737	39.3
2	3.127	47.2
3	2.260	52.8
4	2.187	58.3
5	1.936	63.1
6	1.742	67.5
7	1.593	71.5
8	1.416	75.0
9	1.087	77.7
10	1.072	80.4
11	.988	82.9
12	.848	85.0
13	.783	86.9
14	.709	88.7
15	.630	90.3
16	.557	91.7
17	.489	92.9
18	.430	94.0
19	.410	95.0
20	.404	96.0
21	.315	96.8
22	.273	97.5
23	.232	98.1
24	.205	98.6
25	.172	99.0

is treated as a separate cluster, and the two closest clusters, in terms of a minimal increase in the error sum of squares, are fused. This step-by-step fusion process continues until a specified number of clusters has been reached. We used this procedure initially to produce 24 clusters, at which point we allowed a local optimization step to be added after each fusion of two clusters. (The local optimization step was not added earlier in the clustering process because of the additional cost involved.) The rationale for employing a local optimization is to take account of the fact that after a new cluster has been defined by fusion some of the elements of the new cluster may now be closer to the centroid of another cluster and, similarly, some elements of other clusters may now be closer to the centroid of the new cluster.

In Table 4.3 we present some statistics from the cluster analysis as it moves

TABLE 4.3

Change in the Error Sum of Squares and a Test Statistic for the 14–18-Cluster Solutions

Number of Clusters	Change in ESS	Test statistic	P
18	70.125	60.867	.001
17	91.125	75.138	.001
16	83.813	84.694	.001
15	112.325	93.482	.001
14	130.325	95.249	.001

from 18 to 14 clusters. In deciding at what point to stop the fusion of clusters two criteria should be considered: the statistical significance of the increase in the error sum of squares and the substantive meaning of the fusion. A test statistic can be calculated for these fusions (see Kaufman, 1981) based on a weighted change in the error sum of squares, where the weights are the inverse of the variance of the factors. This test statistic is distributed as $\chi^2(25)$, but it is not very useful in our case because every cluster fusion to less than 35 clusters is significant ($p < .001$). We chose to stop at 16 clusters for two reasons. First, the change in the error sum of squares appeared to level off at 16 clusters before it sharply increased for 15 clusters. Second, as we discuss next, the 16 clusters had a conceptual appeal in terms of the differences between clusters on some key industrial characteristics.

We offer this categorization as a framework for operationalizing key differences in industrial structure. We do not present this result with the claim that it represents a definitive and final solution to the question of how to operationalize economic segmentation in the U.S. economy. We believe that this categorization is superior to prior attempts to operationalize economic segmentation in that it fully reflects the multidimensionality of economic segmentation. This multidimensionality has long been apparent in the conceptual apparatus of this field but has heretofore been inadequately handled, both theoretically and empirically. This level of detail also allows flexibility and choice for future research applications. In addition to being used at the full level of detail, this categorization can be collapsed across distinctions that researchers believe to be theoretically unimportant to their particular research problem.

Interpreting the New Industrial Sector Classification

The conceptual sense of the 16-cluster solution can be seen from an examination of Tables 4.4 and 4.5. Table 4.4 lists the industries in each of the 16

TABLE 4.4

Classification of Industries into 16 Sectors

Sector	Industries
Oligopoly	Office and accounting machine mfg.
	Electronic computing equipment mfg.
	Motor vehicle and equipment mfg.
	Photographic equipment mfg.
	Drug and medicine mfg.
	Petroleum refining
	Misc. petro and coal products mfg.
Core	Crude petro and natural gas extraction
	Glass and glass products
	Cement and plaster products
	Structural clay products
	Pottery and related products
	Misc. stone products
	Blast furnaces, steel works and mills
	Other primary iron and steel mfg.
	Primary aluminum mfg.
	Other primary nonferrous mfg.
	Cutlery and hardware metal mfg.
	Fabricated structural metal mfg.
	Metal stamping mfg.
	Misc. fabricated metal mfg.
	Engines and turbines mfg.
	Household appliance mfg.
	Electrical machinery mfg. n.e.c.
	Cycles and misc. transport equipment mfg.
	Meat products mfg.
	Dairy products mfg.
	Canning and preserving
	Grain mill products mfg.
	Bakery products mfg.
	Confectionary products mfg.
	Beverage mfg.
	Misc. food products mfg.
	Knitting mills
	Dyeing and finishing textile mfg.
	Floor covering, except hard surface, mfg.
	Yarn, thread and fabric mills
	Apparel and accessory mfg.
	Pulp and paper mills
	Misc. paper and pulp products
	Paperboard containers mfg.
	Printing and publishing, except newspaper
	Industrial chemical mfg.
	Plastics, synthetics and resin mfg.

(continued)

TABLE 4.4—*Continued*

Sector	Industries
Wholesale	Synthetic fiber mfg.
	Soap and cosmetic mfg.
	Paints, varnishes, etc. mfg.
	Agricultural chemical mfg.
	Misc. chemical mfg.
	Not-specified chemical mfg.
	Farm machinery mfg.
	Construction equipment mfg.
	Metalworking machinery mfg.
	Railroad locomotive and equipment mfg.
	Mobile dwellings mfg.
	Legal services
	Engineering and architectural services
	Accounting and bookkeeping services
	Misc. professional and related services
	WHOLESALE:
	Motor vehicle and equipment
	Drugs and chemicals
	Dry goods and apparel
	Food and related products
	Farm products—raw materials
	Electrical goods
	Hardware, plumbing, heating supplies
	Not-specified electrical and hardware products
	Machinery equipment and supplies
	Metals and minerals, n.e.c.
	Petroleum products
	Scrap and waste materials
	Alcoholic beverages
	Paper and paper products
	Lumber and construction materials
	Wholesalers, n.e.c.
	Not-specified wholesalers
Periphery	Metal mining
	Coal mining
	Nonmetallic mining
	Logging
	Sawmills
	Misc. wood products
	Screw machine products
	Radio, TV, communication equipment mfg.
	Aircraft and parts mfg.
	Ship and boat building
	Scientific instruments
	Optical and health service supplies mfg.

TABLE 4.4—*Continued*

Sector	Industries
	Watches and clocks mfg.
	Misc. manufacturing
	Misc. textile products
	Misc. fabricated textile products
	Rubber products
	Misc. plastic products
	Tanned and finished leather mfg.
	Leather products, except footwear
	Department stores
	Limited-price variety stores
	Vending machine operators
	Direct-selling stores
	Misc. general merchandise stores
	Dairy products retail
	Retail bakeries
	Food retailing, n.e.c.
	Advertising services
	Services to buildings
	Commercial R&D and testing services
	Employment agencies
	Business management and consulting services
	Computer programming services
	Detective and protective services
	Business services, n.e.c.
	Auto services, except repair
	Auto repair services
	Electrical repair services
	Misc. repair services
	Hotels and motels
	Other lodging places
	Laundering and garment services
	Beauty shops
	Barber shops
	Shoe repair shops
	Dressmaking shops
	Misc. personal services
	Theaters
	Bowling alleys and pool parlors
	Misc. entertainment services
Small Shop	Furniture and fixture mfg.
	Newspaper printing and publishing
	Footwear, except rubber, mfg.
	RETAIL:
	Lumber and building materials
	Hardware and farm equipment

(*continued*)

TABLE 4.4—*Continued*

Sector	Industries
	Grocery stores
	Motor vehicle dealers
	Tire, battery, and auto accessories
	Gas service stations
	Misc. vehicle dealers
	Apparel and accessories
	Shoe stores
	Furniture and home furnishings
	Household appliances, TV and radio
	Eating and drinking places
	Drug stores
	Liquor stores
	Farm and garden supplies
	Jewelry stores
	Fuel and ice dealers
	Retail florists
	Misc. retailing
	Not-specified retail
	Offices of physicians
	Offices of dentists
Core utilities and finance	Radio and TV broadcasting
	Electric light and power
	Electric and gas utilities
	Gas and steam supply systems
	Banking
	Credit agencies
	Insurance
Periphery utilities	Water supply
	Sanitary services
	Other and not-specified utilities
Core transport	Railroads and railway express
	Street railways and bus lines
	Water transport
	Air transport
	Telephone services
	Telegraph and misc. communication services
Periphery transport	Trucking services
	Warehousing and storage services
	Pipe lines, except natural gas
	Services incidental to transport
Local monopoly	General building contractors
	Other general contractors
	Special trade contractors
	Taxicab services
	Offices of chiropractors

TABLE 4.4—*Continued*

Sector	Industries
	Hospitals
	Convalescent institutions
	Offices of health practitioners, n.e.c.
	Health services, n.e.c.
Educational and nonprofit services	Private households
	Elementary and secondary schools
	Colleges and universities
	Libraries
	Educational services, n.e.c.
	Not-specified educational services
	Museums, art galleries, and zoos
	Religious organizations
	Welfare services
	Residential welfare facilities
	Nonprofit membership organizations
Agriculture	Agricultural production
	Agricultural services
	Horticultural services
	Forestry
	Fisheries
Brokers	Security, commodity brokerage, and investment companies
Real estate	Real estate
Ordnance	Ordnance
Tobacco	Tobacco mfg.

clusters,[9] and Table 4.5 shows the cluster means for some key industrial characteristics. The discussion of these results can best be organized around a series of profiles for each cluster.[10]

Oligopoly

The oligopoly sector has the highest values on almost every characteristic. In particular, it has the highest values on the size measures, on two of the three concentration measures, on foreign involvement, on profit, and on federal purchases. On capital intensity, it is exceeded by only two of the utilities and transport sectors. The seven industries in this cluster contain firms that are among the very largest multinationals (e.g., IBM, GM, Kodak, Lilly, Exxon) and that are oligopolies in the American economy. Compared with the core sector, the oligopoly sector has considerably higher values on all the measures except unionization. Workers in this sector are expected to have relatively high wages.

TABLE 4.5

Means of Some Key Industrial Characteristics[a] by Sector

Sector	Eight-firm employment concentration	Eight-firm assets concentration	Sales[b] concentration	Assets[b] per firm	Employ-ment[b] per firm	Foreign[b] dividends	Percentage incorporated	Assets[b] per employee	Net income[c] per assets	Federal[d] purchase per firm	Percent-age union
Oligopoly	64.30	29.54	4.46	3.31	5.16	7.04	91.46	.52	12.5	7.39	33.72
Core	37.55	18.50	3.67	1.28	4.59	4.72	84.76	-1.11	8.0	1.59	48.12
Wholesale	13.27	10.81	1.09	-.34	2.74	2.23	73.09	-1.46	8.2	.16	21.31
Periphery	24.83	29.73	-.50	-.43	2.53	1.41	50.43	-1.92	6.7	2.65	25.23
Small shop	12.72	10.97	-.00	-1.43	1.94	-2.50	44.41	-2.05	8.3	.01	12.35
Core utilities and finance	—	10.10	—	3.32	—	2.19	—	1.06	2.9	.16	29.69
Periphery utilities	—	6.55	—	-.55	—	1.90	—	-1.86	3.7	.36	56.45
Core transport	—	21.38	—	1.97	—	2.25	—	-.82	2.9	2.96	67.03
Periphery transport	9.10	10.42	-4.61	.15	2.25	1.79	70.48	.55	6.0	.70	47.07
Local monopoly	6.65	10.50	1.49	-1.03	1.98	-.52	30.18	-2.96	5.2	.05	26.52
Education and nonprofit	—	13.58	—	-2.11	—	-1.53	—	-3.87	8.2	.12	4.82
Agriculture	—	7.82	—	-1.43	—	-2.09	—	-2.42	6.9	-.21	1.78
Brokers	—	4.06	—	.65	—	2.54	—	1.61	4.3	.00	1.82
Real estate	—	2.83	—	-.98	—	-2.90	—	.32	2.9	.01	18.86
Ordnance	68.94	34.37	3.04	1.23	6.00	2.37	86.73	-2.87	6.4	267.50	51.40
Tobacco	83.93	96.76	4.50	3.41	5.93	6.14	80.95	.30	11.4	.00	60.70
Total	26.43	18.70	1.19	.06	3.18	1.76	64.57	-1.56	7.0	2.73	29.70

[a] For the definition of these variables see Appendix A.
[b] Logarithmic scale.
[c] Multiplied by 100.
[d] In $100,000s.

Core

The core sector has the second highest values on two of three size measures and on foreign involvement. On unionization it is exceeded by only core transport and periphery utilities. This sector is composed solely of manufacturing industries. Contrasted to the wholesale, periphery, and small shop sectors, it is higher for almost every comparison, except profit, for which it has a roughly similar value. Workers in this sector are expected to have wages that are potentially as high as those in the oligopoly sector.

Wholesale

This sector has a relatively low level of concentration, but it is roughly average on the size measures and has higher than average levels of foreign involvement, capital intensity, and profit. In addition to all the wholesale industries, this sector contains a few machinery manufacturing and professional service industries. Compared with the periphery sector, the wholesale sector is less concentrated but has larger firms, more foreign involvement, greater capital intensity, and higher profits. Compared with the small shop sector, wholesale is about equally concentrated but has higher values on all the other major dimensions. Workers in this sector are expected to have earnings near the median level.

Periphery and Small-Shop

The periphery sector, somewhat surprisingly, has an above-average level of concentration but is below average on all the other dimensions. This sector is composed of a variety of industries: a large number of service industries, a few durable and nondurable manufacturing industries, most of mining, and those retail industries typified by chain stores. The small-shop sector has an above-average profit rate,[11] but it is below average on all the other dimensions. This sector is composed of retail industries, three manufacturing industries typified by small-scale production, and offices of physicians and dentists. Although both these sectors have lower than average values on almost all dimensions of industrial structure, the periphery sector has higher values than the small-shop sector on all the dimensions except profit. In particular, the periphery sector is much more concentrated than the small-shop sector. For the most part, the difference between these sectors is one of degree. But on the criterion of concentration, the sectors appear to be qualitatively distinct. Many of the industries in the periphery sector contain some dominant firms of national scale, whereas few, if any, of the industries in the small-shop sector contain firms that operate outside of local markets. Wages in both of these sectors are expected to be well below average, with those in the small-shop sector significantly lower than those in the periphery.

Core Utilities and Finance; Periphery Utilities

The core utilities and finance sector is typified by extremely high assets per firm and by capital intensity. It has relatively low levels of concentration, profit, and foreign involvement. The industries comprising this sector are the electric and gas utilities, radio and television broadcasting, and three finance industries. The periphery utilities sector, composed of miscellaneous utilities, is typified by low values on all major dimensions, except unionization. In contrasting these two sectors, we see that, whereas both have relatively low levels of concentration and profit, they are sharply different on the dimensions of asset size and capital intensity. These two sectors produce similar products but employ vastly different amounts of capital in their production. In differentiating the core utilities and finance sector from the oligopoly and core sectors we see that the core utilities and finance sector has lower foreign involvement, a lower profit rate, less concentration, but higher assets and capital intensity. These differences result from greater government regulation of utilities and finance and from differences in the nature of the product (e.g., the production of utilities is tied to a given geographic region and to high plant and equipment costs, thus limiting the development of national and international ties). In contrasting the periphery utilities sector with the periphery and small shop sectors, we see that these sectors are similar, being based primarily on production in small enterprises operating in local product and labor markets. However, the periphery utilities sector is differentiated by a lower profit rate and a much higher degree of unionization. These differences reflect close government regulation on the one hand and the high skill requirements of production in the periphery utilities sector on the other. Because the core utilities sector has characteristics similar to those of the core sector, wages are expected to be high. The periphery utilities sector has corporate structure characteristics similar to those in the periphery sector, except that it has a very high level of unionization; the wage expectation under these conditions is largely indeterminant.

Core Transport and Periphery Transport

The core transport sector is typified by relatively high levels of concentration, asset size, and capital intensity and by a low profit rate. It has the highest value of any sector on unionization. This sector is composed of railroad, bus, air, and water transport, and telephone and telegraph services. The periphery transport sector is characterized by low values for concentration, asset size, and profit but high values for unionization and (somewhat surprisingly) for capital intensity. This sector is composed of trucking, warehousing, and pipeline transport industries. In contrasting these two sectors, we see that they are again typified by a "core/periphery" relationship in terms of size, concentration, and unionization. But the periphery transport sector has a surprisingly high level of capital intensity. This discrepancy results from the nature of the service produced by this sector, which requires large investments in land, buildings, and equipment. The comparison of core transport to the core and oligopoly sectors and the periphery transport to the periphery and small shop sectors is similar to that discussed previously for the core and periphery utilities sectors. However, the core and periphery transport sectors are additionally differentiated from other sectors by extremely high rates of unionization, resulting from the historical importance of the Teamsters' Union in these industries. Workers in the core transportation sector are expected to have high average wages. The high values of the periphery transportation sector on capital intensity and unionization may also be sufficient to determine high wages for these workers.

Local Monopoly, Education and Nonprofit Services, and Agriculture

These three sectors are characterized by low values on all the major industrial characteristics. Within this group, the local monopoly sector is highest on asset size and unionization. The education and nonprofit sector has the lowest levels of capital intensity and asset size. The agriculture sector has the lowest levels of concentration and unionization. All three sectors are typified by extremely small-scale labor-intensive operations. However, the highly variable nature of the production processes for the industries in these sectors results in their differentiation as three distinct sectors. Low wages are expected to be prevalent in all three sectors.

Brokers, Real Estate, Ordnance, and Tobacco

These four sectors are each composed of a single-industry outlier. The brokerage industry appears as an outlier because of its extremely low values on some dimensions and extremely high values on others. It had low levels of concentration, profit, federal purchases, and unionization but high levels of foreign dividends, asset size, and capital intensity. This industry consists of many competitive brokerage houses dealing with large volumes of financial capital. In contrast to brokers, the real estate sector has even lower levels of concentration, profit, federal purchases, and unionization and has very low levels of foreign dividends and asset size. However, real estate has among the highest values of any sector for capital intensity, owing to investments in land and buildings. The ordnance sector has among the highest values of any sector for concentration and size and has especially high values for federal purchases and unionization. However, it has among the lowest values for capital intensity because of its utilization of a large amount of skilled labor. The tobacco sector is a large positive outlier on *all* the dimensions except federal purchases. Indeed, on some measures it is roughly equal to the oligopoly sector, and on other measures it has considerably higher values. Because of the outlier nature of these four sectors, we must remain somewhat cautious in our expectations about employees' earnings. However, the high values of the brokerage sector on assets and foreign involvement and the high value of the ordnance sector on capital intensity may be sufficient to determine relatively high wages in these sectors. The pattern of industrial characteristics in the real estate sector indicates that wages in this sector may be at or below the median level. Finally, in contrast to the expectation that would be derived from everyday knowledge about the tobacco industry, its pattern of high values on a variety of industrial characteristics indicates that we should expect relatively high wages in this sector.

In reviewing the sector profiles and contrasts just outlined, we can see that there is some utility to a core-versus-periphery distinction. However, such a contrast does not hold across the entire industrial spectrum. Rather, it is a distinction that is reproduced within some of the broad industrial product types and that is inadequate for conceptualizing a large portion of the economy. We also find that many of the dimensions on which theorists have relied to differentiate core and periphery sectors do not consistently demonstrate a pattern of high and low values grouping separately. For example, the wholesale sector is competitive but is based on production in large firms, with much foreign involvement and great capital intensity.[12] Moreover, many of the outlying sectors demonstrate a pattern of extremely high values on some dimensions matched with extremely low values on others.

The differentiation of a true oligopoly sector from a larger core sector provides a final interesting point of contrast. Arguments about whether or not a "core" sector is based on monopolistic practices may be informed by this finding. Once a truly monopolistic sector is distinguished from the core sector, we find that the core and periphery sectors are differentiated more by size and foreign involvement than by concentration.

Reservations and Anomalies

Before accepting these sector placements we should consider possible problems with our data and method. Four types of problems seem most relevant. First, some of the variables used may reflect unique historical circumstances of the year in which they were collected rather than some more lasting aspect of industrial structure. Profit rates provide a good example of this potential problem. Second, some variables may have different meanings in different industries. For example, "asset size" has a different meaning in real estate than in manufacturing, and "assets per employer" has a different meaning in insurance than in utilities. Third, certain industries may lie in a boundary area where two sectors overlap. Their sector placement then becomes arbitrary and is determined by potentially insignificant numeric differences. Fourth, because all 40 dimensions of industrial structure were weighted equally, industries may have been placed in a certain sector on the basis of secondary characteristics.

There also exist in sector placement certain apparent anomalies that deserve consideration. Most textile industries, except fabricated textiles, appear in the core sector, whereas we generally think of these as peripheral industries. The reason lies in the large size, particularly the large employment size, of textile plants. Conversely, in the periphery sector are several industries that we might ordinarily think of as core industries: "aircraft and parts mfg.," "ship and boat building," and "rubber products." When we consider these industries we may think of a few key giant corporations. However, each of these industries also has a large contingent of small businesses engaged in parts manufacture, repair, and, in the case of rubber products, in the manufacture of miscellaneous products such as gloves and tubing.

Included in the wholesale sector we find several categories of professional services, such as engineering and architectural services. In terms of the organizational and financial characteristics on which industries are sorted into sectors, these professional service industries represent medium-sized establishments with low levels of concentration, just as is the case for the wholesale industries themselves. It is important not to confuse the organizational and financial characteristics of an industry with its occupational composition. This example again highlights the importance of using sectoral classifications in conjunction with occupational and class categories.

Doctors are placed in the small-shop sector, whereas lawyers, whom we may imagine as having a similar work organization, are included in the wholesale sector. The category "offices of physicians" includes only doctors' private practices; the large enterprises with which doctors are sometimes associated are listed as a separate industry, "hospitals." The industrial category "legal services," however, includes private law practices as well as huge corporate law firms. These differences in definition explain this otherwise anomalous placement.

Finally, in the education and nonprofit services sector we find both universities and domestic services. The financial assets, sales, and profits of many of the nonprofit enterprises in this sector, including some universities, are constrained to a very low level, which explains the placement of universities in this sector. Domestic services likewise operate on a very low profit rate as well as on a very small scale. However, domestic services might just as well have been placed in the small-shop sector as in the education and nonprofit sector. For this industry, the choice between these two sectors seems somewhat arbitrary.

In reviewing these problems and anomalies we see that many of them result from the use of industries as a unit of analysis. Others, however, result from our selection of data or from our choice of method in constructing industrial sectors.

In sum, we believe that these anomalies and problems represent only the type of difficulties that any use of industries or industrial sectors as analytic constructs must face. With these caveats in mind, we shall proceed with the utilization of this sectoral classification in our study of labor force outcomes.

An Aggregate Six-Sector Solution

The grouping of detail industries into the clusters presented above is based on a completely empirical and statistical procedure. Theoretical considerations enter this process only through the selection of variables to be included in the analysis. However, our selection of the 16-cluster level as a stopping point for the analysis was a decision based on the interpretability of the results. In the choice of this level we relied on our knowledge and intuition about specific aspects of the industrial structure of the United States.

The choice of the 16-cluster level as a stopping point maximizes the interpretability of the results; however, it also creates some potential problems. Sixteen clusters are awkward to work with in certain kinds of statistical analysis. This is particularly the case for regression analysis, where we might want either to enter the clusters as dummy variables in a regression equation as the predictors of some workplace outcome or to stratify the sample for analysis within sectors. To have allowed the clustering process to converge further would have produced uninterpretable results because of the numeric process involved in the clustering. This process takes account of neither the spread within a given cluster nor qualitative differences that the evaluation of "distances" between clusters may overlook. Nevertheless, we felt a need to collapse the 16-sector scheme into fewer categories for use in parts of the subsequent analysis. To do this, we again examined the means of key component variables by sector (see Table 4.5). Utilizing this empirical base, we further grouped clusters in such a way as to maintain the interpretability of results. The outcome of that process was the somewhat more manageable six-sector categorization described below.

Oligopoly (Oligopoly, Tobacco)

The tobacco industry has extremely high values for the variables that delineate the oligopoly sector—concentration, foreign dividends, assets, profit, and value-added. In fact, tobacco is a positive outlier on all these dimensions, having even more extreme values than the oligopoly sector. For this reason, tobacco, as a single-industry outlier, was grouped with the oligopoly sector. This combined oligopoly sector can be thought of as dominated by the largest and most concentrated multinational corporations.

Core (Core, Wholesale, Ordnance)

The core group is typified by an extremely high degree of unionization and higher than average levels of foreign involvement and asset size. In addition, the core ranks immediately below the oligopoly sector on the criterion of profit rate. The core is dominated by large firms with a high degree of foreign involvement, high profits, and a heavily unionized work force. It differs from the oligopoly sector chiefly on the dimension of concentration.

Periphery (Periphery, Small Shop, Real Estate)

Low ratings on unionization, asset size, and foreign involvement typify the periphery group of industries, which are dominated by small establishments operating with limited capital and a nonunion labor force in local or regional markets.

Core Utilities (Core Utilities and Finance, Core Transportation, Brokers)

The industries included in the core utilities group share the characteristics of relatively high foreign dividends and high assets but low profits. In addition, these industries produce highly similar products and therefore have many technologies in common. The uniformly low rate of reported profit is probably a result of close government regulation of these industries. This sector is based on large-scale, high-technology production. It differs from the oligopoly sector chiefly on the criteria of concentration and profit rate.

Periphery Utilities (Periphery Utilities, Periphery Transportation)

Although the periphery utilities group shares a common product with the core utilities, the two sectors are differentiated on the basis of firm size and foreign involvement. The periphery utilities have much lower values on these two variables than the core utilities. Production in this sector is based on smaller-scale enterprises, which operate primarily in local markets. It is differentiated from the periphery sector proper by its close subordination to state regulation and by the relatively high-technology service, rather than a low-technology production or distribution function, that it provides.

Trades (Local Monopoly; Education and Nonprofit; Agriculture)

The trades sector is composed of those industries with the lowest values on asset size, concentration, and foreign involvement. This sector, even more than the periphery sector, can be thought of as being composed of very small producers, employing a minimum of capital, and operating only in local product and labor markets.

The 6-category sectoral scheme just outlined obviously does not preserve all the distinctions embodied in the 16-category scheme. Nevertheless, we feel that it taps the major dimensions highlighted by the literature on economic segmentation (e.g., size, concentration, foreign involvement, and profit rate). Therefore, much of the analysis to be presented in subsequent chapters will utilize this 6-sector categorization. Results from the analysis using the 6-sector categorization should prove much easier to present and interpret than results employing the full 16-sector scheme.

The results presented in this section demonstrate that patterns of industrial alignment do not form a consistent dichotomy. The multidimensional nature of economic segmentation must be given serious consideration in future work, both theoretical and empirical. Although the dual economy approach has served a purpose as a heuristic device, and it has been important in focusing attention on the economic basis of inequality, it is time to break out of the simple dualistic mold. The 16- and 6-sector models provide alternative operationalizations of economic segmentation that other researchers may find useful. However, we do not propose these results as a final solution to the operationalization of industrial segmentation. Rather, we hope that they will promote further serious conceptual and empirical work in this field.

COMPANY DATA

Company data are more difficult to collect than industry data. This is true for several reasons. First, a much larger number of units of analysis are involved—in the present case we searched for information on the employers of 6602 persons, whereas the industry data utilizes only 213 categories. Second, companies that are privately owned are not required by law to report publicly financial data that can then be compiled in usable sources. This is particularly a problem with small companies, on which data are almost impossible to find. Because of these problems we severely limited the number of variables we sought for companies, hoping to be successful in collecting a limited set of variables for as many of the companies as possible.

Coding the Employers' Company Names

On the Wisconsin survey questionnaire administered in 1975 the respondents were asked "What is the name of the place where you work?" Responses to this question served as the basis for the identification of employers' company names. The coding instructions utilized for this project are reported by Hodson (1980). In general, respondents answered this question clearly and with good detail. Surprisingly few people refused to answer the question (see section entitled "Missing Company Data").

Our major coding problem was ensuring that identical places of employment were coded as such. That is, once we had listed a given large factory it was likely that we would later find other respondents employed in the same place who gave similar, though not necessarily identical, answers to the question "What is the name of the place where you work?" This problem was typically solved by comparing the addresses of the plants. In fact, without the additional information on street address, city, and state of place of employment that was ascertained on the questionnaire, we would have frequently been unable to distinguish one "Joe's Bar" or "Smith's Plumbing," or "Acme Manufacturing" from the next! To eliminate problems of identification caused by similarly named companies, the full company name, street address, and city and state were appended to each respondent's data record. The use of long-distance directory assistance was also invaluable in verifying questionable or unclear company names and addresses.

An additional problem was presented by respondents who reported a brand name instead of a company name. This might, for instance, happen in the case of a "Chevrolet Parts" plant, where the company name is General Motors. The data coders were alerted to this kind of problem and were instructed to add the company name to a listing if they knew it, for example, General Motors in this case. Other instances were more problematic. Sometimes a coder did not know that a reported name was only a brand name or realized this but did not know the company's formal name. This problem created a small amount of inaccuracy in our coding of company names. However, almost all of this inaccuracy was later cleared when we collected the actual company data by utilizing sources that linked brand names to specific companies. Throughout the company name-coding procedure we were aided by the fact that the majority of the respondents still lived and worked in Wisconsin. The coders became closely familiar with many of the larger Wisconsin employers and the myriad ways that respondents might designate them when answering the question "What is the name of the place where you work?"

When coding the names of places of employment we made no effort to determine if there was a larger owning unit than the one reported. We coded the response as given, making use of whatever information and sources we could to clarify that response. Thus, different plants of the same company were coded as different places. In the company data-coding stage discussed next, one of our principal activities was determining the ultimate ownership of a place of employment.

Coding the Company Data

Once the name of place of employment was attached to each respondent's data record, we were faced with the question of what sample to choose for the collection of company data. We attempted to be as comprehensive as possible. However, the data we were seeking were neither relevant nor available for government workers. Accordingly, we excluded all persons reporting public administration as their industry and all teachers who reported themselves as employed by the government. This reduced the sample of persons for whom we sought data on employers to 6602.

Included in this sample are categories of persons later excluded from the analysis. These categories are self-employed persons, persons working without pay on family farms or business, and government workers outside of public administration and teaching. Because these company data are appended to the ongoing Wisconsin longitudinal study of schooling and attainments, it is hoped that the degree of comprehensiveness that we attained will aid possible future users of these data who may wish to analyze a different sample or to further develop the data base.

The unit of analyses employed in this part of the data-collection process is the company. However, the sample is of persons, and the units in which place of employment is recorded are plants, for example, specific factories or stores. This somewhat confusing array of people working for specific companies in specific locations was handled in the following way. The machine-readable person-level data set was sorted by company name and by address within company names. Selected information was then printed in a format suitable for the addition of company data. Thus, 6602 entries were printed with column headings specifying the data to be collected and blanks formatted and underlined to contain the company data. Each entry contained a numeric person code that would later be used to match the company data to a person record. Each entry also contained the full company name and address. Additional data were extracted from each person's record and displayed as an informational aid to the coders. This information was the industry of employment reported by the respondent, the class of worker of the respondent, and the number of people the respondent reported as working in the place where he or she worked. If several persons reported working in the same plant, these persons would all be listed together. If there were respondents who worked in several plants of the same company, these would appear consecutively. Data coding was thus rendered much easier because we only needed to code data for companies once, even though a given company might employ several respondents. Data for subsequent entries were machine-duplicated. The effective sample of companies for which data were searched was thus smaller than the 6602 persons in the sample. There were approximately 4200 different companies named by the respondents.

The routine that we developed for searching and obtaining company data can now be described. The overall sample was broken into industry subsamples. Thus, we had a subsample of manufacturing companies, retail companies, hospitals, service companies, and so on. The reason for this procedure was to ensure maximum effectiveness in the use of data sources. Some sources were applicable only to a very limited set of companies. It would have been tremendously inefficient to search the entire list of companies utilizing these sources. Other sources were applicable across the entire range of industries and were utilized with each subsample.

The process was started by selecting a source and searching through an industry subsample with it. Because the coverage in any one source was never complete, the companies in a subsample not found in the first source would be searched later with another source. Thus, the continually decreasing unfound residual of any subsample might be searched repeatedly 10 or even 15 times until we had exhausted all our possible sources. We employed first those sources that we believed included the most reliable data and that had the best coverage of companies.

We collected company data on the largest owning unit of a place of employment. Thus, all subsidiaries were allocated the data for their parent companies. This choice was made because in discussions of the effects of industrial structure on workplace outcomes, the unit most commonly designated (or implied) is the ultimate owning company. During a pretest stage of data collection we considered the idea of coding two duplicate sets of data for each company— one for the reported company and, if it was a subsidiary, another for its owning company. This idea had to be rejected because when a company is majority-owned by another company financial data are rarely if ever reported separately for it.

The company measures that we collected are listed in Table 4.6. As with the industry measures, certain concepts are tapped by multiple empirical measures. Measures for only 5 of the 10 industrial structure concepts developed in Chapter

TABLE 4.6

Enterprise Structure Concepts and Variables

Factor	Concept	Variable
Internal	Size	Employment
		Sales
		Net income
		Assets
		Net worth
		Existence of plants outside the local area
		Fortune magazine list of leading corporations
Technical	Capital intensity	Assets per employee
Market	Profit	Net income per sales
	Corporate autonomy/dominance	Subsidiary of another company
		Number of domestic subsidiaries
		Number of total subsidiaries
	Foreign involvement	Number of foreign subsidiaries

3 could be collected at the company level. We were able to collect measures of size, capital intensity, profit, corporate autonomy, and foreign involvement but not productivity, unionization, government regulation, concentration, and growth. However, each of the major areas of industrial structure (internal, technical, and market factors) is represented by measures tapping at least one of its component concepts. The measures that we developed represent clearly some of the most important dimensions of industrial structure discussed in the literature. Because of these factors, we feel that the trade-off between the range of available variables and the detail of coverage, necessitated by the nature of corporate-level data, has been a profitable one. Details on the operationalization of the company-level variables are available in Appendix B. The data sources that we utilized are listed in the References, and a discussion of these sources can be found in the work of Hodson (1980).

Missing Company Data

A serious problem of missing data exists in the company data set. Although we utilized a great number of data sources, many of the companies were simply too small to be listed in any publicly available sources. Table 4.7 reports the number of missing data cases for three samples of interest: the total sample for which we

TABLE 4.7

Missing Company Data, 1975 Wisconsin Survey

Variables	Total sample searched[a]		Private workers[b]		Private workers reporting earnings of $100 or more[c]	
	Number missing	%	Number missing	%	Number missing	%
Employment	2299	34.82	1186	23.07	965	21.48
Sales	3315	50.21	1982	38.56	1653	36.79
Income	4308	65.25	2880	56.03	2455	54.64
Assets	3946	59.77	2588	50.35	2203	49.03
Worth	3389	51.33	2083	40.53	1738	38.68
Plants outside local area	1913	28.98	904	17.59	725	16.14
Domestic subsidiaries	3470	52.56	2138	41.60	1803	40.13
Foreign subsidiaries	4144	66.86	2738	53.27	2338	52.04
Fortune	72	1.10	40	0.78	24	0.53
Subsidiary	3035	46.00	1748	34.01	1450	32.27

[a] $N = 6602$.
[b] $N = 5140$.
[c] $N = 4493$.

sought company data, private workers (the sample of theoretical interest), and private workers who reported earnings (the sample that we shall utilize throughout the analysis). Note that missing data problems are reduced but not eliminated when we select private workers from the more extensive sample.

For the sample of private workers, the *Fortune* (1975a–c) list variable has no missing data except for respondents who declined to report the name of the place where they worked. This is because companies were coded as either present on the *Fortune* lists or not present. The variable measuring plants outside the immediate area has slightly less than one-fifth missing data. Employment has slightly more than one-fifth missing data. The rest of the company variables have substantial missing data up to and including about half of the cases. These data cases cannot be ignored because that would badly bias the results. Our analysis would then be about variation within companies large enough to be listed in publicly available sources. Also, because a case tends to be missing several variables if it is missing any, conventional data-estimation techniques are of little avail.

Two strategies were chosen to confront this problem. For two qualitative variables later used in the construction of corporate sectors (plants outside the immediate area and presence of any subsidiaries), missing data were given the assumed value of zero. That is, we assumed that if information on a company's number of subsidiaries had not been found, it had none, and that if information on plants outside the immediate area had not been found, there were none. Missing data cases were also given assumed zeros for the subsidiary status variable; that is, we assumed that companies with missing data on this variable were not a subsidiary of some larger company. Our reasoning for this procedure is as follows. Judging from our intensive and repeated search procedures, we felt that almost all companies large enough to have subsidiaries were located in some source. "Number of subsidiaries" is a variable we were able to code from almost every source. Similarly, any company for which we were unable to find information on plants outside the local area was assumed to have none. In general, this procedure is grounded on the belief that companies for which we were not able to find these basic qualitative variables were, indeed, "too small to find" rather than missing in some less-defined sense.[13] Having closely supervised the entire data-coding operation and having personally coded substantial parts of the data, we feel that we can make this assertion with some confidence. However, it is only an assertion and the reader should note that on these variables a significant percentage of cases have zero values that have been assigned rather than measured.

For quantitative variables, missing data were replaced with a constant (the mean of the variable's distribution), and a binary variable was constructed denoting whether the data had been originally missing or present. The variable was then used in conjunction with this quality-of-data dummy to capture as much as possible of its true effect (see G. S. Maddala, "Econometrics," 1977:202, for a discussion of this technique). In addition, several of the company-size variables were combined into an index to alleviate problems of missing data and multi-collinearity. The construction of this index is discussed in detail in Chapter 6.

A Sectoral Model at the Corporate Level

As with the industry-level data, many of the company variables described in Table 4.6 will be used in Chapter 6 to construct a continuous-variable model of industrial structure and workers' earnings. However, we are also interested in evaluating a company-level sectoral model of industrial structure. Because of the more limited set of company variables available, the technique utilized for constructing company-level sectors will be somewhat simpler than the one used in the case of the industrial-level sectors.

A diagram of our operationalization of company-level economic sectors is presented in Table 4.8. This operationalization rests primarily on the specification of qualitatively distinct positions along the major corporate dimension of size. The criteria used in allocating companies to sectors are having plants outside the local area, having subsidiaries, and appearance on one of the three *Fortune* lists of 1975. A six-sector model was initially constructed but can readily be collapsed to fewer categories. The six-sector model includes each of the *Fortune* lists as a separate category, distinguishes between non-*Fortune*-listed companies with and without subsidiaries, and distinguishes between non-subsidiary companies with and without plants outside the local area. The three-sector categorization distinguishes among the *Fortune*-listed companies as a whole, companies with plants outside the local area, and companies with only

TABLE 4.8

Definition of Corporate Economic Sectors

Characteristics	Sectors		
	Six	Three	Two
Listed with *Fortune*'s "500 Largest Industrialists"	Monopoly 1		
Listed with *Fortune*'s "2nd 500 Largest Industrialists"	Monopoly 2	Monopoly	
Listed with *Fortune*'s "50 Largest Banking, Insurance, Financial, Retailing, Transportation, and Utilities Firms"	Monopoly 3		Multiplant
Not on any *Fortune* list, but has subsidiaries	National	Multiplant	
Not on any *Fortune* list, has no subsidiaries, but has plants outside the local area	Regional		
Has no plants outside the local area	Local	Local	Local

local plants. The two-sector categorization distinguishes between companies with and without plants outside the local area. The final selection of a company-level sectoral model from among those presented in Table 4.8 will be made on the basis of the explanatory power of each scheme. If the two- or three-category scheme adequately explains earnings differentials, then we shall utilize one of these simplified categorizations.

INDIVIDUAL-LEVEL VARIABLES EXTRACTED FROM THE WISCONSIN SURVEY AND THE CURRENT POPULATION SURVEY

Our purpose in collecting the many company- and industry-level measures described previously cannot be achieved until we combine these measures of industrial structure with individual-level measures of workplace outcomes for the study of employees' earnings. Therefore, we shall now turn to a brief description of the individual-level variables to be utilized in this study. Most of the central variables for this analysis were contained in both the CPS and in the Wisconsin survey and were coded in similar or identical fashions. Other variables were available or meaningful in only one of the surveys. The abbreviations "Wisconsin" and "CPS" will be used in these variable descriptions to indicate from which surveys the variable was taken.

EARNINGS (WISCONSIN, CPS)   The earnings variable is measured as the total wages and salaries earned in the previous year. It does not include unearned income such as pensions, disability pay, or profits. This variable was transformed by the natural logarithm function for use in most of the analysis.[14]

RACE (CPS)   This variable is coded 1 if the respondent is black and 0 otherwise.[15]

SEX (WISCONSIN, CPS)   The sex of the respondent is coded 1 if female and 0 if male.

EDUCATION (WISCONSIN, CPS)   This variable is coded as years of education completed. Recall that in the Wisconsin sample this variable has a minimum value of 12.

WEEKS (WISCONSIN, CPS)   This variable is coded as the number of weeks worked last year.

HOURS (WISCONSIN, CPS)   This variable is coded as the number of hours worked last week.

OCCUPATION (WISCONSIN, CPS)   The occupations of the respondents were collapsed into four categories denoting managers, professionals, white-collar workers (clerks and salespersons), and manual workers.

UNION (WISCONSIN, CPS)   This variable is coded as 1 if the respondent is a member of a labor union and 0 otherwise.

EXPERIENCE (CPS)   Experience is computed as age minus education minus six and measures the maximum number of years that the respondent might have spent in the labor force. Note that this measure would be completely collinear with education if applied to the Wisconsin survey respondents who are all of the same age cohort.

EXPERIENCE SQUARED (CPS)   This variable is computed as the square of experience and is used to measure curvature in the effects of experience.

TENURE (WISCONSIN)   This variable is a measure of the number of months of tenure the respondent has at his or her current job. It is adjusted for time away from the job for education, military service, and pregnancies.

CLASS (WISCONSIN)   This is an alternative measure to occupation and is coded in categories denoting managers, supervisors, autonomous workers, and workers.[16] This scheme is patterned after that of Wright (1979). See Appendix C for a detailed description of the construction of this variable.

PLANT EMPLOYMENT (WISCONSIN)   Plant employment is the number of people the respondent reported as working at his or her place of employment. This variable was transformed by the natural logarithm function to reduce the problem of large numeric outliers.

An additional group of variables is of less central interest than these and was utilized only in specific sections of the analyses. This group, available only in the Wisconsin survey, concerns mainly socioeconomic background and is listed next.

SIZE OF PLACE OF ORIGIN   This variable is a nine-level integer scale representing population size of the town in which the respondent attended high school. The categories range from "rural" (1) to "greater than 150,000" (9).

FARM   The dummy variable "farm" is coded 1 if the respondent's father was a farmer when the respondent graduated from high school and coded 0 otherwise.

BROKEN HOME   This dummy variable is coded 1 if the respondent was not living with both parents most of the time until his or her senior year of high school. It is coded 0 otherwise.

PARENTAL INCOME   Parental income is measured in the respondent's senior year of high school and was based primarily on information taken from the Wisconsin income tax records. If information from this source was unavailable, the information was taken from the respondent's 1975 retrospective report of parental income. The variable is truncated at 15,000 in 1957 dollars to eliminate the problem of large numeric outliers.

FATHER'S OCCUPATIONAL STATUS   This is a continuous measure of so cioeconomic status based on the work of Duncan (1961). The measure was compiled from the respondent's 1957 report of father's occupation. For information on the construction of this variable see Sewell and Hauser (1975).

FATHER'S EDUCATION   Father's education is measured as number of years of schooling completed and was based on data taken from the respondent's 1975 retrospective report of father's education. If information from this source was unavailable, the information was taken from the respondent's 1957 report of father's education.

HIGH SCHOOL RANK   This measure, the percentile grade rank of the respondent within his or her high school, is based on information gathered from the respondents' high school records.

IQ   This variable is the percentile rank of the respondent on the Henmon–Nelson IQ test, which was taken in his or her junior year of high school. The percentile rankings are based on the scores of the entire 1957 cohort of Wisconsin high school graduates.

OCCUPATIONAL ASPIRATION   This variable is based on the respondent's report of his or her intended occupation at the time of high school graduation. It was scaled in terms of the Duncan socioeconomic index (see "Father's occupational status").

VOCATIONAL SCHOOL ASPIRATION   This dummy variable is coded 1 if the respondent planned, at the time of high school graduation, to go to a vocational or other training school. It is coded 0 in all other cases.

COLLEGE ASPIRATION   This variable is coded 1 if the respondent planned, at the time of high school graduation, to go to a state or liberal arts college, a teacher's college, or a university. It is coded 0 in all other cases.

THE SAMPLE TO BE STUDIED

The sample used throughout this analysis consists of private workers with $100 or more in yearly earnings. Private workers were selected because the company- and industry-level financial measures, and the theory linking these to workplace outcomes, are largely inapplicable to government and self-employed workers. Workers with less than $100 annual earnings were excluded because it is not likely that they were fully engaged in the labor force, even in part-time or marginal positions. It is possible that inclusion of these outlying cases would produce misleading statistical results.

For ease of presentation various subsamples of the CPS and the Wisconsin survey are enumerated in Table 4.9. The number of respondents lost in selecting each subsample is reported, as is the percentage of the total sample represented by each subsample. We see that a larger percentage of the Wisconsin survey

TABLE 4.9

Selection of Subsamples to Be Analyzed from Wisconsin Survey and CPS

N	Description of sample	Number lost	% Residual
Wisconsin survey			
10,317	One-third random sample of Wisconsin high school graduates of 1957	—	100.00
9,138	Respondents to 1975 survey	1,179	88.57
7,428	Experienced civilian labor force (ECLF)	1,710	72.00
6,602	Exclude government teachers and public administrators	826	63.99
5,140	Private workers in ECLF	1,462	49.82
4,846	Exclude respondents with missing earnings reports	294	46.97
4,493	Exclude respondents with reported earnings less than $100	353	43.55
CPS			
42,490	Representative sample of U.S. population	—	100.00
20,643	Private workers in the experienced civilian labor force (ECLF)	21,847	48.58
20,007	Exclude respondents with reported earnings less than $100	635	47.09

TABLE 4.10

Means of Key Variables for Subsamples of ECLF Private Workers by Level of Reported Earnings, 1975 Wisconsin Survey

Variable	ECLF private workers		Reported earnings of $100 or greater		Reported earnings less than $100		Earnings data missing	
	Mean	Standard deviation	Mean	Standard deviation	Mean	Standard deviation	Mean	Standard deviation
Company employment	53,284	142,130	53,820	145,139	52,986	118,367	45,441	119,955
Self-reported employment	942	3,614	1,004	3,801	233	671	762	2,314
Company size index[a]	-.3011	.8567	-.2948	.8644	-.3630	.7904	-.3233	.8126
Plants outside local area	.5111	.4976	.5248	.4994	.3314	.4714	.5170	.5006
Total subsidiaries	12.62	41.88	12.84	40.70	10.26	48.21	12.04	50.66
Profit rate	4.62	2.98	4.63	2.97	4.38	3.35	4.79	2.68
Weeks worked	44.36	11.15	47.30	10.72	5.84	14.92	45.64	12.26
Percent female	44.14	.48	40.13	.49	91.22	.28	48.98	.50
Education	13.10	1.90	13.10	1.91	12.90	1.79	13.27	1.94
N	5,140		4,493		353		294	
Percentage	100		87.41		6.87		5.72	

[a] The computation of this index will be discussed in Chapter 6.

respondents is in the ECLF than is the case for the CPS respondents. This is because the Wisconsin respondents are all in their prime working ages, whereas the CPS sample represents the entire age distribution. Note also that extremely low and unreported earnings account for a greater percentage of lost cases in the Wisconsin sample than in the CPS sample. In the Wisconsin data, where there are 5140 private workers, we lose 294 cases because of missing earnings data and 353 because of yearly earnings less than $100. From 20,643 private workers in the CPS, we lose 29 zero earners and 607 who earned less than $100, leaving us with a sample size of 20,007. This discrepancy is a result of the different data-handling techniques used in the two surveys.[17]

To assess the impact of possible bias resulting from the loss of missing and low earners in the Wisconsin sample, we examined the means and standard deviations of selected key variables for missing and low earners. These statistics are reported in Table 4.10, along with comparable statistics for the total sample of private workers in the ECLF and for our selected analysis sample, which eliminates missing and low earners. Beyond the obvious fact that low earners worked fewer weeks than other workers, two possible sources of bias are evident in these results. First, a large percentage of low earners are women. Second, based on the self-report of size of place of employment, both low and missing earners appear to work in smaller places than average. In eliminating low and missing earners we trade off the exclusion of cases that could potentially produce misleading statistical results against the creation of these possible biases. Although we do not believe this sample selectivity to be a serious problem, the reader should be aware of its existence.

CONCLUSIONS: THE TASK OF COLLECTING COMPANY AND INDUSTRY DATA

The plans we conceived for collecting company and industry data from archival sources were, by and large, completed successfully. A small grant from the Department of Labor was essential for the completion of this data collection task. However, the amount of resources required was not tremendous, and quite a large body of data was collected. If later chapters convince the reader that the results were worth obtaining, then social scientists should be aware of the data possibilities available in this field. In the emerging body of research on labor market segmentation, data that tap corporate structure can be obtained without the expenditure of prohibitively large resources. In the current research project the collection of company-level data required the outlay of perhaps twenty times as many hours and resources as did the collection of the industry-level data. Thus, company-level data are harder to collect than industry-level data, but the task is not by any means impossible.

We were able to collect company- and industry-level data measuring a great many concepts of current interest in the literature on economic and labor market segmentation. Many, if not most, of these measures, however, are based on employment figures or on financial data. There remain groups of concepts not directly measured by the variables we collected. For instance, we did not collect measures of regional market power. Weiss (1966), in a study of workers' earnings and market concentration, takes great pains to correct concentration measures for regional monopoly power. He believes that concentration ratios based on share of the national market are imprecise measures of true monopoly power because such power occurs within markets that may not be national in scale. Indeed, Weiss obtains improved statistical results with measures corrected for the scale of the market for specific industry products.

Perhaps more importantly, the literature on corporate bureaucracy and internal organizational structure remains largely untapped by our measures (see Child, 1973; Pugh, Hickson, Hinings, and Turner, 1968). These studies typically conclude that corporate size is a key organizational variable affecting, if not dominating, other measures. We are fortunate in being able to measure organizational size in a multitude of ways in the present study. However, we do not have any direct measures of other internal organizational concepts such as degree of bureaucratization, standardization, and centralization.

Measures of these and other concepts of importance to the field of labor market segmentation can again be obtained without the application of prohibitively large resources. Some of these variables can be obtained utilizing data collection methodologies similar to the ones employed in the present study. Additional data can be extracted from the sources that we utilized, and further sources can be developed. The collection of data on other variables will require different methodologies. Good measures of the organizational characteristics of companies probably cannot be developed without starting from a sample of companies (rather than a sample of persons) and securing information directly from these companies.

In the emerging field of labor market segmentation, good data are readily available from a variety of sources. From the standpoint of data availability, we do not need to be restricted to dualistic categorizations of industries. Limiting our investigation to such categories and to only the industry level of measurement restricts the interaction of theory, concepts, and measurement so important for the development of social science. From a methodological as well as a theoretical standpoint, such limitation is totally unnecessary in the present case.

NOTES TO CHAPTER 4

1. The Experienced Civilian Labor Force is defined as all persons 14 years or older who are not currently in the military or in an institution and who are working or who have worked in the past and are actively seeking employment.

2. This solution works well for variables computed from data taken entirely from one source where all the variables are at the same level of aggregation. However, calculations made using components taken from different sources created special problems. When the components of a variable came from sources with noncompatible levels of aggregation, we increased the level of aggregation of one component until the aggregated data pertained to comparable industry units across both sources. This increased the level of aggregation in variables that were calculated using data from more than one source.

3. This problem is distinct from the *nonreporting* of a variable for a specific industry otherwise covered by a source. This latter problem affected less than 1% of the observations and was largely a result of an agency's obligation to maintain the privacy of large reporting corporations. Most of these missing data were replaced by estimated or interpolated values.

4. Because we are using the principal components factor analytic technique, the first 11 eigenvalues presented in Table 4.2 are the exact eigenvalues for an 11-factor solution.

5. Based on the 11-factor solution, the communalities for the variables in the size concept group (listed in the order in which they appear in Table 4.1) are .94, .98, .91, .88, .86, .90, and .81. The communalities for the variables in the concentration concept group are .85, .82, .60, .65, .88, and .78.

6. The weighting procedure used to handle missing data was

$$F_{Aj} = \frac{40}{N_A} \sum_{k=1}^{N_A} f_{jk} \, x_{Ak},$$

where N_A is the number of nonmissing variables for case A, F_{Aj} is the factor score for case A for factor j, f_{jk} is the factor score coefficient for factor j on variable k, and x_{Ak} is the standardized value of variable k for case A.

7. The seven "not-specified" manufacturing industries for which factor scores could not be computed were construction machinery, metal machinery, electrical machinery, professional equipment, food, and the general "not-specified" manufacturing industry.

8. We used the 25 factors in their original unweighted construction. Alternatively, a weighting scheme giving more weight to the factors with more explanatory power could have been utilized. This option was rejected because our goal was to reproduce the original variable space in an orthogonal space, and any weighting scheme would have distorted that space.

9. We changed the cluster placement of 3 of the 202 industries (crude petroleum extraction, ship and boat building, and miscellaneous petroleum products manufacturing). Each of these three industries was a large outlier in clusters where the other industries were tightly grouped, and each was almost as close to another cluster in which it was conceptually more reasonable to place the industry. A test statistic can be calculated for these changes in placement (see Kaufman, 1981). This test statistic was not significant for any of the three changes ($p > .10$).

10. In profiling the major industry clusters and discussing their rank orderings on the variable means, we exclude from consideration the four single-industry outliers.

11. This finding may result from the difficulty of compiling accurate measures of profit across different industries. (See Weiss, 1974, on this point.)

12. It is interesting to note that some of the industries in the wholesale sector are classified as core and some as periphery by both Hodson (1978) and Tolbert, Horan, and Beck (1980). However, these researchers do not agree as to which of these industries are to be included in the core and which are to be included in the periphery.

13. Missing data on the *Fortune* list variable were also assumed to have a value of zero, that is, not on any of the lists. These missing data represent cases in which the name of place of employment was coded as missing. Assuming a value of zero for these cases is justified because most of these cases were not "refusals" but were unclear or incomplete names of small shops. We pursued such

cases diligently at the company name-coding stage in an attempt to determine a specific company name. Again, directory assistance and Wisconsin city telephone directories were our major aids in this attempt. For large plants we could often make a verification of the company name based on the address plus the incomplete response. In other cases, we could make no such verification. Such plants were assumed to be "too small to find." This allocation of missing data involved only 24 cases in the final-analysis sample, representing about .5% of that sample.

14. When an earnings variable is transformed by the natural logarithm function, changes in this variable are interpretable as percentage changes in earnings. This transformation is the one most commonly used in earnings equations for two reasons. First, it reduces statistical problems caused by extremely high earners. Second, it is commonly argued that people think of differences in income in percentage terms rather than in absolute dollar terms. The use of a logged dollar function also makes possible the direct comparison of earnings coefficients across time and across nations without adjustments for inflation or currency. (See Coleman and Rainwater, 1978; Jencks, 1979; and Rainwater, 1974; for a counterargument in favor of the unlogged dollar function, see Wright, 1979.) Two alternative earnings functions will also be discussed and evaluated in Chapter 6.

15. A race variable will not be utilized with the Wisconsin data because of the extremely small number of blacks and other minorities in this sample.

16. The literature on economic segmentation argues that authority-based class relations are the key to understanding the impact of economic structure on the workplace (Reich, Gordon, and Edwards, 1973; Edwards, 1979). Such authority relations provide the basis for the operationalization of class positions used in the analysis of the Wisconsin data. However, the CPS does not include the type of data that would allow us to construct measures of true class position. Instead, we are forced to use broad occupational categories in the analysis of the CPS data. Occupations are defined as different technical functions in production. These different job tasks are related to class (position in the authority structure), but in an inexact and changing manner. Nevertheless, occupational categories have a long tradition of usage in the social sciences. Their use in the present context does not substantially detract from the analysis and, as we shall see, may even shed further light on certain theoretical arguments.

17. In the CPS, missing data, including earnings, are given allocated values.

5

Distribution of Poverty, Union Membership, Class Positions, and Race and Gender Groups across Economic Sectors

In this chapter we shall discuss the distribution of several labor force and labor market characteristics across the industry- and enterprise-level economic sectors developed in previous chapters. The characteristics selected for presentation are ones that have been named as key correlates or outcomes of economic segmentation by the literature in this field: poverty, unionization, class position, and race and gender. In this chapter we seek to achieve two goals. First, we wish to evaluate some specific expectations about the labor force composition and labor market characteristics of the various sectors. Second, we wish to gain an overview of the characteristics of the various sectors to provide a basis for our interpretation of more complex models to be presented in subsequent chapters.[1]

POVERTY

The explanation of poverty has been a critical issue in the economic segmentation literature throughout its development. This concern results from the importance of this issue in American society and from the strong relationship between poverty and industrial segmentation.

In an attempt to study this relationship we shall utilize several alternative individual-level measures of poverty. Although poverty is most appropriately measured as an attribute of families, the focus of the present study on individuals makes such operationalizations difficult to integrate. The measures developed here are based either on individual annual earnings at a rate below the minimum wage or on earnings below the single-person or family poverty lines.

POVERTY 40/35   This measure represents earnings of less than the minimum wage ($2.30 in 1973 and in 1975) for 35 hours a week, 40 weeks a year. A 35-hour week and a 40-week year are the CPS definition of year-round full-time employment. The cutoff point for this measure is $3220.

POVERTY 50/40   This poverty line also represents year-round full-time work at the minimum wage. Here the 40-hour week and the 50-week year are the base and the cutoff point is $4600.

POVERTY–S   This measure is based on the official poverty line for single-person families. For 1973 the cutoff point is $1947; for 1975 the cutoff point is $2101 (*World Almanac* 1975).

TABLE 5.1

Distribution of Persons across Union Membership and Poverty Status by Industrial and Company Sectors[a]

Sector	Union (%)	Poverty 40/35 (%)	Poverty 50/40 (%)	Poverty-S (%)	Poverty-F (%)	YRFT[d] Poverty-F (%)
Industrial[b]						
Oligopoly	46.3	10.3	14.0	6.7	12.0	1.3
Core	31.2	18.8	28.1	12.0	22.7	6.4
Periphery	18.1	45.3	55.8	32.6	50.4	14.9
Core utilities	29.9	15.1	25.0	9.6	17.9	4.0
Periphery utilities	42.8	20.2	25.7	13.1	22.4	6.3
Trades	19.1	46.9	56.6	35.7	51.5	18.5
Total	24.6	34.2	43.9	24.5	38.5	10.5
Company[c]						
Monopoly	37.5	8.2	10.9	5.8	10.1	0.9
Multiplant	26.6	14.2	19.8	10.4	18.8	3.0
Local	13.3	25.0	32.1	18.5	30.9	6.1
Total	24.0	17.3	22.6	12.7	21.6	3.5

[a] Sample is private employees with annual earnings of at least $100.
[b] Data taken from CPS ($N = 20,007$).
[c] Data taken from Wisconsin survey ($N = 4493$).
[d] Year-round full-time labor force, $N = 10,911$ (CPS); $N = 2841$ (Wisconsin survey).

POVERTY–F   This measure is based on the official poverty line for families of four persons. For 1973 the cutoff point is $3944; for 1975 the cutoff point is $4247 (*World Almanac* 1975).

Looking at Table 5.1 we see that poverty earnings are sharply differentiated across industrial sectors.[2] For each definition of poverty, periphery workers are about twice as likely to be below the poverty line as core workers are. In turn, core sector workers are twice as likely to be below the poverty line as oligopoly sector workers are. Core and periphery utilities workers fare about as well as workers in the major core sector, with periphery utilities workers being slightly more likely to experience poverty than are core utilities workers. Workers in the trades sector fare similarly to those in the periphery sector. Even for persons with full-time year-round jobs, 15% of those in the periphery and 18% of those in the trades sector earn less than enough to support a family of four above the poverty line. In the core sector this figure is reduced to 6%, and in the oligopoly sector such poverty is virtually unknown. This pattern of findings is in close accord with the expectations developed in Chapter 4 for earnings levels within these sectors.

Examining the second panel of Table 5.1 we see a similar pattern of poverty reproduced across company-level economic sectors. Monopoly sector workers experience the least poverty. Multiplant sector workers are about twice as likely and local sector workers about three times as likely to experience poverty as monopoly sector workers. Even for year-round full-time workers in this select sample of 35-year-old high school graduates, 6.1% of those employed in the local sector earn less than enough to support a family of four at the absolute minimum level of existence.

UNION MEMBERSHIP

Union membership measures the degree of self-organization of labor in response to the working environment. It is the most commonly discussed working class organizational correlate of economic segmentation. Workers in large enterprise sectors of the economy are thought to be more unionized than other workers because of the organizational possibilities available in large plants and the alienating conditions of labor in these sectors.

The first column of numbers in the top half of Table 5.1 presents the percentage of union membership across industrial-level economic sectors. We see that the degree of labor force organization differs sharply across economic sectors. Only about one-fifth of the labor force in the periphery is organized, whereas one-third is organized in the core and nearly half is organized in the oligopoly sector. The core and periphery utilities sectors are also heavily unionized. The core utilities sector is organized at about the level of the core, and the periphery utilities sector is even more highly unionized. The high rate of unionization in the periphery utilities sector results from the inclusion of transportation workers in this sector and from the organizational power of the Teamsters' Union. The trades sector has a low overall rate of unionization despite the inclusion of the construction industry in this sector. This highlights the diversity of working environments represented by this small-enterprise, labor-intensive sector.

Turning to the company-level model presented in the second half of Table 5.1, we see that unionization rates are again sharply differentiated across sectors along the dimension of corporate size. Monopoly-sector workers enjoy the highest rates of unionization, and the sector that is composed of only locally based firms has the lowest rate of unionization. These findings again clearly indicate the centrality of organizational size in the successful growth of trade unionism.

CLASS POSITIONS

Theories of economic segmentation frequently include a discussion of the dynamics of class development that accompany the emergence of economic sectors. The monopoly or large-firm sector is generally thought to give rise to the growth of the new middle class of salaried professionals and white-collar workers. This argument is articulated by both Marxist analysts (e.g., Poulantzas, 1975) as well as by more mainstream theorists (e.g., Bell, 1973). By surveying the distribution of class positions across economic sectors, we may be able to shed some light on these propositions.

Examining the top half of Table 5.2, we see that the oligopoly and core industrial sectors have less than their share of managerial and white-collar employees and only a slightly greater than average percentage of professional employees. These core sectors, however, employ very large proportions of manual workers. The company-level monopoly sector also has fewer managers and more workers than the average across sectors.[3] These findings clearly do not support the hypothesis that the large-firm monopoly sector is the birthplace of the new middle class of salaried employees.

The periphery and small-shop sectors, as dependent or satellite sectors, are often thought of as primarily employing manual labor, especially service workers. This proposition, however, is again not supported. The peripheral industrial sector is typified by lower white-collar employment, and the local and multiplant corporate sectors are typified by large numbers of managers, supervisors, and autonomous workers.[4]

In summary, the core sectors contain a greater proportion of manual workers than do the periphery sectors. They demonstrate an extreme polarity of class positions much more akin to the traditional Marxist analysis of the class structure

TABLE 5.2

Distribution of Persons across Class Positions by Industrial and Company Sectors[a]

	Occupation				
Industrial sector[b]	Managers (%)	Professionals (%)	White collar (%)	Manual (%)	Total N (100%)
Oligopoly	6.3	12.2	15.3	66.2	593
Core	7.8	9.1	19.8	63.3	5,403
Periphery	9.9	5.5	30.5	54.1	7,619
Core utilities	13.0	6.9	54.1	26.0	1,805
Periphery utilities	7.4	1.4	15.8	75.4	383
Trades	5.1	15.5	10.2	69.2	4,181
Total	8.4	8.8	24.7	58.0	19,984[d]

	Class				
Company sector[c]	Managers (%)	Supervisors (%)	Autonomous (%)	Working (%)	Total N (100%)
Monopoly	14.3	28.8	8.4	48.5	1,528
Multiplant	19.8	30.8	11.9	37.5	875
Local	16.6	35.0	15.0	33.4	2,090
Total	16.4	32.1	12.2	39.3	4,493

[a] Sample is private employees with annual earnings of at least $100.
[b] Data taken from CPS (N = 20,007).
[c] Data taken from Wisconsin Survey (N = 4493).
[d] Twenty-three cases have missing values on the industrial sector variable.

of capitalism than do modern-day Marxist or mainstream identification of the monopoly sector with the rise of the new middle class. Conversely, the periphery economic sectors are typified by a predominance of white-collar and other middle-level positions.

To understand this seemingly anomalous pattern, recall the argument from the literature of complex organizations that the administrative ratio is in fact smaller in large enterprises, an argument that appears to be more in accord with the distribution of positions just described.[5] The large-plant and monopolistic sectors have a much smaller contingent of managers and supervisors than do the periphery and local sectors. This pattern indicates that, although the growth of the broad new middle class of salaried employees may be associated with the rise of industrialism and monopoly capital, this class does not emerge predominently in the monopoly sector itself. Instead, the growth of the new middle class appears to occur in subordinate and ancillary sectors of the economy.

These findings and the interpretations offered of them may be in better accord with certain aspects of the thesis of labor market segmentation than current constructions of that thesis would allow. The location of large bodies of working class positions in the large-plant and monopolistic sectors highlights the organizational power of the working class in these sectors. The lack of such masses of working class positions in the growing service and satellite sectors partially explains the historic difficulty of the labor movement in organizing workers in dependent, small-shop, and peripheral sectors of the economy.

RACE

Employment discrimination against blacks in core sectors has long been an important theme in the literature on economic segmentation. This topic is not our principal focus in the present research, so we will not spend a great deal of time developing and analyzing sophisticated models of discrimination. However, to gain at least an initial appraisal of this issue within a multisector framework, it will be useful to survey the percentage of black job holders across occupational positions within the various industrial sectors.

Looking at the percentages given in Table 5.3, we see that the hypothesis of the exclusion of blacks from the core and oligopoly sectors must be rejected. The core sector employs a greater percentage of blacks than the periphery does, and the oligopoly sector employs a considerably higher percentage of blacks than either the core or the periphery does. Indeed, the position with the highest percent of black employment is the oligopoly manual class. In addition, the

TABLE 5.3

Percentage of Blacks across Occupational Categories by Industrial Sector[a]

Industrial sector	Occupation				
	Managers	Professionals	White collar	Manual	Total N
Oligopoly	10.5	1.4	11.0	17.6	14.1
Core	0.2	2.8	2.8	11.6	8.2
Periphery	2.1	2.6	4.5	10.8	7.5
Core utilities	1.3	2.4	8.3	8.7	7.1
Periphery utilities	0.0	0.0	5.0	11.1	9.1
Trades	0.9	7.1	7.0	16.7	13.4
Total	1.6	4.3	5.2	12.6	9.1

[a] Data taken from March–May match 1973 CPS. Sample is private employees with annual earnings of at least $100; ($N$ = 20,007.)

oligopoly managerial class contains over 10% blacks, the highest black representation in any sector's managerial class. The strong representation of blacks in the oligopoly managerial class may be a result of the high visibility of these positions and public and government pressure for affirmative action hiring practices. The strong representation of blacks in the oligopoly manual class may be a result of the workings of similar forces as well as a result of the employment of large numbers of blacks in heavy manufacturing industries in response to historical and ecological factors (see Bonacich, 1976). Table 5.3 indicates that blacks are strongly stratified into lower positions in the occupational hierarchy, but the same assertion does not hold for stratification across sectors of the economy.

It is certainly the case that blacks on the average have inferior jobs to whites, but this does not appear to be a result of the employment of blacks in peripheral sectors of the economy.[6] In fact, the core and oligopoly sectors are among the largest employers of blacks. These findings indicate that the inferior employment positions of blacks cannot be attributed to discrimination between industrial sectors but must be seen as primarily resulting from occupational segregation. (See Kaufman, 1981, for a more detailed analysis of the issue of racial employment discrimination across industrial sectors and occupational categories.)

TABLE 5.4

Percentage of Females across Class Positions by Industrial and Company Sectors[a]

Industrial sector[b]	Occupation				
	Managers	Professionals	White collar	Manual	Total N
Oligopoly	7.9	9.7	46.2	15.0	18.7
Core	8.4	10.3	55.3	26.8	29.4
Periphery	25.8	32.9	73.3	37.4	47.0
Core utilities	19.6	19.4	69.7	6.6	43.3
Periphery utilities	27.6	40.0	51.7	1.0	11.7
Trades	18.4	62.7	85.2	38.4	45.9
Total	19.3	35.8	69.0	31.6	40.2

Company sector[c]	Class				
	Managers	Supervisors	Autonomous	Working	Total N
Monopoly	6.9	17.0	25.6	35.2	25.1
Multiplant	7.8	36.0	46.0	52.9	37.9
Local	22.7	46.6	70.5	63.3	51.8
Total	14.7	35.6	55.5	49.7	40.1

[a] Sample is private employees with annual earnings of at least $100.
[b] Data taken from CPS ($N = 20,007$).
[c] Data taken from Wisconsin survey ($N = 4493$).

GENDER

The selection of women into lower-paying positions and stereotyped "women's jobs" is a topic of increasing concern in sociological literature. Both class and sectoral discrimination are strongly implicated in this process. Statistics on the percentage of women employed in occupational positions and in authority-based classes across industrial and company sectors are presented in Table 5.4. It is evident that women occupy few positions in the core sectors of the economy and many positions in the peripheral and the small-shop sectors.[7] In addition, women rarely attain higher occupational and class positions. Women are greatly underrepresented in the managerial and professional occupations and in the managerial and supervisory classes. Conversely, women fill more than their share of white-collar occupations and autonomous and working class positions.

The dynamics producing the exclusion of women from jobs high in the authority and skill hierarchies and from jobs in the core economic sectors overlap to produce an extreme exclusion of women from managerial positions in the leading economic sectors. The representation of women is less than 10% in these jobs. For women, the hypothesis of strong selection out of these key positions in the economy is firmly upheld.[8]

CONCLUSIONS

We have seen that the economic structure of industries and companies is reflected in the organization of the work force in a variety of ways. However, these structures are not always reflected in the ways that the literature suggests.

On the issue of differential poverty across sectors, the findings are very strong and entirely in the expected direction. The periphery sector is, indeed, the home of the working poor, a sector where "losing one's job is not much more catastrophic than keeping it" (Bluestone, 1970:26). The degree of union membership is also differentiated across sectors in the expected manner. Monopoly- and core-sector workers are highly unionized, whereas periphery- and local-sector workers remain relatively unorganized.

Concerning the distribution of class positions across sectors, many of our expectations were in error. The oligopoly, core, and monopoly sectors are typified by large numbers of working class positions, but the superordinate positions are filled by professionals rather than by managers. The periphery and small shop sectors are typified by a less divergent class structure. These satellite sectors have all the major class and occupational positions well represented, rather than embodying a sharp divergence between class positions. We believe that this class structure results from the more direct modes of labor control employed in these peripheral sectors. That is, whereas the monopoly sector appears to rely heavily on technological and bureaucratic modes of control that demand a large contingent of professional workers, the competitive sector appears to rely more on direct personal modes of control that demand a larger supervisory labor force (see Edwards, 1979).

Expectations derived from the segmentation literature on the allocation of blacks into peripheral economic sectors were shown to be in serious error. Blacks are selected into, not out of, the oligopoly and core sectors. Blacks are strongly selected out of higher occupations but not out of core economic sectors. Women, on the other hand, are strongly selected *both* out of dominant class and occupational positions and out of key economic sectors. The dynamics of discrimination in operation here are very powerful, resulting in the near exclusion of women from managerial positions in key economic sectors. These findings suggest that it is perhaps to this arena that we can most fruitfully direct future research efforts on economic segmentation and labor market discrimination.

In this chapter we have surveyed the labor market characteristics and labor force composition of economic sectors defined at both the industry and enterprise levels. This survey has provided us with important background information on the nature of working conditions in the different sectors and has also allowed us to evaluate important expectations derived from the literature on economic segmentation. Some of these expectations have been supported but others have not. In this evaluation we have, we hope, learned something about the processes that produce the outcomes we have observed in the different sectors. The inadequacy of theoretical work relating class and race to economic segmentation has been noted, as has been the key neglected issue of gender selection into the various economic sectors.

In interpreting these findings we have relied heavily on the dimension of corporate size as a key element of organizational structure. However, the dimension of capital intensity of production has also been indicated as an important aspect of organizational structure, especially in relation to the sorting of race and gender groups into jobs in the various sectors. We have seen that the use of sectoral operationalizations at both the industry and enterprise levels adds depth to many of the interpretations offered as well as provides a built-in reliability check for key findings. In the next chapter we shall turn to the analysis of employee earnings, again utilizing sectoral models but also developing new continuous-variable models that will allow analysis of the separate effects of the many dimensions of industrial structure.

NOTES TO CHAPTER 5

1. Throughout this chapter the six-sector industrial classification and the three-sector enterprise classification will be utilized for ease of presentation. It is hoped that these models will provide an adequate basis for the overview and evaluation sought in this chapter.

2. The distribution of private sector employees across the sectors is as follows. In the industrial classification the three largest sectors are the periphery (38%), the core (27%), and the trades sector (21%). (See Table 5.2 for the corresponding sample sizes.) A total of 86% of the labor force is employed in these three sectors. The remaining three sectors, core utilities (9%), oligopoly (3%), and periphery utilities (2%), employ about 14% of the labor force. Workers are distributed somewhat more evenly across the three sectors of the company-level model. The largest employer is the local sector (46%), the next largest is the monopoly sector (34%), and the smallest employer is the multiplant sector (20%). (See Table 5.2.)

3. Examining the marginal distributions of class and occupational positions in Table 5.2, it is obvious that manual occupations are not coterminous with working class positions. There are many more employees in manual occupations than in working class positions. Cross tabulations of occupational positions by industrial sectors for the Wisconsin sample and for a similarly constrained CPS subsample are presented in Appendix Table D.1. In both the Wisconsin sample and the CPS subsample, more employees have managerial, professional, and white-collar positions and fewer have manual positions than in the more inclusive CPS sample. Nevertheless, the occupational distributions are highly similar across these two samples of middle-aged high school graduates, indicating again that the Wisconsin sample respondents are reasonably representative of a similarly constrained national sample. It seems reasonable, therefore, to compare the distribution of class positions in the Wisconsin sample with the distribution of occupational positions in either the Wisconsin sample or the constrained CPS sample without fear of confounding conceptual differences with sample differences. In this comparison the manual and working classes are roughly equal in number at about 42% of the labor force. However, many fewer employees are classified as autonomous than as either professional or white collar by occupation. Finally, many more employees are classified in the managerial and supervisory classes than in the managerial and professional occupations. In other words, a large number of professionals and white-collar employees occupy managerial and supervisory positions, but relatively few occupy truly autonomous positions in the hierarchy of authority. A direct cross-classification of occupational and class positions might shed additional light on these relationships but would be largely tangential to the project at hand.

4. The core utilities sector is also typified by a disproportionate number of white-collar workers. The periphery utilities sector, on the other hand, is typified by an unusually high proportion of working class positions. Again we see that the inclusion of these economic sectors in the larger core and periphery sectors would tend to obscure important relations by conceptually equating highly dissimilar working environments. The trades sector is typified by large numbers of both professional and manual positions, again testifying to the heterogeneity of systems of production within this economic sector.

5. Part of the discrepancy between the theory of a small administrative ratio in large firms and the theory of the large firm as the home of the new middle class concerns the gray area between the two concepts employed. The administrative ratio refers to a much smaller set of positions than the new middle class does. Administrators are basically top- and middle-level management. The "new middle class" is generally considered also to include professional as well as some lower-white-collar positions. Thus, a given corporation may have a relatively small administrative ratio while having relatively large proportions of supervisory, professional, technical, sales, and clerical positions.

6. The thesis of racial employment discrimination in the dual labor market literature rests on the selection of blacks into marginal, secondary, and irregular jobs in the ghetto. These jobs, however, represent a relatively small portion of the economy. When attempting to understand racial employment discrimination in a broader context, it is important to distinguish these truly marginal jobs from the diverse employment situations in sectors that may be typified by any of a variety of dimensions of peripheral and subordinate status. Many of the truly irregular workers and jobs highlighted by the dual economy literature (see especially Gordon, 1972) may, in fact, be unrepresented in the CPS. Such individuals are difficult for enumerators to locate and, as a result, are often underrepresented in social science surveys. In addition, our industrial classification lacks a truly

marginal or "irregular economy" sector. As a result, we lack both the category and many of the respondents needed to study marginal positions. The study of these truly marginal positions and workers must not rely on large-scale representative sample surveys but on other methods, such as detailed case studies and participant observation. On any account, however, it is important to distinguish truly marginal positions from the jobs held by the majority of both black and white workers.

7. Women are strongly represented in the core utilities sector and the trades sector but are underrepresented in the periphery utilities sector. The employment of women in the many lower-white-collar jobs in financial institutions and in large utility companies is responsible for the high female representation in the core utilities sector. The importance of "women's jobs" in the educational and nonprofit firms of the trades sector accounts for the high female representation in this sector. Conversely, the virtual exclusion of women from manual jobs in transportation is responsible for their underrepresentation in the periphery utilities sector. Again, these findings highlight the importance of utilizing a multisector approach to the study of economic segmentation and labor force outcomes.

8. Bridges (1980) argues on the basis of empirical findings that women are selected into labor-intensive sectors of the economy but not necessarily into jobs dominated by other characteristics of industrial marginality, such as small size. This finding gives rise to the thesis that cheap female labor is used as an alternative to capital investment. The sectoral operationalizations utilized here are dominated by the size dimension (especially the company-level model), and because small corporations are also typically more labor-intensive, this may produce the apparent sorting of women into sectors dominated by small-scale enterprises. However, this relationship may be somewhat misleading. Under Bridges's argument, women are employed in these sectors because of the labor-intensive systems of production in small-scale enterprises, not because of the "marginality" of small size per se.

6

Enterprise- and Industry-Level Models of Employees' Earnings

INTRODUCTION

In this chapter we shall investigate the relationship between industrial structure and employees' earnings, again utilizing the categorical models developed in Chapter 4 as well as developing new continuous-variable models. In the development of the continuous-variable models of employees' earnings and industrial structure, we shall rely primarily on inductive tests of statistical significance. This strategy is taken because we are not engaged in strict, formal testing of a specific theory. Rather, we are comparing the utility of several competing theories that focus on different dimensions of industrial structure. The inductive method will provide us with the greatest ability to differentiate among the interpretations offered by these competing theories.

In the development of both industry- and company-level continuous-variable models of employee earnings, we encountered problems of extreme multicolinearity among many of the predictor measures. Frequently, these problems were so severe as to prevent the inversion of a correlation matrix containing all possible predictors. This denied us the ability to use standard regression selection procedures such as forward, backward, or stepwise selection. We confronted this problem in two ways. First, we combined similar measures into indices of major concepts. Second, we entered, tested, and retained or discarded variables against relatively simple models before progressing to more elaborate models. The resulting selection procedure is somewhat less elegant than conventional methods. However, because of the knowledge gained about these data sets through the evaluation of literally hundreds of models, we feel confident that the final models that we selected depict the major forces at work in an accurate fashion. As a further check on the validity of the models selected, all of the variables that had been rejected from earlier models were retested against the final models. In no case did these tests alter our initial model selection.

This chapter consists of two major parts. In the first part, we shall evaluate the categorical model of industrial structure as an explanation of employees' earnings and shall select and evaluate a final continuous-variable model. The second part will pursue an identical chore at the company level. The chapter will conclude with a comparison of the industry- and company-level models.

A SECTORAL INDUSTRY MODEL

The mean annual earnings and mean log annual earnings of private workers in each industrial sector are presented in Table 6.1. The mean earnings are generally in accord with the expectations derived in Chapter 4. Oligopoly sector workers have the highest earnings of workers in any major sector. These earnings exceed core sector earnings by over $3000 annually. The extremely high levels of capital intensity, foreign involvement, and concentration prevalent in the oligopoly sector set the stage for the attainment of some of the highest average wages in America. The core sector, with more moderate values on these characteristics, lags far behind in earnings, in spite of its higher level of unionization. The average core sector worker, nevertheless, annually earns over $2000 more than does the average periphery sector worker. This substantial gap can be attributed to the large differences in average establishment size between these two sectors. The industrial structure of the aggregate core utilities and periphery utilities sectors is typified by high levels of assets, capital intensity, and unionization. As a result, workers in these sectors have average earnings above even those of workers in the aggregate core sector.[1] The trades group has the lowest average earnings of any major sector, a finding in accord with its extremely low values on most of the industrial characteristics associated with high wages.[2] Each of these patterns is reproduced in the dollar, as well as in the log dollar, metric.

Subsectors within the six-sector classification have mean earnings similar to those in their sector as a whole. The particular patterns of earnings within these broader sectors reinforce prior expectations. Based on its small establishment size, the small-shop sector has earnings even lower than those in the periphery sector proper. The large establishment size and capital intensity of production in the wholesale and ordnance sectors determine earnings that are even higher than those in the core sector, with which they are grouped in the six-sector classifica-

TABLE 6.1

Mean Earnings and Mean Log Earnings in 16 Industrial Sectors[a]

Sector	Earnings	Standard dev.	Log earnings	Standard dev.	N	% of Sample
Oligopoly (total)	10,559	6,153	4.44	0.77	593	2.96
Oligopoly	10,875	6,091	4.50	0.72	555	2.77
Tobacco	5,966	5,197	3.67	1.05	38	0.19
Core (total)	8,250	6,314	4.08	0.95	5,403	27.01
Core	7,794	5,731	4.04	0.93	3,575	17.87
Wholesale	9,112	7,321	4.14	1.02	1,769	8.84
Ordnance	9,698	4,388	4.46	0.52	59	0.29
Periphery (total)	5,382	5,768	3.39	1.25	7,619	38.09
Periphery	5,686	5,587	3.47	1.24	3,748	18.73
Small shop	4,913	5,611	3.28	1.24	3,646	18.22
Real estate	7,772	9,280	3.67	1.33	225	1.12
Core utilities (total)	8,801	6,319	4.18	0.91	1,805	9.02
Core utilities and communication	7,964	6,135	4.05	0.94	1,104	5.52
Core transportation	9,730	5,353	4.38	0.75	624	3.12
Brokers	13,281	11,364	4.41	1.19	77	0.38
Periphery utilities (total)	8,627	5,741	4.12	1.01	383	1.19
Periphery utilities and communication	6,207	7,957	3.19	1.67	24	0.12
Periphery transportation	8,788	5,541	4.18	0.93	359	1.79
Trades (total)	5,338	5,808	3.28	1.39	4,181	20.90
Agriculture	2,834	3,918	2.60	1.31	534	2.67
Schools, nonprofit, personal service	3,489	4,840	2.65	1.47	1,408	7.04
Local monopoly	7,098	6,155	3.83	1.09	2,239	11.19
Missing	6,916	6,332	3.69	1.30	23	0.10
Total sample	6,670	6,204	3.67	1.23	20,007	100

[a] Data taken from March–May match 1973 CPS. Sample is private employees with annual earnings of at least $100; $N = 20,007$.

tion. The trades sector exhibits the greatest internal variability of any of the major sectors. Included in this sector are employees in the local monopoly sector, who earn slightly more than average, as well as employees in agriculture, who receive the lowest average earnings of workers in any sector.

Three of the outlier sectors—brokers, ordnance, and real estate—are typified by high levels of assets, foreign involvement, and capital intensity. The earnings of employees in each of these sectors are generally higher than the earnings in the broader sectors with which they are grouped. The low earnings of employees in the tobacco sector, however, are not in accord with the extremely high values on many of the industrial characteristics associated with high wages. This anomaly again suggests the necessity of utilizing models of industrial structure in conjunction with class and occupational models.

In summary, the earnings patterns observed across our categorization of industrial sectors support prior expectations. Large gaps in mean earning are observed between sectors, particularly between oligopoly sector workers and core sector workers and between both of these categories and periphery sector workers. Also, workers in both the core and periphery utilities sectors are observed to earn more than do workers in the core sector proper. These findings reinforce our argument that dichotomous industrial categorizations are inadequate as a basis for understanding the role of industrial structure at the workplace.

The dimensions of size, capital intensity, concentration, and foreign involvement appear to be key characteristics defining sectors with radically different patterns of earnings. The role of unionization in this process receives somewhat more mixed support. Unionization appears to contribute to the relatively high earnings of workers in the utilities sectors, but the high level of unionization in the core does not appear sufficient to overcome the substantial earnings gap between this sector and the oligopoly sector. To gain a better appraisal of the distinct roles of each of these dimensions, we now turn to the development of continuous-variable models of industrial structure and earnings, which specify each dimension as a separate variable.

A CONTINUOUS-VARIABLE INDUSTRY MODEL

Variables to be entered into this analysis were selected from the set listed in Table 4.1. Selections were made on the basis of the degree to which a given variable represents a key theoretical construct. In addition, the zero-order correlations of the variables with log mean industrial earnings were also examined as an aid in this selection procedure. The variables selected are listed in Table 6.2 along with their means, standard deviations, and correlations with log earnings.

All of the variables under the "Size" heading in Table 4.1, except net income and establishments per company, were selected. The two variables that we discarded do not correlate highly with the remainder of the group and were rejected as representing secondary aspects of corporate size. All of the variables under the "Concentration" heading, except advertising, were selected.[3] Advertising was rejected, both because it has low correlations with the other variables in this group and because it has a low correlation with log individual earnings. Rather than attempt to include a competing and secondary measure of monopoly power in a data set already overburdened with multicollinearity, we excluded advertising expenditures before proceeding with the analysis. All of the measures of foreign involvement were retained.

TABLE 6.2

Means, Standard Deviations, and Correlations with Log Individual Earnings of Industry Variables[a]

Variable	Mean	Standard dev.	Correlation with log earnings[b]
Internal factors			
Size	0.04	0.95	.29
Sales per company	2.24	1.95	.22
Assets per company	−0.08	1.84	.31
Value added per company	0.89	1.80	.33
Employment per company	3.24	1.77	.15
Companies that are corporations (%)	61.44	26.68	.22
Productivity			
Net national product per employee	16.30	12.96	.11
Technical factors			
Capital intensity/labor intensity			
Assets per employee	−1.67	1.46	.28
Part-time employment (%)	−2.75	1.08	−.23
Market factors			
Concentration	−0.03	0.89	.23
50-Firm employment concentration	40.20	30.80	.15
50-Firm sales concentration	43.17	30.77	.16
50-Firm assets concentration	42.28	25.37	.20
Sales in firms with over			
$250M sales (%)	1.88	2.74	.06
Assets in firms with over			
$250 assets (%)	32.27	30.78	.28
Growth			
New capital expenditures per company	−2.41	2.40	.29
Profit			
Net income per sales	0.05	0.03	.09
Corporate Autonomy			
Industry work force employed by companies operating primarily in that industry (%)	82.77	13.69	−.19
Foreign involvement	0.02	0.89	.32
Foreign dividends per company	1.00	3.16	.31
Foreign tax credits per company	−0.80	2.75	.31
Exports per company	−2.63	2.31	.27
Industry production exported (%)	−1.22	2.36	.27
Log individual earnings	3.37	1.23	—

[a] Data taken from March–May match 1973 CPS. Sample is private employees with annual earnings of at least $100; N = 20,007.

[b] All correlations are significant at the .01 level.

Six other variables measuring key concepts were also selected: net national product per employee (which measures productivity), assets per employee and percentage of employment that is part-time (which measures capital intensity or, conversely, labor intensity), new capital expenditures per company (which measures growth), net income over sales (which measures profit), and percentage of industry work force employed by companies operating primarily in that industry (which measures corporate autonomy). These variables represent our best measures of the remaining key concepts developed in the economic segmentation literature. Unionization will be introduced at a later stage in the analysis because we consider it an essential measure to be included in the analysis, no matter what the outcome of the selection procedure. Government regulation, although it is important for such labor force outcomes as discriminatory hiring practices, is considered less important in the analysis of earnings. In addition, none of the government regulation measures correlates significantly with log mean industrial earnings. For these reasons, none of the government regulation measures was retained.[4]

The multiple measures grouped under size, concentration, and foreign involvement were combined into summary scales. The variables that we utilized in constructing a given index have high intercorrelations and similar zero-order correlations with individual earnings (see Table 6.2 and Table D.2 in the Appendix). We first standardized each component variable by subtracting its mean and dividing by its standard deviation. Next, the variables were summed and divided by the number of variables present for each data case. Thus, each scale value is simply the arithmetical average of its components. These indices greatly lessen problems of collinearity, help on the problem of missing data (much less of a problem here than in the company data), and create measures smoothed across the kinds of measurement error that might be entailed in any one measure.

All of the industry variables that we selected have significant positive correlations with log individual earnings except for the measures of labor intensity, which has a significant negative relationship as expected, and corporate autonomy.[5] The negative relationship of corporate autonomy and individual earnings provides something of an anomaly because this variable was expected to be positively related to earnings. However, it will be retained and tested further in a multivariate context against more complex models. Most of the industry variables have zero-order correlations with log earnings of between .2 and .3. In the study of individual earnings, such correlations are substantial and reenforce the idea that subsequent analysis will yield substantively interpretable results.

Selecting an Industry-Level Model

The correlation matrix for the set of variables from which we shall select the final industry-level model is presented in Table D.3 in the Appendix. (This matrix also includes correlations for a component variable utilized later in the analysis.) Utilizing this set of three scales and six additional variables, we are presented with the problem of constructing a model of employee earnings. Many of the measures still exhibit a high degree of multicollinearity in spite of our scaling efforts. This reaffirms the need for a cautious stepwise selection procedure to avoid drawing conclusions based on erroneous tests of statistical significance resulting from severe multicollinearity. Accordingly, we shall enter the variables by stages, eliminating insignificant variables whenever possible. (Multiple regressions among the independent variables were also performed for each equation that we estimated, and the intercorrelation, or Multiple R, among a set of predictors never exceeded .90, a level that is an acceptable rule of thumb for the detection of severe multicollinearity.)

We also made use of an R^2 test for differences between regression coefficients to determine whether apparent differences were statistically verifiable. If one suspects that j regression coefficients are in fact indistinguishable in an equation, one may test this by summing the variables and entering the new variable in place of the j variables in a second equation. The test statistic for this procedure is, then,

$$\frac{(R_1^2 - R_2^2)/j}{(1 - R_1^2)/(n - k - j - l)}$$

distributed $F_{j,n-k-j-l}$, where k is the number of other predictor variables in the equation (see Cohen, 1968). We shall use this test during the selection procedure to justify combining two variables whose effects are distinguishable.

The three scales representing size, concentration, and foreign involvement are first entered simultaneously into a regression equation, and all are observed to have significant effects on earnings.[6] (See Table 6.3.) However, at this point the coefficient for concentration becomes negative, drastically altering its interpretation. The negative net effect of concentration on employee earnings was not evident from an examination of zero-order correlations because of the close association of concentration with dimensions of industrial structure that are positively related to earnings (e.g., size).

The remaining six variables are tested for significance one at a time as the last-entered variable in a model that includes the three scales (see Table 6.3, Models 2–7). Profit and labor intensity are dropped as insignificant at this stage. The other four variables have significant coefficients in the expected direction (all positive). Note that at this stage the sign for corporate autonomy switches to positive as expected. Probably the reason for this is as follows. Construction, agriculture, and many service industries have high values on this variable (little domination) because of their semiautonomous nature. This contributes to the negative zero-order relationship of autonomy with earnings. When the effect of these small-firm industries on earnings is eliminated by controlling for size, the sign of autonomy switches to positive as initially expected.

The three scales and four remaining variables are next entered into one model

TABLE 6.3

Regression of Log Earnings on Industry Variable Models, Stage 1[a]

Variable	Model						
	1	2	3	4	5	6	7
Size	.1598	.1402	.1610	.1595	.1435	.0615	.1813
	(.0178)	(.0216)	(.0207)	(.0178)	(.0181)	(.0188)	(.0236)
Concentration	−.1132	−.1159	−.1110	−.1130	−.0869	−.0777	−.1060
	(.0168)	(.0196)	(.0196)	(.0169)	(.0175)	(.0169)	(.0199)
Foreign involvement	.3876	.3497	.4349	.3852	.3728	.3365	.3862
	(.0174)	(.0234)	(.0223)	(.0175)	(.0175)	(.0175)	(.0202)
Growth		.0251					
		(.0080)					
Autonomy			.0047				
			(.0010)				
✗ Profit				[.2562]			
				(.2500)			
Productivity					.0037		
					(.0007)		
Capital intensity						.1155	
						(.0073)	
✗ Labor intensity							[.0286]
							(.0149)
Intercept	3.65	3.71	3.26	3.64	3.59	3.85	3.73
R^2(×100)	10.50	10.56	10.64	10.50	10.63	11.60	10.52
Standard deviation	1.16	1.16	1.16	1.16	1.16	1.16	1.16

[a] Data taken from March–May match 1973 CPS. Sample is private employees with annual earnings of at least $100; $N = 20,007$. Regression coefficients, unless enclosed in square brackets, are significant at the .01 level. Standard errors are reported in parentheses beneath each regression coefficient.

(see Table 6.4, Model 1). Both productivity and size are insignificant in this model. Productivity is removed first because its effect is smaller than its standard error, whereas the size effect is larger than its standard error. The equation is refit as Model 2 of Table 6.4, and we find that the effect of size is now significant at the .05 level but not at the .01 level. Based on the theoretical importance of the size dimension, we were reluctant to remove size from the model on the basis of this marginal test. Therefore, we considered the possibility that the results of these tests were influenced by entering too many collinear measures, which compete with each other for explanation of the same earnings variance, into one model. To test this possibility we examined all possible variable combinations in this six-variable model to determine whether we could in fact distinguish their coefficients. Of these 15 tests only one could not be rejected. That combination (presented in Model 3 of Table 6.4) sums size and growth and actually produces

TABLE 6.4

Regression of Log Earnings on Industry Variable Models, Stage 2[a]

Variable	Model			
	1	2	3	4
Size	[.0359]	[.0754]		
	(.0227)	(.0232)		
Concentration	−.0766	−.1290	−.1773	−.2349
	(.0205)	(.0200)	(.0188)	(.0193)
Foreign involvement	.3270	.3373	.3061	.1147
	(.0250)	(.0249)	(.0229)	(.0268)
Autonomy	.0044	.0043	.0061	.0088
	(.0010)	(.0010)	(.0010)	(.0010)
Capital intensity	.1117	.1417	.1254	.0364
	(.0087)	(.0090)	(.0089)	(.0127)
Growth	.0349	.0292		
	(.0089)	(.0081)		
Productivity	[.0006]			
	(.0009)			
Size scale			.2540	.4677
			(.0214)	(.0257)
(Size scale)^2				−.1171
				(.0116)
(Foreign involvement)^2				.1210
				(.0152)
(Capital intensity)^2				−.0440
				(.0039)
Intercept	3.56	3.61	3.36	3.21
R^2($\times$100)	11.80	12.64	13.27	14.57
Standard deviation	1.16	1.15	1.15	1.14

[a] Data taken from March–May match 1973 CPS. Sample is private employees with annual earnings of at least $100; $N = 20{,}007$. Regression coefficients, unless enclosed in square brackets, are significant at the .01 level. Standard errors are reported in parentheses beneath each regression coefficient.

an *increase* in explained variance. The zero-order correlation of growth (new capital expenditures per company) with size is .8, and perhaps it should have been included in the size index initially. Our measure of new capital expenditures, intended to tap industry growth, appears to be dominated by a corporate size component. In any event, the relationship of size and new capital expenditures to log earnings is indistinguishable in a multivariate model of industrial structure. Accordingly, they are combined into a new measure, labeled "Size scale" in Table 6.4.

Model 3 of Table 6.4 is selected as our final model of industrial structure and employee earnings. It provides a readily interpretable pattern of effects, all of which are significant at the .01 level. This model contains measures of size, concentration, foreign involvement, capital intensity, and corporate autonomy. All variables excluded at previous stages were retested against this final model and none was found to have a significant effect on earnings.

At this point we considered the possibility of curvatures or nonlinearities in the earnings effects of the industrial structure variables. Prior theoretical and empirical work was inadequate to specify a priori the correct functional form for these variables; therefore, we again relied on inductive exploratory procedures. Squared terms for all five variables were initially considered. However, the squared term for autonomy was immediately rejected because it correlated .99 with autonomy itself. In addition, the squared term for concentration was rejected because its effect was insignificant in a model containing only size, concentration, and foreign involvement. The remaining three squared terms were entered, one at a time, to the five-variable industry model. Each was highly significant and had a negative slope, indicating declining returns to the base variables (size, foreign involvement, and capital intensity), which all have positive effects.

When entered into the model simultaneously, the three curvature terms are all still highly significant, and the overall explained variance increases from 13.27 to 14.57%, an improvement of about 10%.[7] However, when all three terms are entered simultaneously, the sign for the curvature of foreign involvement switches from negative to positive, indicating increasing earnings returns to foreign involvement (see Model 4 of Table 6.4).

Before discussing the final industry-level model, it will be useful to display the effects of the variables with curvature terms in a more easily interpretable manner. The slope at any point on a curve can be found by evaluating the first derivative of that curve at the desired point. The first derivative of a simple quadratic is $a + 2bx$, where a is the regression effect of the linear component, b the regression effect of the squared term, and x the value of the variable at the point at which the slope is to be evaluated. Table 6.5 reports slopes for each of the three variables with nonlinear effects evaluated at the tenth, thirtieth, fiftieth, seventieth, and ninetieth percentiles of their respective distributions. Inspecting these slopes, we see that size has a gradually decreasing positive slope that does not approach zero within the range of values of this variable. Capital intensity has a somewhat more rapidly decreasing positive slope that does approach zero at the upper end of its distribution. Foreign involvement actually has a mildly negative slope at the low end of its distribution, increasing rapidly by the midpoint of this distribution. This anomalous pattern for the effect of foreign involvement is probably a result of the low earnings of workers in certain high-export sectors, such as agriculture. Because exports are one component of our measure of foreign involvement, the moderately high value of this variable for these sectors, combined with the low earnings of workers in these sectors,

TABLE 6.5

Evaluation of Curvature in Basic Industry Model[a]

Cumulative % of distribution	Value of size	Slope	Value of foreign involvement	Slope	Value of capital intensity	Slope
10	(−1.07)	.718	(−1.03)	−.135	(−3.50)	.344
30	(−0.83)	.662	(−0.77)	−.072	(−2.37)	.245
50	(0.30)	.397	(−0.08)	.095	(−1.62)	.179
70	(0.47)	.358	(0.43)	.219	(−1.23)	.145
90	(1.43)	.133	(1.27)	.422	(0.03)	.034

[a] See Model 4 of Table 6.4. Data taken from March–May match 1973 CPS. Sample is private employees with annual earnings of at least $100; $N = 20,007$.

probably produces this oddly curved pattern from what would otherwise be a positive linear effect. This finding may well speak of too much conceptual heterogeneity in our foreign involvement variable, which combines measures of exports with measures of multinational links, such as foreign dividends and foreign tax credits.

Interpreting the Industry-Level Model

The industry-level model of earnings that we have selected is composed of five variables, three of which have nonlinear effects.[8] Size has a positive decreasing effect and is one of the most important variables in the model.[9] In relatively small companies, a one-unit increase in size produces a 72% increase in workers' earnings (see Table 6.5). At the other end of the scale, in large companies, a unit increase in size produces only a 13% increase in earnings. Across the entire range of companies, a unit increase in size produces, on average, a 25% increase in earnings (see Model 3 of Table 6.4). The effect of size can be interpreted either as indicating that employers use the greater discretionary resources provided by organizational size to increase wages as a means of labor control or as indicating that worker power is enhanced by large organizational size through such mechanisms as economies of scale for union-organizing drives. The positive effect of organizational size on earnings supports expectations derived from each of the theoretical traditions reviewed in Chapter 3.

Capital intensity also has a positive decreasing effect. In relatively labor-intensive industries a 1% increase in capital intensity produces a .34% increase in workers' earnings. In relatively capital-intensive industries a 1% increase in capital intensity produces only a .03% increase in earnings. Across the entire range of industries, a 1% increase in capital intensity produces, on the average, a .13% increase in earnings (see Model 3 of Table 6.4). The positive effect of capital intensity can be interpreted in a similar fashion to that for size. The responsibility for expensive production equipment necessitates the payment of high wages to ensure a stable and reliable work force. This finding is in accord with the theoretical expectations of institutional economics, industrial sociology, and Marxist analysis.

Organizational size and capital intensity both tap aspects of industrial structure that are of direct importance to the production process. Accordingly, size and capital intensity are major components of the workplace environment. That both variables exhibit patterns of decreasing returns indicates that workers benefit from increases in these factors at a decreasing rate. Whether this results from declining marginal returns to scale and capital investment or from declining increments to workers' ability to win higher wages in larger and more capitalized shops, we are unable to ascertain solely from the statistical analysis presented here. However, the insignificance of productivity and profit in the model points to the latter interpretation.

Three market factors are also included in the final model: foreign involvement, concentration, and corporate autonomy. Foreign involvement has a positive and increasing slope over most of its range. Along with size it is one of the most significant variables in the model. In Model 3 of Table 6.4, which does not include curvature terms, a one-unit increase in foreign involvement produces a 31% increase in workers' earnings. In the model that includes curvature terms, at low levels of foreign involvement a one-unit increase actually produces a 14% loss in workers' earnings. By the midpoint of foreign involvement a one-unit increase produces a 10% increase in earnings, and at high levels of foreign involvement, a one-unit increase produces a 42% increase in workers' earnings. The increasing return to this variable may indicate a trickle-down effect of some of the super-profits of American multinational corporations to their labor forces. A portion of the profits from that foreign involvement appears to be repatriated to American workers. This finding supports the argument, derived from institutional economics and Marxist analysis, that a certain segment of American labor benefits directly from United States imperialism. The finding of a positive individual earnings return to foreign involvement says nothing, of course, about rising unemployment among American workers and other structural effects resulting from multinationals moving plants overseas in the search for cheap labor.[10] Foreign involvement probably has its primary positive effects on individual earnings through the marketplace rather than through the process of production.

The negative effect of concentration exclusive of other measures of industrial structure is perhaps our most interesting finding. A one-unit increase in market concentration produces a 23% reduction in workers' earnings (see Model 4 of Table 6.4). This finding indicates that the market position of large oligopolistic corporations provides them with the ability to exploit their work forces to a greater extent than would otherwise be possible. That is, the discretionary resources provided by market power are utilized to undermine wages rather than to increase them. The neoclassical expectation that concentration brings greater earnings to workers is clearly mistaken. Rather, the suggestion from labor and institutional economics that concentration may impede wage gains is supported (see Levinson, 1967; Weiss, 1966). It appears that the insulation of these industries from market relations gives them greater power in dealing with their labor forces than that possessed by their fellow giant corporations that only have size on their side. Whereas size brings earnings benefits to workers, concentration may well rob them of these higher earnings. It is noteworthy that this effect is not revealed until multivariate controls are introduced for other dimensions of industrial structure.

This is perhaps the most compelling evidence discovered so far in support of the multivariate approach to industrial structure. Theories based on *assumed* communalities among the effects of the various dimensions of economic segmentation must be rejected. The negative net effect of concentration strongly indicates that dual economy models err by aggregating the effects of this variable with those of other dimensions of industrial structure. Only when we control for other dimensions of industrial structure do the true effects of concentration emerge.[11]

The final variable in the industry-level model, corporate autonomy, operates in the expected fashion, exhibiting a positive linear effect on earnings. A unit (1%) increase in autonomy produces an .88% increase in workers' earnings. Autonomy is the least-significant variable in the model of industrial structure and employees' earnings, having a standardized regression coefficient only about a third the magnitude of those of organizational size and foreign involvement. This finding nevertheless supports the institutional economic thesis that satellite firms and their work forces are exploited by the large conglomerates (Averitt, 1968). It should also be noted that even this effect was not revealed until multivariate controls were introduced.

The Industry Variables Rejected

Consideration of the variables that we have rejected is perhaps as interesting as analysis of the ones we have retained.[12] Corporate profit is observed to have no significant direct effect on employees' earnings. The supposed effects of this variable are largely spurious and can be explained by other variables in the model. This is the key variable in the market factors concept group, and its insignificance provides strong negative evidence for the neoclassical theory of how corporate structure might affect wages. Although profit may be important for corporate actors, its effect on workers' earnings disappears when more proximate measures are taken into account.

Productivity is also rejected from the final model of industrial structure and employee earnings. Because productivity is a central concept in the institutional economics interpretation of wage differentials, the finding that it has no direct effect on earnings seriously calls into question interpretations based solely on this approach.

The insignificance of profit and the negative effect of concentration on earnings provide a possible solution to the question of how to interpret the positive effect of size. If the discretionary resources provided by concentration are used to undermine wages and not to raise them, then we have no reason to believe that the discretionary resources provided by large size would not be used in the same manner. This suggests that the higher earnings associated with large size result from the constraints placed on large corporations by size, not from the generosity of the owners of large firms or from the use of wages as a mechanism of social control. Similarly, the insignificance of profit in the final earnings model undermines the interpretation that companies with excess profits use a portion of those profits to increase wages to create more stable and reliable work forces. (See also the previous interpretation of the declining returns to size and capital intensity.) These findings may not demonstrate that the control argument is false, but they do suggest that this is not the only factor at play. Size operates as a resource for workers to secure higher wages, regardless of its effects on company profits or its relationship to concentration.

Summary of the Continuous-Variable Industrial Model

Sociological, Marxist, and institutional economic theories of the workplace all gain support from the large positive earnings effects of organizational size, capital intensity, and foreign involvement. The positive effect of corporate autonomy and the negative effect of concentration predicted by institutional and labor economics provide further support for these theories. However, productivity, a major variable in the institutional approach, was observed to have an insignificant net effect and was eliminated from the model. Profit is a key variable in the neoclassical interpretation of the workplace, and the finding that it has no direct role in employee earnings seriously undermines interpretations based on this theory. The finding of a negative impact of concentration also indicates that we should question many of the propositions about industrial structure and employee earnings arising from this field.

The important roles of size and capital intensity in our final model suggest that internal organizational and technological factors that are more proximate to the workplace are important determinants of outcomes for workers. This does not indicate that market structure is irrelevant to employees' earnings; indeed, one of the largest effects in the model is that for foreign involvement. However, we have shown that organizational and technological variables are also important components of industrial structure. More importantly, we have shown that certain key variables in the economic interpretation of the role of industrial structure (e.g., profit and productivity) have only a spurious relationship with employees' earnings. We have also shown that some of the variables in the market category (e.g., concentration) are better interpreted in organizational terms relevant to the workplace than in economic terms relevant to the marketplace.

The resource perspective suggested in Chapter 3 has been shown to provide valuable insights into the interpretation of these results. This perspective has been buttressed by the findings on size, capital intensity, and concentration. These factors appear to act as resources both for labor and for capital in their mutual struggle at the workplace, rather than serving as the basis for unilateral manipulation by the capitalist class.

In selecting our final industry-level model we have followed an inductive procedure of selection based largely on tests of statistical significance. Such a procedure does not allow for the direct testing of formal hypotheses. Formal tests of our model against some other model must await further conceptual work and the development of competing measures and data sets by other researchers. For the present, we shall accept it as one industrial structure model that appears to capture major expected relationships in an interpretable manner, and we shall utilize it in Chapters 7 and 8 in our investigation of how industrial structure effects are realized in the workplace as mediated by social class, unionization, and individual-level characteristics.

APPLICATION OF INDUSTRY-LEVEL MODELS TO THE WISCONSIN SAMPLE AND THE RESTRICTED CURRENT POPULATION SURVEY SAMPLE

In the next section we shall develop models of economic segmentation based on company-level data applied to the Wisconsin sample. In comparing those models to the industry-level models just developed, we may have difficulty in determining whether differences are due to different levels of measurement of economic structure or to sample differences. To confront this problem, we shall evaluate the industry-level models on the Wisconsin sample and on a similarly constrained CPS subsample. The Wisconsin sample respondents are all high school graduates, were about 35 years old in 1975, when the survey was taken, and about 70% of them still lived in Wisconsin at that time. The national CPS subsample chosen was high school graduates in their 30s. Comparison of results for these two samples with the overall CPS results should aid us in determining whether any differences between the company- and industry-level models are a result of different samples. Such sample differences might result from the restriction of attention to high school graduates or from the nonrepresentativeness of the Wisconsin sample.

The mean log earnings in each sector for each comparison sample are presented in Table 6.6. Note first that these means are higher than those presented in Table 6.1 for the total CPS sample. This is because the mean earnings reported in Table 6.6 are for samples of workers who graduated from high school and are in their prime working ages. The sector mean log earnings ranks observed in the total CPS sample are largely reproduced in the two comparison samples. The oligopoly sector has the highest earnings, followed by the core sector. The two utilities sectors have earnings at or above the level of the core sector. Earnings in the periphery sector are lower than in the core by a substantial gap, and the trades sector has average earnings near the level of the periphery. Earnings in the Wisconsin sample are higher by a small margin than in the similarly constrained national CPS sample. This results from low unemployment in Wisconsin, the relative prosperity of the area, and the absence of lower-earning blacks in this sample.

Examining the distribution of the labor force across sectors shown in Table 6.6, we see that the two comparison samples have almost exactly equal distributions. However, both samples differ from the overall CPS sample in that fewer

TABLE 6.6

Mean Log Earnings in Six Industrial Sectors[a]

| Sector | CPS[b] | | | Wisconsin survey[c] | | |
	Log earnings	N	% of sample	Log earnings	N	% of sample
Oligopoly	4.71 (0.56)	134	5.15	4.89 (0.58)	248	5.52
Core	4.43 (0.83)	790	30.35	4.67 (0.81)	1501	33.41
Periphery	3.91 (1.14)	839	32.23	3.91 (1.25)	1350	30.05
Core utilities	4.45 (0.80)	341	13.10	4.61 (0.88)	505	11.24
Periphery utilities	4.35 (0.97)	43	1.65	4.85 (0.79)	98	2.18
Trades	3.85 (1.21)	452	17.36	4.05 (1.15)	720	16.02
Missing	4.38 (0.86)	4	0.15	4.77 (0.68)	71	1.58
Total sample	4.18 (1.00)	2603	100	4.35 (1.01)	4493	100

[a] Means are presented with their standard deviations reported beneath in parentheses. Sample is private employees with annual earnings of at least $100.

[b] CPS high school graduates in their thirties ($N = 2603$).

[c] Wisconsin survey ($N = 4493$).

workers are employed in the lower-paying trades and periphery sectors, and more are employed in the core and oligopoly sectors. Given the nature of the constraint of these samples to high school graduates in prime working ages and the ability of these groups to monopolize better-paying positions, this finding is hardly surprising. In general, we feel that these contrasts have shown the CPS subsample and the Wisconsin sample to be highly comparable. To the extent that there are differences between the overall CPS sample and the Wisconsin sample, it is because of the restriction of the Wisconsin sample to high school graduates, not because the Wisconsin sample fails to be representative of a similarly constrained national sample.

We also evaluated the continuous-variable industry-level model on the Wisconsin sample and on the CPS subsample (see Table 6.7). The results are

TABLE 6.7

**Regression of Log Earnings on
Final Industry Model**[a]

Variables	CPS[b]	Wisconsin survey[c]	t Test for difference in slopes
Size	.3134	.3195	−0.07
	(.0676)	(.0547)	
Concentration	−.2733	−.3206	0.74
	(.0493)	(.0406)	
Foreign involvement	.1692	.3243	−1.91
	(.0631)	(.0513)	
Capital intensity	[−.0217]	[−.0071]	−0.40
	(.0273)	(.0243)	
Autonomy	.0053	.0053	0.00
	(.0023)	(.0017)	
(Size)^2	[−.0398]	−.0547	0.40
	(.0293)	(.0226)	
(Foreign involvement)^2	[.0307]	[.0069]	0.55
	(.0337)	(.0273)	
(Capital intensity)^2	−.0512	−.0374	−1.19
	(.0088)	(.0076)	
Intercept	3.90	4.03	
R^2 (×100)	12.09	14.25	
Standard deviation	0.97	1.00	
Mean log earnings	4.18	4.35	

[a] Sample is private employees with annual earnings of at least $100. Regression coefficients, unless enclosed in square brackets, are significant at the .05 level. Standard errors are reported in parentheses beneath each regression coefficient.
[b] CPS high school graduates in their thirties (N = 2603).
[c] Wisconsin survey (N = 4493).

very similar to those reported for the more comprehensive CPS sample. In no case are differences between the industrial structure coefficients for the restricted CPS sample and the Wisconsin sample statistically significant at the .05 level. All three scale variables (size, concentration, and foreign involvement) have positive effects and are still highly significant. The linear component of capital intensity is no longer significant in either of the samples and registers a trivial negative effect. However, because capital intensity has a significant negative curvature and is scaled to be negative throughout almost all of its range, these coefficients evaluate as a positive, rapidly decaying slope that becomes negative at the upper end of the distribution, a situation not that much different from that observed in the larger CPS sample. An additional difference is that, although the curvature terms for size and foreign involvement have signs consistent with those observed in the larger CPS sample, the only curvature term for these variables which is significant is that for size in the Wisconsin sample. Overall, we feel that the basic similarity of these results with those observed in the larger CPS sample leads to the conclusion that any differences observed between the industry- and company-level models must be attributed primarily to differences in the level of measurement of economic segmentation, not to differences in labor force samples. It is to the selection and evaluation of these company-level models that we now turn.

A SECTORAL COMPANY MODEL

The Wisconsin sample to be utilized in this section is limited to high school graduates about 35 years old in 1975, most of whom were still living in Wisconsin at the time of the survey. However, we have seen that this sample accurately reflects processes of economic segmentation observable in a similarly constrained national sample. The company data to be employed in this section are superior to the industry data in level of detail but suffer from substantial missing data. The analysis in this section will proceed in an identical fashion to that in the industry section. We shall first evaluate sectoral models of economic segmentation. Next, we shall develop and evaluate a continuous-variable model of economic segmentation. Finally, we shall compare these company-level models with the industry-level models previously developed.

In Chapter 4 we outlined a corporate-level categorical model of economic segmentation and two possible collapses of that model. Table 6.8 reports the results of a dummy variable regression of log earnings on these three competing models. Over one-third of the sample is employed by companies appearing on one of the *Fortune* magazine lists of leading American corporations. On the other hand, nearly half the respondents in this sample work for companies with no plants outside the immediate local area.

TABLE 6.8

Regression of Log Earnings on Corporate Economic Sectors[a]

Model	b	Standard error	N	% of sample
Six-sector				
Monopoly 1	.7033	.0406	963	21.43
Monopoly 2	.5842	.0743	217	4.83
Monopoly 3	.3049	.0603	348	7.75
National	.3351	.0500	549	12.22
Regional	.3537	.0620	326	7.26
Local	—	—	2090	46.52
Intercept	4.08			
R^2 ($\times 100$)	6.88			
Standard deviation	1.04			
Three-sector				
Monopoly	.5957	.0352	1528	34.01
Multiplant	.3421	.0421	875	19.47
Local	—	—	2090	46.52
Intercept	4.08			
R^2 ($\times 100$)	6.10			
Standard deviation	1.05			
Two-sector				
Monopoly	.5033	.0314	2403	53.48
Local	—	—	2090	46.52
Intercept	4.08			
R^2 ($\times 100$)	5.41			
Standard deviation	1.05			

[a] Data taken from 1975 Wisconsin survey. Sample is private employees with annual earnings of at least \$100; $N = 4493$.

People working for companies on the *Fortune* top 500 industrial companies list receive the highest income by a wide margin. There is, however, considerable spread within the three *Fortune*-listed groups. In fact, workers in companies on the *Fortune* list of the top 50 companies in various nonmanufacturing industries have average earnings similar to workers in the national and regional sectors. Workers in companies with only local plants earn far less than workers in any other sector.

Examining the results for the three- and two-sector collapses, it appears that the three-sector categorization will prove the most useful. Only .78% of explained variance in log earnings is lost between the six- and three-sector designs, and three degrees of freedom are saved. Between the three- and two-sector designs, an additional .69% of explained variance is lost, but only one additional degree of freedom is saved. A reasonably good distribution of workers is generated by the three-sector design, and the regression coefficients are patterned in the expected manner. For these reasons, we shall select the three-sector design as our categorical model of corporate-level economic segmentation and utilize it throughout the remainder of the analysis.

The pattern of earnings across these three sectors supports the argument that size is a key dimension of industrial structure in relation to workplace outcomes. Earnings are sharply differentiated across these three qualitatively different sectors. Workers in companies that are entirely locally based receive the lowest earnings. Workers employed in companies that have plants outside the immediate local area receive substantially higher earnings. Finally, the employees of large, nationally prominent companies receive by far the highest average earnings of workers in any sector.

A CONTINUOUS-VARIABLE COMPANY MODEL

The analysis in this section will proceed in a manner similar to that in the industry-level section. First, the variables to be utilized in the model-selection process will be reviewed. A summary index of size will be constructed to alleviate problems of multicollinearity. Finally, a model of corporate structure and employee earnings will be selected in a stepwise procedure and theoretically interpreted.

The means, standard deviations, and correlations with log earnings of the company-level variables to be considered in our model selection are presented in Table 6.9. These variables include measures of company size (employment, sales, income, assets, and net worth), plant size (employment), capital intensity, profit, corporate autonomy/dominance (subsidiary status, number of domestic subsidiaries, and number of total subsidiaries), and foreign involvement (number of foreign subsidiaries). Except for subsidiary status, the correlation of each of the variables with earnings is in the expected direction (positive) and is significant at the .05 level. Subsidiary status, which also has a significant positive relationship with earnings, is a measure of conglomerate domination, and it is expected to have a negative relationship to employee earnings. This apparent anomaly is a result of the close relationship between size and subsidiary status and disappears when controls are added for company size. Note that for the company size variables the average correlation increases from .1 to .2 with the natural logarithm transformation. Plant size has the highest zero-order correlation with log earnings of any variable, at .33 in the log form. (Note also that these zero-order correlations are somewhat smaller than those observed for the industry data. More will be said on this issue later in the chapter.)

TABLE 6.9

**Means, Standard Deviations, and Correlations with Log
Individual Earnings of Company Variables**[a]

Variable	Mean	Standard deviation	Correlation with log earnings[b]
Employment	53,284	162,039	.09
Sales ($100,000s)	26,152	61,486	.09
Income ($100,000s)	2,142	5,928	.10
Assets ($100,000s)	40,140	121,919	.10
Net worth ($100,000s)	14,816	50,286	.09
Employment (log)	7.52	3.26	.20
Sales (log)	7.73	2.70	.17
Income (log)	7.88	0.76	.13
Assets (log)	8.39	2.26	.20
Net worth (log)	7.60	1.80	.16
Company size	−0.29	0.96	.23
Plant size (log)	4.99	2.18	.33
Profit (× 100)	4.62	4.53	.10
Capital intensity	6.21	2.02	.21
Domestic subsidiaries	1.40	1.60	.10
Foreign subsidiaries	1.02	1.69	.10
Total subsidiaries	1.78	1.79	.13
Subsidiary status	0.30	0.46	.07
Log earnings	4.35	1.08	—

[a] Data taken from 1975 Wisconsin survey. Sample is private employees with annual earnings of at least $100; $N = 4493$. Missing data are not replaced with mean values.

[b] All correlations are significant at the .05 level.

The five major company size variables (employment, sales, income, assets, and net worth) are highly intercorrelated (see Table D.5 in the Appendix). In addition, the zero-order correlations of these variables with log earnings are very similar. Because of these factors a company size index was constructed using these five variables in standardized form. The index is the average of whichever variables are present. Thus, it includes from one to five standardized variables and can be computed whenever any of the five variables is present. If *no* size measure is present for a particular case, the size index is assigned its own mean, and this fact is registered in a quality-of-data dummy, which will be used in conjunction with the index. (In approximately one-fifth of the cases none of the company size index components was present.) In general, we regard this quality-of-data dummy as differentiating between companies large enough to have publically available data and companies that are so small that data are unavailable.[13] The size index helps accomplish three goals. First, it smooths the measurement of company size over possible measurement error entailed in any one single measure. Second, it helps reduce the problem of missing data. Third, it reduces problems of collinearity with the measurement of company size. The company size index correlates .2255 with log earnings. This correlation is higher than those of any of its components and confirms the success of our scaling operation.

Selecting a Company-Level Model

The correlation matrix for the set of company variables from which we shall select our final model is presented in Table D.7 in the Appendix. Because of the high intercorrelations among these variables, it was again necessary to use stepwise procedures to select a final model. In addition, for each equation evaluated, we regressed each independent variable simultaneously on all other independent variables as a test for multicollinearity. Never did the multiple R of any of these equations exceed .90, a level below which, we have argued, multicollinearity is not a serious problem. The possible variables to be entered into the selection process are: company size, plant size, profit, subsidiary status, domestic subsidiaries, foreign subsidiaries, total subsidiaries, and capital intensity. In addition, a quality-of-data dummy, which differentiates valid data cases from cases in which missing data has been replaced by the variable mean, was constructed for each of the variables except plant size.

The first set of equations that we evaluated tests the zero-order effect of each variable net of its quality-of-data dummy. All the effects are in the expected direction (all positive except for subsidiary status, which is negative) and are statistically significant. The quality-of-data dummy for each variable has a large positive net effect, showing an upward jump in employee earnings between companies for which information on this variable was found and companies that were so small that no information could be found.

Selected models from the final stages of the company-level model selection process are presented in Table 6.10. Model 1 finds that a curvature term for size has a significant effect. This curvature term is retained in Model 2, which tests the addition of plant size. In Model 2, plant size is highly significant, but the curvature term for company size is not and is rejected at this stage. The three size variables—company size, company size dummy, and plant size—form a baseline model against which additional variables are tested.

The next two variables to be added to the model are profit and subsidiary status (see Table 6.10, Model 3).[14] Subsidiary status is not significant in this model and is rejected at this point. Subsidiary status was expected to have a large net effect because this dummy variable indicates whether the rest of the company data really applies to the respondent's employer or to a larger owning company.

TABLE 6.10

Model Selection for Regression of Log Individual Earnings on Company Variables[a]

	Model							
Variable	1	2	3	4	5	6	7	8
Company size	.2290	.0959	.0888	.1173	.0783	.1102	.0852	.0894
	(.0180)	(.0198)	(.0216)	(.0302)	(.0245)	(.0321)	(.0199)	(.0197)
Size dummy	.5305	.1860	.2006	.2338	.1906	.2246	.1886	.1891
	(.0417)	(.0469)	(.0440)	(.0503)	(0448)	(.0513)	(.0427)	(.0427)
(Company size)^2	−.0521	[.0126]						
	(.0145)	(.0149)						
Plant size		.1305	.1295	.1288	.1293	.1295	.1347	.1345
		(.0086)	(.0082)	(.0082)	(.0082)	(.0082)	(.0082)	(.0082)
Profit			.0149	.0142	.0155	.0142	[.0075]	
			(.0052)	(.0052)	(.0053)	(.0053)	(.0054)	
Subsidiary status			[−.0046]					
			(.0411)					
Domestic subsidiaries				[−.0212]				
				(.0163)				
Foreign subsidiaries					[.0095]			
					(.0142)			
Total subsidiaries						[−.0137]		
						(.0154)		
Capital intensity							.1093	.1167
							(.0204)	(.0197)
Intercept	4.03	3.62	3.55	3.55	3.55	3.55	3.66	3.71
R^2 (×100)	6.87	11.56	11.72	11.75	11.72	11.73	12.29	12.25
Standard deviation	1.04	1.01	1.01	1.01	1.01	1.01	1.01	1.01

[a] Data taken from 1975 Wisconsin survey. Sample is private employees with annual earnings of at least $100; $N = 4493$. Regression coefficients, unless enclosed in square brackets, are significant at the .05 level. Standard errors are reported in parentheses beneath each regression coefficient.

(The interactions of subsidiary status with each of the other variables was also tested and none was found to be significant.) Profit, however, does enter the equation as a significant predictor of employee earnings. Holding company size constant, profit rate has a positive impact on individual log earnings.

The model now contains three size measures and profit rate. This model serves as the baseline for testing the remaining variables: number of subsidiaries (foreign, domestic, and total, each tested separately) and capital intensity (see Table 6.10, Models 4–7). None of the three subsidiary variables enters these equations in a statistically significant manner, and all are eliminated from further analysis. Capital intensity enters the equation as a highly significant variable and eliminates the positive effect earlier attributed to profit rate. All variables rejected from earlier models were retested at this stage, and none was found to be significant.[15] The final company-level earnings model at which we arrive is presented as Model 8 of Table 6.10, and includes measures of company size, company size quality-of-data, plant size, and capital intensity.[16]

Interpreting the Company-Level Model

The final company-level model that we selected includes three measures of size—company size, company size dummy, and plant size—and a measure of capital intensity. A one-unit increase in company size produces a 9% increase in workers' earnings.[17] In addition, in companies large enough to have data available for constructing the company size index, the employees benefit from an additional 19% increase in earnings. Net of these effects, a 1% increase in plant size produces a .13% increase in workers' earnings. A 1% increase in capital intensity produces a net increase in workers' earnings of .12 percent. Plant size has the largest effect of any variable in the company-level model. Its beta coefficient is approximately 3.5 times as large as that for company size.[18] Large shop size gives workers resources to attain higher wages through opening such possibilities as collective bargaining. Plant size makes a greater contribution to earnings than does company size because it directly increases workers' power to struggle for higher wages and earnings. Working in a large company may be a mixed blessing for workers. It often implies large plant size and may bring along the higher earnings and benefit levels associated with the organizational arrangements of large companies, but it also increases employers' power to undercut wages and earnings through runaway shops, union-busting activities, strike resistance, and so on.[19]

These findings have important theoretical implications. The finding that plant size benefits workers' earnings strengthens the interpretation that size impacts the workplace through allowing the possibility of greater collective action on the part of workers. The large magnitude of this effect suggests that this is the predominant role of size. However, the finding that company size also has an independent positive effect on workers' earnings supports the interpretation that large companies may use at least part of their discretionary resources to increase workers' earnings as a means of labor control.

Other than size, the only variable included in the final company-level model is capital intensity. This too is an important finding and can be interpreted as indicating that the nature of the work environment (measured by capital intensity) is more important than the financial success of the company (measured by profit rate) for employee earnings. This effect may be actualized through such factors as the provision by advanced technology of greater worker resources to be used in the struggle for higher earnings or through the necessity of developing a more highly educated and rewarded labor force to operate high-technology plants.

The Rejected Company Variables

Three sets of variables were rejected from the final company-level earnings model selected in this section. These variables are profit, three measures of corporate autonomy, and foreign involvement. Consideration of these variables should again lead to additional insights about the implications of the model selected. The rejection of profit from the final model indicates that corporate profits have no direct effect on employee earnings. This reaffirms a similar finding in the industry-level data and further undermines interpretations of economic structure and workplace outcomes that rely on neoclassical explanations of the forces at work.

All three measures of corporate autonomy (subsidiary status and number of domestic and total subsidiaries) were eliminated from the final company-level model. This result gives no support to the thesis that center firms exploit their dependent subsidiaries, at least insofar as that exploitation is carried over into wage differences for the employees of these firms. The measure of foreign involvement (number of foreign subsidiaries) was also rejected in the final company model, contradicting the thesis that U.S. workers receive a direct subsidy from imperialist exploitation abroad. However, industry-level measures of both corporate autonomy and foreign involvement were found to be significant predictors of employees' earnings. It is possible that corporate autonomy and foreign involvement influence wages primarily by setting industry standards for wages and conditions, and that company-level measures of these concepts do not tap these standards directly because of the predominance of cross-industry conglomerates in these sectors. For now, these findings leave us with a somewhat ambiguous interpretation of the role of these institutional factors in the determination of workplace outcomes.

Summary of Continuous-Variable Company Model

In reviewing the final company-level model, it is apparent that size is the key component. Company size and plant size have the two largest effects in the model, and of these, plant size is by far the larger. The only concept other than size retained in the model is capital intensity. In an interpretation similar to that employed with the industry-level model, we can characterize these variables as important components of the organizational and technical environment of production. The size of the company is important for such issues as degree of bureaucratization, organizational style, modes of social control, and so on. Plant size and capital intensity have an obvious impact on such issues as union viability and power and the production technology that is utilized.

By contrast, the concepts rejected from our model—profit rate, corporate autonomy/dominance, and foreign involvement—can be thought of as operating chiefly through market relations rather than through production relations. Such market relations may well be important for corporations, but they do not appear to have equal impact on employee earnings. Theories of economic segmentation that have stressed such concepts may be forced to examine more closely the theoretical and empirical links between such variables and workplace outcomes. In the company-level model, the variables that are most important in determining employee earnings are those that reflect directly on the workplace, rather than those that reflect on the corporate environment.

The importance of size and capital intensity in this model gives strong support to the sociological, Marxist, and institutional theories that stress the role of these factors in determining workplace outcomes. The finding that company profit has no direct role in determining an individual's level of earnings seriously calls into question neoclassical interpretations of the workplace because profits are the primary allocational mechanism specified by this theory. The finding that corporate autonomy and foreign involvement have no direct effect on earnings in the company-level model raises questions about institutionally based economic and Marxist theories concerning both domestic and international exploitation between firms, which argue that the employees of domestic center firms recieve a share of the profits of exploitation between capitalist competitors.

In summary, the company-level model gives strong support to the theoretical argument that the internal organizational and technical factors proximate to the workplace are more important determinants of outcomes for employees than are the more distant market forces of profit and loss. The importance of these more proximate factors of production also gives support to the resource interpretation of industrial structure, which argues that workers are able to utilize certain elements of industrial structure to their advantage. In particular, the finding that plant size has by far the largest effect of any variable in the company-level model indicates that the size dimension operates primarily as a resource to employees, rather than providing organizational resources for manipulating employees to produce a more stable and compliant work force.

In analyzing the company-level data to select a model of individual earnings, we encountered substantial problems of missing data and multicollinearity. These problems were eventually resolved by combining several measures of company size into a single scale and by using allocated data in conjunction with quality-of-data dummies. The final continuous-variable model at which we arrive contains measures of company size, plant size, and capital intensity. This is a new model in the literature, and we feel it deserves serious consideration. Because the model was selected by inductive procedures, verification against specific alternative models is needed before it can be accepted as a formal model of the relationship between company-level organizational structure and employee earnings. However, evaluation of the model has provided many insights into the nature of earnings determination at the workplace. Use of the model in conjunction with individual-level factors in Chapters 7 and 8 will provide a basis for further appraisal of its utility.

COMPARISON OF COMPANY- AND INDUSTRY-LEVEL RESULTS

In planning this research project we sought to collect variables that could be directly compared across the company and industry levels of measurement. We were largely successful in this attempt, though we were able to collect many more industry-level variables than company-level variables. The comparison of industry- and company-level measures of the same concepts provides one of the most interesting and worthwhile parts of this analysis. Similar findings across levels of measurement offer validation of these findings. Divergent findings across levels of measurement lead us to question either our measurement attempts or the theory that argues for these effects.

Our research design has also allowed us to extend this comparison by applying the industry-level model to the Wisconsin sample. That comparison, along with the application of the industry model to a similarly constrained national CPS sample, produced similar results across samples. With this in mind, we can attribute observed differences in the industry- and company-level models either to differences in our ability to measure industry- and company-level economic segmentation or to differences in the effects of structural dimensions of segmentation across levels of economic organization, rather than to sample differences.

The sectoral model we developed utilizing company-level data is based primarily on size. The industry-level scheme is based on 40 variables that tap most of the major dimensions of economic segmentation discussed in the literature. Both categorizations behave as expected in terms of differentiating mean earnings levels. Unfortunately, these sectoral classifications are not directly comparable. (In findings yet to be presented we shall discuss the correlation between these classifications in terms of the distribution of employees across sectors as one way to evaluate their relationship.)

The company- and industry-level continuous-variable models produce results that are more directly comparable. Size and capital intensity are key elements in both the company- and industry-level models. In addition, size has its greatest effect at the plant level. These findings cross-validate our conclusion that internal organizational and technical factors of production are key mechanisms in the determination of workplace outcomes. Profit rate, however, was eliminated as insignificant from both the industry- and company-level models. Because this variable has the key role in economic based interpretations of the workplace, its insignificance in these models strongly supports the argument that such market-based corporate factors are of secondary importance in determining workplace outcomes for employees. Concentration, where we were able to measure it at the industry level, is observed to have a negative effect on employees' earnings exclusive of the effects of other measures of industrial structure. This is one of our most exciting findings. In much of the literature on economic segmentation, size and concentration are assumed to have similar or identical effects on the workplace. We have shown that they have separable and opposite net effects. This finding clearly supports arguments in favor of analyzing the dimensions of industrial structure in terms of their distinct roles. This finding also supports the resource perspective, in that concentration must be interpreted as a resource for the capitalist class only, whereas size provides resources for both employees and for the capitalist class.

The two models produce conflicting results concerning the roles of foreign involvement and conglomerate domination. Neither of these variables is significant as a company-level measure in the Wisconsin data, but both are significant as industry-level measures in the CPS data. If we return to Table 6.7 and examine the application of the industry model to the Wisconsin and restricted CPS samples, we see that both variables have significant effects in the expected direction in these samples. This leads to the conclusion that differences in sample do not produce these observed differences in the final models. Rather, differences in the role of, or the measurement of, these factors at the company and industry levels are indicated as probable causes of the observed differences in the models.

One possible explanation is that the company variables are inadequately measured. Many of them suffer badly from missing data. Although our dummy variable quality-of-data technique for handling this situation prevented our results from being biased, it is incapable of preventing the erosion of variance and covariance that results from the replacement of missing data with a constant value.

A second possible explanation is that company-level measures have different meanings than do industry-level measures of the same concepts. The company-level measures in our final model all tap dimensions important for production. The industry-level model contains these variables as well as variables that are important chiefly through market relations. Perhaps these market relations only have an effect on labor force outcomes through the setting of conditions that operate on the industry as a whole. These same market relations, operating only for specific companies, would have relatively little impact on workplace outcomes.

This argument has importance for future discussions of the appropriate level of measurement for economic segmentation. This is a question to be taken seriously as a theoretical problem, and not simply decided on the basis of whether or not data are readily available at a given level of measurement. It appears that variables measuring organizational and technical aspects of economic production are important at both the company and industry levels, whereas variables measuring market relations operate only at the industry level. In the final analysis, we cannot definitively say whether the observed differences in the company- and industry-level models are a result of differential measurement error or of different processes operating, respectively, at the level of companies and the level of industries. (We need not feel totally defeated by this constraint; it is a rare instance in which we are able to distinguish assuredly issues of measurement from substantive interpretation in the social sciences.)

In conclusion, we are pleased with the ability of our analysis design to sort out possible competing explanations for the observed industry- and company-level effects. We feel that we have learned substantially more about the impact of economic structure on workplace outcomes than we would have learned by utilizing only one level of measurement and one operationalization of economic segmentation. Overall, the industry-level and company-level models selected are very similar. To the extent that the models agree, the effects they demonstrate are confirmed. Size and capital intensity are important components of our corporate structure earnings models at both the industry and company levels. Rate of profit is not significant in either model. On the issues of conglomerate domination and the role of foreign involvement, the models differ, but we are able to narrow the range of possible explanations for these differences—they result either from differences in measurement error or from differences between what is important about working for a given company and what is important about working in a given industry. In either event, we have seen that American workers receive an earnings benefit from the foreign involvement of the industry in which they work, regardless of whether they receive higher earnings from foreign involvement by the company for which they work. Similarly, workers receive an earnings benefit from industrial autonomy, if not from corporate autonomy.

We may be able to gain additional insight about the relationship of the company- and industry-level models by directly examining their cross tabulations and correlations. The top panel of Table 6.11 presents a cross-classification of industrial sector by company sector for the Wisconsin sample. The observed relations are entirely as expected. However, it is also important to ask how strong these relationships are. In the oligopoly industrial sector, 84% of the workers are employed by *Fortune*-listed firms (the corporate-level monopoly sector). In the trades industrial sector, 92% of the employees work in companies with only local plants. These relationships seem very strong indeed. However, 32% of core workers are employed by locally based companies, and 25% of periphery workers are employed by *Fortune*-listed companies. Although it is true that a greater percentage of core as opposed to periphery workers are employed in *Fortune*-listed firms and a greater percentage of periphery as opposed to core workers are

Table 6.11

Comparison of Industry- and Company-level Sector Classifications and Correlations of Industry- and Company-level Continuous Variables[a]

	Industrial sector						
Company sector	Oligopoly	Core	Periphery	Core utilities	Periphery utilities	Trades	Total
Monopoly	209	728	337	208	15	7	1504
	(84.3)	(48.5)	(25.0)	(41.2)	(15.3)	(1.0)	(34.0)
Multiplant	18	286	244	174	51	53	826
	(7.3)	(19.1)	(18.1)	(34.5)	(52.0)	(7.4)	(18.7)
Local	21	487	769	123	32	660	2092
	(8.5)	(32.4)	(57.0)	(24.4)	(32.7)	(91.7)	(47.3)
Total	248	1501	1350	505	98	720	4422[b]
	(5.6)	(33.9)	(30.5)	(11.4)	(2.2)	(16.3)	(100)

	Industry-level measure				
Company-level measure	Size	Concentration	Foreign involvement	Capital intensity	Autonomy
Company size	.42	.51	.41	.27	−.21
Size dummy	.38	.36	.36	.30	−.28
Plant size	.51	.51	.52	.20	−.45
Capital intensity	.20	.01	−.02	.42	−.02

[a] Data taken from 1975 Wisconsin survey. Sample is private employees with annual earnings of at least \$100; $N = 4493$. Numbers reported in parentheses beneath cell frequencies are column percentages.

[b] Values are missing for 71 cases on the industrial-sector variable.

employed in the locally based corporate sector, the relationship is not as strong as that depicted for the oligopoly and trades sectors. Similarly, 41% of core utilities workers are employed by *Fortune*-listed companies, whereas only 15% of periphery utilities workers are employed by *Fortune*-listed companies. However, the majority of the remaining periphery utilities workers are employed in multiplant enterprises rather than in locally based companies.

Examining the correlations presented in the second panel of Table 6.11, we see that the company-level measure of capital intensity has its highest correlation with industry-level capital intensity. However, the three company-level measures of size correlate just as highly with the industry-level concentration and foreign involvement measures as they do with the industry-level measure of size. Recalling that these three industry scales are themselves highly intercorrelated, this is hardly surprising, but neither does it give us much confidence in the ability of these scales to differentiate size from other components of organizational structure at the industry level.[20]

In Table 6.12 we present models that directly contrast the industry- and company-level models of economic segmentation.[21] Model 6 simultaneously evaluates the company- and industry-level sectoral models. All of the coefficients for each model have consistent signs, and all are statistically significant. With the exception of the effect for the periphery (industrial) sector, the absolute values of the coefficients are uniformly reduced by anywhere from 25 to 50% of their

TABLE 6.12

Comparison of Industry- and Company-Level Sectoral and Continuous-Variable Regression Models of Individual Log Earnings[a]

	Model						
Variable	1	2	3	4	5	6	7
Company variable							
Company size	.0894				[.0053]		.0581
Size dummy	.1891				[.0701]		.0501
Plant size	.1345				.1323		.1183
Capital intensity	.1167				.1244		[.0215]
Company sector							
Monopoly		.5957			.2362	.3530	
Multiplant		.3421			.1276	.1855	
Local		—			—	—	
Industry variable							
Size			.1501				[.0795]
Concentration			−.2509				−.3270
Foreign involvement			.4146				.3618
Capital intensity			.0839				.1057
Autonomy			[.0033]				.0050
Industry sector							
Oligopoly				.8457		.5519	
Core				.6168		.4273	
Periphery				−.1388		−.2433	
Core utilities				.5657		.3735	
Periphery utilities				.8022		.6688	
Trades				—		—	
Intercept	3.71	4.08	4.13	4.05	3.69	4.04	3.51
R^2 (×100)	12.25	6.10	13.48	11.84	12.52	13.46	18.24
Standard deviation	1.01	1.05	1.00	1.01	1.01	1.00	0.98

[a] Data taken from 1975 Wisconsin survey. Sample is private employees with annual earnings of at least $100; N = 4493. Except where enclosed in square brackets, regression coefficients are significant at the .05 level.

values in equations evaluating each model alone (compare Models 2, 4, and 6 of Table 6.12). As indicated in the examination of the cross-tabulation of these sectors (Table 6.11), there is considerable overlap between the industry- and company-level sectoral models, and they appear to offer competing explanations for roughly the same earnings variance.

Turning to the final model presented in Table 6.12, which simultaneously evaluates the company- and industry-level continuous-variable models, we see that the company-level size variables still have large positive effects but that the effect of company-level capital intensity is strongly reduced. For the industry model, all the variables have strong and consistent effects, except for size, which is sharply reduced. It appears that the organizational size dimension of economic structure is realized primarily through company- and plant-level effects, and only secondarily through industrial environment effects. However, the effects of capital intensity and the market structure variables appear to be realized primarily through the setting of an industrywide workplace environment.

CONCLUSIONS

In this chapter we have evaluated the sectoral models of economic structure developed in Chapter 4 in terms of their ability to explain labor force earnings. We have also selected and evaluated company- and industry-level continuous-variable models of economic structure. In this process we have clearly seen that economic structure is an important determinant of employee earnings. The company-level continuous-variable model includes three measures of size and a measure of capital intensity, all of which have positive net effects on employee earnings. The industry-level continuous-variable model also contains measures of size and capital intensity, as well as measures of foreign involvement, corporate autonomy, and market concentration. All of the variables in this model have positive effects on labor force earnings except market concentration, which is observed to have a negative net effect on earnings. When the company- and industry-level models are evaluated against three different earnings functions, they exhibit a high degree of stability, buttressing our confidence in the selection of these models and in their stability when evaluated under different statistical conditions.

The central role of size and capital intensity in both the industry-level and company-level models supports sociological, Marxist, and institutional theories of the workplace that specify internal organizational and technical factors at the workplace as key determinants of labor force outcomes. The finding that profit and productivity do not have direct effects on labor force earnings indicates that economic interpretations that rely on these factors as crucial mechanisms in determining workplace outcomes must be seriously questioned. Such theories do not appear to give us adequate guidance in our efforts to understand the mechanisms through which organizational factors influence people's working lives. The negative earnings effect of concentration in the industry-level model also supports institutional theories but suggests that certain market-based factors may also have important influences on labor force outcomes. However, the influence of these factors is again best interpreted as operating through institutional, rather than purely market, mechanisms. Finally, the inclusion of corporate autonomy and foreign involvement in the industry-level model indicates that relationships of exploitation between companies have important implications for labor force earnings, at least insofar as these factors influence industrywide standards of wages and working conditions. In sum, the findings in this chapter indicate that sociological and institutional interpretations of the role of industrial structure in influencing labor force outcomes may be more important than the type of economic factors specified by much of the previous literature on segmentation, including those specified by the dual economy approach.

The resource perspective suggests that size and capital intensity are important organizational characteristics that may provide workers with potential resources to use for the attainment of higher wages. The finding that these are key characteristics in both the company-level and industry-level models strongly supports this interpretation. The negative effect of concentration and the insignificance of profit in these models seriously undermines the alternative "control" interpretation of the effects of size and capital intensity. This interpretation suggests that under the conditions of large firm size or capital-intensive production, both of which require stable planning horizons, capitalists use their organizational resources to increase wages to create a compliant and reliable work force. Under the control interpretation, size and capital intensity would result in high wages only to the extent that these factors are realized through high profits or monopoly position, which by implication results in excess profits. But these factors are shown to have insignificant net effects on employee earnings. The finding that plant size has a much larger effect than company size in the company-level model also strongly implies that the influence of size on labor force earnings operates primarily through the provision of organizational resources to labor.

The findings in this chapter have demonstrated the utility of a research design that employs company-level as well as industry-level measures of key constructs. Key findings, such as the central role of size and capital intensity, have been replicated across measurement levels, thus substantiating their reliability as well as demonstrating the legitimacy of measurement at the industry level for tapping certain key characteristics of economic structure. This research design has also allowed insight into the interpretation of the structural variables being evaluated, by specifying whether they are operational at the industry, company, or plant levels of organizational structure. Capital intensity appears to operate primarily through the determination of an industrywide level of production technology. Similarly, the findings suggest that corporate autonomy and foreign involvement influence employee earnings by specifying industrywide relations of exploitation. Organizational size, however, appears to influence the workplace primarily through the scale of the specific employing company and, even more importantly, through plant size.

Finally, the analysis in this chapter has also demonstrated that the continuous-variable models of industrial structure are somewhat preferable to the sectoral models in that they allow us to interpret the effects of industrial structure in a much more clear-cut manner than is possible with the sectoral models. The continuous-variable models may also be preferable on the statistical grounds of explained variance and stability of coefficients. (See Note 21 and the row reporting explained variance in Table 6.12.) For these reasons we shall rely heavily (but not solely) on the continuous-variable models in Chapters 7 and 8, which investigate the interaction of economic structure with labor force composition and with labor market characteristics in the determination of employees' earnings.

NOTES TO CHAPTER 6

1. Workers in the core utilities sector earn slightly more than workers in the periphery utilities sector do, which is in accord with the more developed industrial structure in the core utilities sector. The greater level of unionization in the periphery utilities sector is apparently unable to offset this disadvantage.

2. Almost 60% of the labor force is employed in the aggregate periphery sector or in the trades sector, both of which record among the lowest average earnings. It is also noteworthy that, whereas the core sector employs 27% of the labor force, the oligopoly sector, which pays the highest wages, is relatively small, employing only about 3% of the labor force.

3. The 50-firm concentration measures were substituted for the 8-firm measures utilized in Chapter 4 because of the higher intercorrelations of these measures with the rest of the variables in this group and because of their higher correlations with log mean industrial earnings.

4. The government regulation measure based on the work of Scherer (1970) was tested against the final model and found to be nonsignificant.

5. The .01 level of statistical significance was utilized in the selection of an industry-level model of earnings for the CPS data because of the large sample size ($N = 20{,}007$). When we move to the selection of a company-level model of earnings for the Wisconsin data ($N = 4493$), we shall utilize the more commonly employed and less restrictive .05 level of statistical significance.

6. These three scales were selected as the first-entered variables because of their heightened reliability owing to the scaling process.

7. The performance of the basic industry model against three functional forms of earnings is evaluated in Table D.4 in the Appendix. The functional forms selected are dollar earnings, log dollar earnings, and cube root dollar earnings. (The cube root function is suggested by Jencks, 1979.) All of the variables in the industry model are significant and have constant signs when evaluated against each of the three earnings functions. The percentage of explained variance under the natural log and cube root transformations is roughly equal at about 14%, whereas the explained variance of the dollar

function is somewhat lower at 9%. The finding of constant effects across all three earnings functions substantiates the validity of the industry model. The remainder of the analysis will continue to use the log earnings function because of its interpretability and its statistical properties, and because convention warrants this choice for the sake of comparison with other research results. (See also discussion in Chapter 8).

8. One must be careful when contrasting ''linear'' and ''nonlinear'' effects to recall that our dependent variables and many of our independent variables are already in the log form. Thus, for example, the linear coefficient for capital intensity is interpretable as indicating a certain percentage change in dollar earnings for each percentage change in capital intensity. Adding a curvature term allows these percentage changes to vary over the range of capital intensity. But, whether these percentage changes vary or not, they are not the same as linear *unit* changes in dollar earnings per some *unit* change in capital intensity. Size, foreign involvement, and concentration are all composite scales formed as the average of several standardized measures, some of which were in unit form and some of which were in log form. Each of these scales has a roughly normal distribution with a mean of zero and a standard deviation of one (size mean = .01; standard deviation = .97; foreign involvement mean = .02, standard deviation = .88; concentration mean = −.03, standard deviation = .89). Thus, a one-unit shift in any of these three variables from the mean moves through about 34% of the distribution of persons on that industrial structure variable, and a four-unit shift from the low end to the high end of the variable traverses over approximately 95% of the distribution of that variable. Autonomy is measured in percentage form by definition and ranges from 31 to 100, with a mean of 83 and a standard deviation of 14. We utilize these variables in these forms becuase of their ease of interpretation and because these functional forms appear to fit the data well. However, the reader should be aware that other transformations are possible and might produce competing interpretations of the effects of the industrial structure concepts that these variables tap. The eventual resolution between such choices depends ultimately on theoretical, rather than statistical, grounds.

9. Comparison of the standardized regression coefficients (betas) from Model 3 of Table 6.4 allows an evaluation of the relative importance of the five industrial structure variables included in the final model. These betas are: size (.20), capital intensity (.14), concentration (−.13), autonomy (.07), and foreign involvement (.22).

10. Even those American workers who receive a share of these profits may not benefit in the aggregate because of the high taxes paid to support the massive military budget required by the system of economic imperialism.

11. This result is analogous to controlling for organizational size and finding that vertical and horizontal differentiation, both of which are associated with large size, are in fact alternative strategies of corporate expansion (Blau and Schoenherr, 1971; Mileti, Gillespie, and Haas, 1977).

12. The regression selection procedures utilized in this chapter are primarily exploratory techniques, not hypothesis-testing techniques. Our interpretation of the findings must, therefore, be read with a certain degree of circumspection.

13. In Table D.6 in the Appendix we compare the means of several company variables for cases with and without a company size index. These variables include plant size, plants outside the local area, appearance on a *Fortune* list of leading corporations, and number of subsidiaries. For each comparison, the employers for which no size index could be computed are shown to be smaller in size than the employers for which an index could be computed. This substantiates the argument that these companies can be thought of as ''too small to find'' rather than simply as representing missing data. The quality-of-data dummy for the size index can, therefore, be interpreted as tapping this particular element of company size. That is, the quality-of-data dummy for the company size index designates those companies that are so small that public data on them are largely unavailable.

14. None of the quality-of-data dummies for variables other than company size is significant in any equation evaluated that also includes company size and its quality-of-data dummy variable. This indicates that the component of size tapped by the quality-of-data dummies for the various measures

is adequately indexed by company size and its quality-of-data dummy. Thus, these controls can be dropped from further models without the introduction of bias in the coefficients.

15. The final variables in the model were also summed in all possible pairs and tested to determine whether each made a unique contribution. The effects of each variable were found to be statistically distinguishable from those of other variables in the model so that no two variables could be combined in the final model. Squared terms were also constructed and tested for each of the variables in the final model. None of these terms was found to have a significant effect.

16. In a parallel comparison to that carried out with the industry-level model, we regressed three popular transformations of earnings on our final company model (see Table D.8 in the Appendix). The dollar form of earnings has a large positive skew. Both the natural log and cube root forms pull these high earners back in toward the center of the distribution. The cube root form does this somewhat less sharply than does the natural logarithm transformation. Comparing standardized beta coefficients across earnings transformations we see that the model produces nearly identical results for each form of earnings. The only exception is that the company size dummy has a statistically insignificant effect in the regression with dollar earnings. Comparing the percentage of explained variance for the three equations, it appears that the log and cube root forms of earnings are equally well predicted by our model, whereas the dollar form is somewhat less well estimated. These R^2 coefficients, however, are misleading in that they indicate the percentage of the variance *of a given distribution* that is explained. A better comparison between these forms would evaluate the explanatory power of the model in the same metric. Using the log form as our base, we calculate an expected $\hat{Y}$ value from each regression equation and transform it to the log form. Thus, the $\hat{Y}$ from the log equation needs no transformation; the $\hat{Y}$ from the dollar equation must be transformed by the natural logarithm function; and the $\hat{Y}$ from the cube root equation must be transformed by the natural logarithm function and multiplied by three. These transformed $\hat{Y}$, all in the same log metric, can then be correlated with log earnings, and these correlation coefficients will be directly comparable. These correlations are all nearly identical, indicating that any of the earnings forms can in fact be fit equally well by our model (see Table D.8). This finding, along with the finding that the company-level model has similar effects when applied to any of these three earnings functions, reinforces our confidence in the selection of this model.

17. The company size index is a composite variable formed as the average of several standardized measures of company size. As such it has roughly a zero mean and a unit standard deviation (company size index mean = $-.29$, standard deviation = .86). Thus, a one-unit shift from the mean of this variable moves through about 34% of the distribution of persons on this variable, and a four-unit shift from the low to the high end of the index traverses over approximately 95% of the distribution. Capital intensity and plant size are both transformed by the logarithmic function. Thus, in equations predicting log earnings, the coefficients for capital intensity and plant size are interpretable as indicating a certain percentage change in dollar earnings for each percentage change in capital intensity or plant size, respectively.

18. The standardized regression coefficients (betas) for the variables in the final company-level model are as follows: company size, .08; size dummy, .07; plant size, .28; and capital intensity, .07.

19. An alternative explanation for the larger effect of plant size relies on the argument that it is better measured than the other variables in the model. However, company size has missing data in only approximately one-fifth of the cases, and this explanation does not seem adequate to account for the extremely large difference in the magnitudes of the effects of these variables.

20. It is unlikely that this problem results from measurement error in the company variables because plant size has very little missing data and company size has valid data for over 80% of the cases.

21. Model 5 of Table 6.12 simultaneously evaluates the company-level continuous-variable and sectoral models. In this evaluation the sector coefficients are reduced by over half but are still

statistically significant with unchanged signs. The company size variable and size dummy variable are reduced sharply and, although still positive, are no longer statistically significant. However, the plant size and capital intensity variables are almost unaltered by the inclusion of the company sector measures. It seems that the company sectors and the company size measures are competing for the same earnings variance. That variance can be explained by a company size dimension whether we operationalize it with categorical or with continuous measures.

A similar comparison can be made at the industry level by simultaneously evaluating the industry-level continuous-variable and sectoral models on the total CPS sample. This comparison is presented in Table D.9 in the Appendix. Comparing Models 1 and 3 of this table, we see that the coefficients for the continous variables are relatively stable, having constant signs and roughly similar magnitudes when evaluated with and without the inclusion of the sectoral model. The only effect that is strongly altered is that of foreign involvement, which is reduced to less than one-third of its original level and becomes statistically insignificant. On the other hand, the signs for the industry sectors change wildly when the continuous-variable model is added to the equation. In Model 2, which includes just the sector variables, the oligopoly and core utilities sectors have the strongest positive earnings effects, whereas in Model 3, which also includes the continuous-variable measures, they have the strongest negative effects. The other three sector coefficients are statistically insignificant in this latter model. In addition, the inclusion of the industry sectors with the continuous-variable model only increases the explained variance by about .5%. These results suggest that the industry-level continuous-variable model may be superior to the sectoral model, not only in terms of interpretability, but also on the statistical grounds of explained variance and stability of coefficients.

7

Economic Structure and the Individual Earnings Attainment Process

INTRODUCTION

In this chapter we shall integrate the models of economic structure and employee earnings developed in previous chapters with individual-level models of earnings attainment. The results of this integration will be used to address two issues. First, how is the role of economic structure in determining employee earnings realized through individual and social structural factors? Second, to what extent are the effects attributed to individual-level earnings determinants and the interpretation of these effects altered by the inclusion of economic structure in earnings determination models?

In Chapters 4 and 6 we selected economic structure models in a context that did not control for other determinants of earnings. This strategy was based on the argument that economic structure preexists the demographic, educational, and skill characteristics of the labor force. Based on this argument, the true effect of economic structure is its total effect. Part of that effect may be indirect via the association of economic structure with individual characteristics, but no part of that effect should be considered spurious in that it arises from prior causal characteristics.

Although it is reasonable to argue that economic structure does exist prior to individuals in the sense just described, clearly certain labor force groups are

150

associated with specific industrial locations. One way in which this may occur is through self-selection into employment positions. For example, women may select themselves into industrial locations that offer part-time employment and, by implication, low earnings. Alternatively, women may be restricted to such sectors by discriminatory hiring practices. Thus, although economic structure preexists the demorgraphic characteristics of a particular cohort of workers, part of the earnings effect attributed to economic structure might just as well be attributed to the demographic characteristics of the work force. In this sense, economic structure and demographic, educational, and skill characteristics interact to determine workers' earnings.

Cross-sectional regression analysis cannot provide a solution to models that contain this kind of codetermination of exogenous variables. If we could a priori specify the nature of these joint effects, then we could solve such complex models of earnings. However, research on these questions has yet to provide us with definitive answers. Nevertheless, prior theory and research do give us suggestions as to how to interpret the various effects in such models.

For demographic characteristics, it can be argued that different social groups are primarily sorted into economic sectors by corporate hiring practices rather than self-selected into given job roles and that this sorting is crucial for the determination of their level of earnings (Bonacich, 1976; Oppenheimer, 1970). Therefore, reductions in the effects of race and sex in models that include a specification of economic structure can be thought of as indicating that a portion of the earnings effects that are attributed to these characteristics in individual-level models are spurious. Similarly, it can be argued that the effects of education and experience can be partially explained by taking into account the economic structure within which such factors specify employee earnings (Boudon, 1974; Edwards, 1979).

Concerning the relationship among economic structure and class, occupation, and unionization, we have less grounds for specifying causal orderings. Because of the shared history of development among these factors, their relationships of interdependence are even more complex than those involving individual characteristics. Historical analysis is able to inform us of many of the details of this development (see Chapter 3) but also warns that the relationship cannot be reduced to simple models of linear causality. Accordingly, the unanalyzed codetermination process among these variables specifies that their shared effects cannot be given an unambiguous causal interpretation.

Finally, labor demand can be more clearly interpreted as an outcome of economic structure. Therefore, any changes in the effects of economic structure variables when controls are added for weeks and hours worked must be seen as decompositions of the overall effect of economic structure into direct and indirect components, not as an alternative explanation of these effects.

Based on the model of determination just outlined, four sets of hypotheses will be evaluated in this chapter. First, we expect the direct effects of economic structure to be reduced, but not eliminated, by the inclusion of labor force composition and other controls in models of earnings attainment. This reduction will be interpretable as due partly to the realization of the effects of economic structure through the provision of labor demand and through the selection of employees with specific labor force characteristics and partly to the intercorrelation of economic structure with class structure and unionization. Conversely, we expect the effects of race and gender to be substantially reduced by the inclusion of economic structure variables in a model of individual-level earnings attainment. The effects of these demographic variables are partially explainable in terms of the selection of workers into specific economic structures. Third, we expect that the effects of education and experience on individual earnings will be similarly reduced. In fact, if one takes seriously arguments that the role of educational credentials is to act solely as a sorting device into jobs with different rates of pay, then the inclusion of a well-specified model of economic structure in an earnings attainment equation should totally eliminate the direct effect of education (see Berg, 1970). Finally, we hypothesize that when a model of social and family background is included in the same earnings equation with the economic structure model, the parameters for these two models will be largely unaltered. That is, the effects of these two different levels of social structure on earnings are hypothesized to be largely independent (see discussion in Chapter 3).

EVALUATION OF THE INDUSTRY-LEVEL MODEL

In Table 7.1 we present models of earnings that are more fully specified than have been the models we have examined so far. These models include demographic, human capital, class, unionization, and labor demand variables as well as the industry-level model of economic structure. Comparing Models 2 and 8 of Table 7.1, which present the industrial structure model with and without controls for race, gender, education, and experience, we see that the basic characteristics of the model are maintained under these controls. All the industrial structure characteristics are still significant with constant signs. However, the coefficients are somewhat reduced. Thus, a portion of the total effects of the industrial structure variables is realized through the demogrpahic and skill characteristics of the labor force. Industrial environments that produce jobs with high wages and salaries also select (and are selected by) groups with privileged social status and superior training and experience. For size, the direct effect is 83% of its original effect, for concentration it is 40%, for foreign involvement it is 23%, for autonomy it is 52%, and for capital intensity it is 55%.[1]

Measures of occupation, unionization, and weeks and hours worked are added in Model 6. Under this specification the coefficient for size is further reduced. However, the effects of the remaining dimensions of industrial structure are largely unaltered, and all the coefficients for the industrial structure variables are still significant and have constant signs. In this model the direct effects are the following percentages of the total effects: 43% for size, 62% for concentration, 28% for foreign involvement, 41% for autonomy, and 41% for capital intensity. Thus, we see that an average of about 43% of the total effects of industrial structure are direct and that the rest are mediated in some fashion by the other variables in this full earnings model.

A larger portion of the indirect effects of industrial structure on earnings appears to operate through the social and skill characteristics of the labor force than through occupation, unionization, and labor demand.[2] Size provides a possible exception to this pattern, a finding that again points to the close association of this dimension of economic structure both with union viability and with the bureaucratic drive toward reliable planning horizons, such as those embodied in a prevalence of full-time stable employment positions.

These patterns are replicated in the comparison of Model 9 with Models 3, 4, and 5, all of which utilize the industry-level model with curvature terms. (See also Table 7.2, which evaluates the slopes for the variables with curvature terms.) Under this specification, the industry-level model again has similar, though reduced, effects when compared with its evaluation without controls. Size and capital intensity have positive decaying effects, concentration has a negative effect, and autonomy has a positive effect. The linear component of the foreign involvement term, however, is no longer significant. The effect of this variable across its range is displayed in Table 7.2 and resembles a bowl shape. (For an interpretation of this anomaly see discussion in Chapter 8, especially Note 6.) With this one exception, both the linear and curvilinear forms of the industry-level model retain their basic characteristics when a full set of controls is implemented. Even the introduction of controls for weeks and hours worked does not remove the strong direct effects of these models on workers' earnings. This is compelling evidence that industrial structure influences job-related outcomes directly as well as through the creation of labor demand and through the matching of workers to jobs.

The industry-level sectoral model of economic structure is evaluated under a full set of controls in Model 7 of Table 7.1. The earnings effects of the sectors are all significant and align in an identical pattern to that observed prior to the introduction of controls. Overall, in this model, the direct sector effects are about 35% of their total effects.[3] Thus, the sector effects are mediated to a slightly greater degree by other earnings determinants than are the effects of the continuous-variable model, again indicating that the continuous-variable model may provide the superior operationalization of industrial structure, at least on statistical grounds.

TABLE 7.1

Regression of Log Earnings on Industry Model with Controls[a]

Variable						Model					
	1	2	3	4	5	6	7	8	9	10	11
Female	-.9058	-.8001	-.7839	-.7153	-.4357	-.4627	-.4949				-.5102
Black	-.1578	-.1472	-.1347	-.0919	-.0885	-.1049	-.1078				-.1129
Education	.1001	.0979	.0991	.0721	.0551	.0536	.0528				.0550
Experience	.1061	.0972	.0964	.0880	.0457	.0471	.0481				.0493
(Experience)²	-.0172	-.0156	-.0154	-.0143	-.0074	-.0077	-.0079				-.0081
Size		.2118	.3161	.2874	.2401	.1082		.2540	.4677		
Concentration		-.0705	-.0882	-.1465	-.1348	-.1103		-.1773	-.2349		
Foreign involvement		.0689	[-.0043]	[-.0158]	[-.0089]	.0864		.3061	.1147		
Autonomy		.0032	.0049	.0035	.0047	.0025		.0061	.0088		
Capital intensity		.0684	.0480	.0622	.0299	.0520		.1254	.0364		
(Size)²			-.0803	-.1083	-.1093				-.1171		
(Foreign involvement)²			.0560	.0891	.0687				.1210		
(Capital intensity)²			-.0119	[-.0066]	-.0144				-.0440		

154

	(1)	(2)	(3)	(4)	(5)	(6)	(7)	(8)	(9)	(10)	(11)
Manager				.7107	.4608	.4538	.4654				.4768
Professional				.5912	.4514	.4270	.4112				.4128
White collar				.2728	.1455	.1454	.1614				.2075
Union				.3489	.2976	.2957	.2900				.3000
Union power				.0039	.0040	.0034	.0043				.0056
Weeks					.0367	.0365	.0365				.0369
Hours					.0093	.0094	.0093				.0099
Oligopoly							.3430	1.1671			
Core							.2463	.8036			
Periphery							.0698	.1090			
Core utilities							.2693	.9002			
Periphery utilities							.1651	.8408			
Intercept	1.91	1.81	1.70	1.81	0.44	0.58	0.57	3.28	3.21	3.36	0.59
R^2 (×100)	41.36	45.19	45.50	49.08	71.65	71.09	70.76	10.14	14.57	13.27	70.12
Standard deviation	0.94	0.91	0.91	0.87	0.66	0.66	0.67	1.17	1.14	1.15	0.67

[a] Data taken from March–May match 1973 CPS. Sample is private employees with annual earnings of at least $100; $N = 20{,}007$. Except where enclosed in square brackets, regression coefficients are significant at the .01 level. The categories of manual workers and the trades sector have been left out of these earnings equations to estimate the effects of occupations and sectors, respectively.

TABLE 7.2

TABLE 7.2

Evaluation of Curvature in Industry Model with Full Controls[a]

Cumulative % of distribution	Size		Foreign involvement		Capital intensity	
	Without controls	With controls	Without controls	With controls	Without controls	With controls
10	.718	.474	−.135	−.150	.344	.131
30	.662	.422	−.072	−.115	.245	.098
50	.397	.175	.095	−.020	.179	.076
70	.358	.137	.219	.050	.145	.065
90	.133	−.072	.422	.166	.034	.029

[a] See Model 5 of Table 7.1. Data taken from March–May match 1973 CPS. Sample is private employees with annual earnings of at least $100; $N = 20,007$.

At this point we can turn to an evaluation of the degree to which the effects of the labor force's social and skill characteristics are mediated by industrial structure. By observing changes in the earnings parameters for race across the models presented in Table 7.1, we can evaluate the mediation of the effect of race by other variables in the model. The effect of race on log earnings in a model of labor force composition (Model 1) is .16. (This value is interpretable as indicating that blacks with equal demographic and skill characteristics earn an average of 16% less than whites.) When industrial structure variables are added to the equation (Model 3), the effect of race is reduced by 15% of its original value, to .13. A larger reduction occurs when class and unionization variables are added to the equation (Model 4): the effect of race is reduced by an additional 27% of its original value, to .09. Finally, when weeks and hours worked are added to the equation (Model 5), the effect of race is only very slightly reduced by an additional 2% of its original value. A final comparison is provided by contrasting Models 5 and 11, which present the individual-level earnings model with and without industrial structure variables. Comparing these two equations we see that the industry-level model of economic structure accounts for 22% of the negative effect on log earnings of being black, above and beyond the mediation of this effect by labor force composition, education, experience, occupation, unionization, and weeks and hours worked. Thus, although industrial structure does not totally account for the effect of race on earnings, it certainly provides an explanation for a substantial part of the negative earnings effect of being black that we have observed in individual-level models of earnings attainment. The dimensions of class and unionization have also been observed to account for substantial portions of the relationship between race and earnings.

When industrial structure variables are added to the labor force composition model, the effect of gender is reduced by 13%, from .91 to .78 (compare Models 1 and 3 of Table 7.1). When class and unionization variables are added to the equation (Model 4), the coefficient for gender earnings inequality is further reduced by 8% of its original value, to .72. When labor force supply variables are added (Model 5), the effect of gender is reduced to an even greater extent, by 31% of its original value, to .43. Again comparing Models 11 and 5, we can observe the mediating impact of industrial structure as the last-added set of variables. In this comparison, the net effect of gender is reduced by 15%.

In sum, industrial structure does explain a substantial part of the effects of race and gender, but it does not explain as great a part of the effect of these demographic variables as other variables in the model. Class and unionization account for more of the correlation between race and earnings than does industrial structure, and weeks and hours worked account for more of the correlation between gender and earnings than does industrial structure.

The effect of education on earnings is reduced by only 2% when industrial structure is added to the basic labor force composition model (compare Models 1 and 3 of Table 7.1). When class and unionization are added to the equation (Model 4), the effect of education is reduced by an additional 26% of its original value. When labor force supply variables are added to the equation (Model 5), the effect of education is further reduced by 17% of its original value. Comparing Models 11 and 5, we see that the effect of education is virtually unaltered by the inclusion of industrial structure as the last-entered set of variables in a fully specified earnings model. For education, industrial structure appears to have little or no mediating effect, whereas class, unionization, and weeks and hours worked explain substantial portions of its relationship to earnings.

Similarly, the linear component of experience is reduced by only 8% of its original value with the addition of industrial structure variables. It is further reduced by 8% when occupation and unionization variables are included, but it is reduced by 40% with the inclusion of weeks and hours worked. These results, which suggest that industrial structure reduces the effects of education and experience only minimally, contrast sharply with arguments from the dual economy perspective, which place great stress on industrial structure's mediation of the effects of human capital characteristics.

By examining the mediation of race, gender, and education effects across a series of models to which industrial structure variables and other controls were added, we see that industrial structure is an important, but perhaps not the most important, explanation of the relationship of these variables with earnings. Part of the effect of race is explained by the inclusion of industrial structure variables in an earnings model, but class and union membership are more important in this regard. Gender effects on earnings are also partially explained by industrial structure but are mediated more significantly by weeks and hours worked. Finally, the effect of education on earnings is substantially unaltered by the inclusion of industrial structure variables. However, this relationship is strongly mediated by class, unionization, and labor force demand variables. In addition, race, gender, and education all retain substantial (and statistically significant) direct effects on log earnings, for which they are the sole and unique explanation.

As a final note we observe that union power has a significant positive effect on wages above and beyond the impact of union membership and a full set of individual-level and organizational-level controls. This indicates that unions are successful in raising the average wage in industries in which they are strong, as well as the wages of the workers who are actually union members. Even nonunionized workers in heavily unionized industries reap some advantage from unionization. This effect can be jointly attributed to a spillover effect for average wage levels and to the actions of employers in raising wages to help ward off organizing drives (Ross, 1957).

The relative importance of the direct effects of the various sets of variables in our fully specified model of earnings can be evaluated by examining the contributions to explained variance presented in Table 7.3.[4] We see that weeks and hours worked and experience make by far the largest net contributions to explained variance. Next, in rank order of importance, are race and gender, industrial structure, unionization, class, and education. One should be careful in interpreting these rankings because they represent only net contributions in the fully specified earnings model and ignore patterns of causation among the variables in the model. In addition, examination of the F statistics for these contributions produces a different ranking because these statistics take account of the number of measures used to tap each component of the model (the number of

TABLE 7.3

Contribution to Total Explained Variance R^2 by Sets of Variables in Industry- and Company-Level Log Earnings Models[a]

	Industry model		Company model	
Variable set	Contribution to R^2	F	Contribution to R^2	F
Race and gender	.0211	743.7	.0458	943.8
Education	.0117	824.8	.0101	208.1
Experience/tenure	.0340	1198.5	.0017	35.0
Economic structure	.0153	134.8	.0064	33.0
Occupation/class	.0129	303.1	.0066	45.3
Unionization	.0132	465.3	.0041	42.2
Labor supply	.2257	7955.6	.2168	2233.8

[a] See Model 5 of Table 7.1 and Model 4 of Table 7.4. All contributions are significant at the .01 level.

degrees of freedom expended). Nevertheless, these findings indicate that industrial structure is an important determinant of workers' earnings, even when considering only its net contribution and ignoring its effects on other variables in the model. It is somewhat astonishing that industrial structure, a concept rarely included in sociological or human-capital models of earnings, has a larger net contribution in a fully specified model of earnings than such commonly used variables as class, unionization, and education. This finding clearly speaks to the need to broaden our theories of earnings determination to incorporate a role for the underlying economic structure of corporations and industries.

In concluding this section, several findings should be highlighted. First, industrial structure makes a unique and important net contribution to the explanation of earnings. Second, its inclusion in a more fully specified earnings model substantially alters the observed effects of race and gender on earnings. Therefore, any model that ignores industrial structure while attempting to investigate the effects of these demographic characteristics is seriously misspecified. Third, industrial structure is not found to influence strongly the effects of other earnings determinants such as education and experience.

EVALUATION OF THE COMPANY-LEVEL MODEL

The company-level model of economic structure is evaluated in Table 7.4 under a set of controls similar to those employed previously with the industry-level model. The company model is reasonably stable under this set of controls. All four of its variables have consistent signs in all the models presented, and all variables except company size maintain statistical significance. However, the effects of the company-level economic structure model are strongly reduced by the introduction of this more fully specified earnings model. Comparing Models 6 and 4, we see that 96% of the effect of company size, 65% of the effect of the size dummy, 72% of the effect of plant size, and 78% of the effect of capital intensity are mediated by other variables in the model. Thus, about 22% of the total effects of company-level economic structure are direct, and about 78% occur through the relationship of corporate economic structure with other variables in the model. A substantial part of this reduction in direct effects occurs when gender and education are added to the earnings equation (see Model 2). However, the direct effects of the economic structure variables are also reduced by the introduction of controls for class and unionization (see Model 3) and are more significantly reduced by the introduction of controls for weeks and hours worked (see Model 4). These findings indicate that the impact of economic structure on earnings occurs both directly and also through labor demand and through the relationship of corporate economic structure with the gender, educational, and class composition of the labor force.

TABLE 7.4

Regression of Log Earnings on Company-Level Model with Controls[a]

	Model							
Variable	1	2	3	4	5	6	7	8
Female	−1.4798	−1.3799	−1.1234	−.6397	−.6421			−.6453
Education	.0545	.0541	.0610	.0656	.0723			.0742
Company size		[.0054]	[.0048]	[.0036]		.0894		
Size dummy		.1312	.1146	.0666		.1891		
Plant size		.0689	.0497	.0378		.1345		
Capital intensity		.0680	.0481	.0254		.1167		
Manager			.5802	.2822	.2672			.2600
Supervisor			.2948	.1427	.1386			.1304
Autonomous			.1038	[.0328]	[.0021]			[−.0061]
Union			.1498	.1658	.1762			.1801
Union power			.0013	.0011	.0017			.0021
Tenure			.0026	.0008	.0011			.0012
Weeks				.0463	.0469			.0470
Hours				.0173	.0172			.0172
Monopoly					.0752		.5957	
Multiplant					.0505		.3421	
Intercept	4.23	3.83	3.25	0.41	0.44	3.71	4.08	0.42
R^2 (×100)	48.64	51.41	56.59	78.27	77.71	12.25	6.10	77.63
Standard deviation	0.77	0.75	0.71	0.50	0.51	1.01	1.05	0.51

[a] Data taken from 1975 Wisconsin survey. Sample is private employees with annual earnings of at least $100; N = 4493. Except where enclosed in square brackets, regression coefficients are significant at the .05 level. The categories of working class positions and the local sector have been left out of these earnings equations to estimate the effects of class and sector, respectively.

Turning to our company-level sectoral model we see that, whereas company-level economic sectors still have significant effects in a more fully specified earnings model, about 87% of the monopoly–local sector earnings contrast is a result of the association of economic sectors with other variables in the model (compare Models 5 and 7 of Table 7.4). Similarly, about 85% of the multiplant–local sector earnings contrast is indirect. Thus, a large portion of the total effect of corporate economic structure on earnings is a result of the number of weeks and hours of work offered as employment, the selection by companies of certain categories of labor, and the selection by labor of sectors and levels of employment. Nevertheless, even beyond these interrelationships, corporate economic structure still has a significant direct impact on workers' earnings that must be attributed solely to it and not to any other variables.

At this point we can again turn to an evaluation of the role of the other variables in the more fully specified earnings model. The effect of gender across these regression models of earnings shows an identical pattern to that observed in the industry-level analysis. The direct effect of gender is somewhat reduced by economic structure and somewhat by class and unionization variables but most importantly by weeks and hours worked (see Models 1–4 of Table 7.4). Comparing Models 4 and 8, which present the fully specified log earnings model with and without economic structure variables, we see that only about 1% of the effect of gender can be uniquely explained by company-level economic structure.

Again comparing Models 4 and 8 of Table 7.4, we see that the direct effect of education is reduced by 12% when the company-level economic structure variables are entered into the equation. However, in the Wisconsin sample the net effect of education is lowest when only gender and economic structure are controlled (Model 2) and actually increases when controls are added for class, unionization, and weeks and hours worked (see Models 3 and 4).[5] We also see that the effect of tenure is virtually unchanged by the inclusion of company-level economic structure in the model of earnings determination (again compare Models 4 and 8).

Turning finally to a consideration of the role of class, unionization, and weeks and hours worked, we see that the introduction of company-level economic structure variables into the earnings model causes only a slight reduction in the direct effects of these variables (again compare Models 4 and 8 of Table 7.4). Recall that this was also the pattern observed in the industry-level analyses with the CPS data.

The net contributions of the various sets of variables in the Wisconsin sample earnings model to the explanation of log earnings are presented in Table 7.3. Again, weeks and hours worked have the largest net contribution. Gender has the next largest contribution, and the net contributions of education, class, economic structure, unionization and tenure follow in rank order. These rankings do not demonstrate great stability across the two models and samples, and probably a great deal of weight should not be put on their interpretation. However, we again see that the economic structure model does make an important net contribution to the explanation to individual earnings, even beyond its relationships of joint determination with other components of the model.

In summary, company-level economic structure is observed to have a significant direct impact on workers' earnings that is unexplainable by any other variables in the model. Also, the inclusion of economic structure in our earnings model does reduce to some extent the direct effect of education. However, company-level economic structure does not reduce the direct effect of gender in the Wisconsin sample.

In comparing the company- and industry-level models of economic structure under the controls of a more fully specified model of earnings, we can draw the following conclusions. First, both models demonstrate strong net contributions to the explanation of workers' earnings that cannot be attributed to any other variables in the model. However, the direct effects of the economic structure variables are reduced from the level of their total effects by the inclusion of other variables in the model, in the company-level model somewhat more strongly than in the industry-level model.[6]

Second, both the industry-level and company-level models offer explanations for portions of the total effects of the demographic and training variables in the more fully specified models. Accordingly, our models of economic structure offer a partial explanation for some of the persistent economic inequalities in American society that are otherwise attributed to these variables. However, the reductions in the effects of these variables that are due uniquely to economic structure are not overwhelmingly large, and the direct effects of these demographic and training characteristics do not disappear from the earnings models. Thus, although part of the effects of the demographic and training characteristics of labor may be explained by economic structure, their total effect on earnings cannot be explained entirely by the role of economic structure in selecting workers and in determining earnings.

SOCIAL BACKGROUND AND ECONOMIC STRUCTURE AS DETERMINANTS OF INDIVIDUAL EARNINGS

A unique contribution to the study of social stratification has been made by sociologists, who have developed models of the impact of social background on attainments later in life. We shall incorporate a model of social background in our earnings equation with two purposes in mind. First, by utilizing this more fully and correctly specified model of earnings, we can evaluate our model of economic structure under as rigorous a set of controls as possible. Second, we shall be able to evaluate the hypothesis of the basic independence of these two models of earnings. This evaluation will be carried out using the Wisconsin data, which contain multiple measures of social background characteristics.

In Model 1 of Table 7.5, we evaluate an earnings equation that contains gender, six measures of social background, and five measures tapping the respondents' high school experience. Of these variables, only gender, high school rank, I.Q., occupational expectations, and parental income have significant direct effects on earnings. In Models 2–5, gender maintains a consistent effect as education, economic structure, occupation, unionization, and weeks and hours worked are added as control variables. The net effect of high school rank is reduced as controls are added, and it becomes insignificant with the inclusion of economic structure. I.Q. retains a small positive direct effect on earnings throughout the models presented and is statistically significant in all the equations except Model 2. The net impact of occupational aspirations is reduced by

TABLE 7.5

Regression of Log Earnings on Social Background Variables, Schooling Variables, Company Model, and Controls[a]

Variable	Model						t Test for slope differences	
	1	2	3	4	5	6	(1 vs. 5)	(5 vs. 6)
Parental income	.0011	[.0009]	.0010	[.0008]	.0010		0.17	
Father's occup.	[−.0011]	[−.0013]	[−.0010]	[−.0005]	[−.0003]		0.85	
Father's educ.	[.0035]	[.0015]	[.0029]	[.0018]	[.0018]		0.31	
Broken home	[−.0221]	[−.0237]	[−.0134]	[−.0157]	[−.0082]		0.26	
Town size	[.0043]	[.0034]	[−.0010]	[−.0019]	[.0011]		0.41	
Rural	[−.0453]	[−.0497]	[−.0553]	[−.0465]	[−.0281]		0.32	
H.S. rank	.0019	.0014	[.0011]	[.0008]	[.0008]		1.53	
I.Q.	.0012	[.0010]	.0013	.0011	.0013		0.14	
Occup. exp.	.0018	[.0016]	[.0010]	[.0010]	.0012		0.64	
College exp.	[.0727]	[.0687]	[.0562]	[.0472]	.0622		0.22	
Tech. school exp.	[−.0143]	[−.0806]	[−.0592]	[−.0709]	−.0773		1.20	
Female	[−1.5577]	−1.5312	−1.4223	−1.1546	−.6731	−.6397	23.75[b]	1.01
Education		.0383	.0371	.0522	.0539	.0656		1.44
Company size			[.0066]	[.0035]	[.0018]	[.0036]		0.12
Size dummy			.1311	.1119	.0630	.0666		0.11
Plant size			.0682	.0481	.0358	.0378		0.30
Capital intensity			.0635	.0454	.0223	.0254		0.20
Manager				.5606	.2559	.2822		0.65
Supervisor				.2808	.1254	.1427		0.59
Autonomous				.0960	[.0234]	[.0328]		0.24
Union				.1625	.1814	.1658		0.46
Union power				.0014	.0012	.0011		0.18
Tenure				.0026	.0009	.0008		0.35
Weeks					.0463	.0463		0.00
Hours					.0175	.0173		0.20
Intercept	4.66	4.25	3.87	3.22	0.37	0.41		
R^2 (×100)	48.96	49.19	51.87	56.89	78.68	78.27		
Standard deviation	0.77	0.77	0.75	0.71	0.50	0.50		

[a] Data taken from 1975 Wisconsin survey. Sample is private employees with annual earnings of at least $100; $N = 4493$. Except where enclosed in square brackets, regression coefficients of Models 1–6 are significant at the .05 level. The categories of working class positions and the local sector have been left out of these earnings equations to estimate the effects of class and sector, respectively.

the inclusion of controls and is insignificant in several of the more fully specified models.

Significant effects are conspicuously absent for several variables in these models. In Model 5, which includes the fully specified earnings model developed earlier in this chapter as well as social background and schooling characteristics, the only social background variable that has a significant direct effect is parental income. However, four of the five schooling variables are significant, including I.Q. and occupational and educational expectations.[7]

A test of the independence of the social background and economic structure models of earnings can be constructed by contrasting the coefficients of each model against those from an equation in which both models are entered simultaneously. Statistical tests for these contrasts are presented in the last two columns of Table 7.5. On the 26 tests of slope differences presented in these two columns, none is statistically significant except the test that measures for a difference in the effect of gender between the social background and schooling effects model and the full earnings model. This finding strongly supports the contention that these two models of earnings determination are, indeed, highly independent.

Table 7.6 reports the contribution to explained variance in log earnings by the various components of our most fully specified earnings equation, presented as Model 5 of Table 7.5. We see that the largest contribution can be attributed to weeks and hours worked, and the second largest can be attributed to gender. Education, economic structure, class, and unionization all make roughly equal but somewhat smaller net contributions. Social background and schooling variables and tenure make by far the smallest net contributions to the explanation of log earnings of any groups of variables in the equation, but even these contributions are significant at the .05 level.

The general hypothesis of the substantive independence of the social background and economic structure models of individual earnings is supported by

TABLE 7.6

**Contribution to Total Explained Variance
R^2 by Sets of Variables in Full
Company-Level Log Earnings Model with
Controls for Social Background and
Schooling Variables[a]**

Variable set	Contribution to R^2	F
Gender	.0463	970.1
Social background	.0011	3.8
Schooling variables	.0029	12.2
Education	.0041	85.9
Economic structure	.0056	29.3
Class	.0053	37.0
Unionization	.0049	51.3
Tenure	.0019	39.8
Labor supply	.2179	2282.7

[a] See Model 5 of Table 7.5. All contributions are significant at the .05 level.

these results. Neither model alters the effects attributed to the other to a significant degree, and both function independently in the determination of earnings. In conclusion, it appears that these two models, arising from distinct theoretical traditions and engendering distinct hypotheses about observable job outcomes, can be independently evaluated without fear of substantial misspecification of models. Also, based on the results presented in Table 7.6, it appears that economic structure has much more direct relevance for the study of workers' earnings than does social background.

CONCLUSIONS

We have seen in this chapter that economic structure retains significant direct effects on employee earnings when controls are introduced for labor force composition, class, unionization, weeks and hours worked, and social background and schooling variables. This finding demonstrates that economic structure has a significant direct effect on employee earnings. Overall, the evaluation of the company- and industry-level models of economic structure against more fully specified individual-level models of earnings attainment has produced highly similar results.[8] The direct effects of both models are somewhat reduced by the introduction of controls. However, except for the linear component of the company-level measure of corporate size, all of the economic structure variables have statistically significant direct effects in the models with full controls. In addition, all of the signs of these effects remain constant (except for the linear component of foreign involvement in the quadratic form of the industry-level model). These findings clearly undermine human capital explanations of earnings inequality that attempt to reduce the process of earnings attainment to individual-level characteristics. These direct effects of economic structure operate through the provision of structural resources for all workers employed in specific industries, companies, or plants, regardless of the individual characteristics of those workers. (In Chapter 8 we shall investigate the possibility that these structural resources may, in fact, operate with different levels of effectiveness for different categories of workers.)

An additional part of the overall impact of economic structure on earnings occurs through the relationship of economic structure with other earnings determinants such as race, gender, education, and class. The inclusion of economic structure variables in models of individual earnings reduces the effects that might otherwise be attributed to demographic characteristics and to education. This reduction ranges from 1 to 22% of the total effect of the variable being analyzed and suggests that part of the effects attributed to these variables in individual-level models of earnings results from the sorting of categories of workers into differentially paid positions in the economic structure. In the industry-level model, economic structure operates chiefly to explain the impact of demographic variables, and in the company-level model, primarily to explain the effect of education. However, the effect of race is more strongly mediated by class and unionization than by economic structure, and the effect of gender is more strongly mediated by weeks and hours worked than by economic structure. The effect of education is strongly mediated by economic structure in the Wisconsin sample, but in the CPS sample its effect is more strongly mediated by class, unionization, and weeks and hours worked than by economic structure. In sum, economic structure is not the most important mediator of the effects of these variables.

These results suggest that, although economic structure does interact with these variables in important and interesting ways, it does not entirely explain their persistent effects on workers' earnings. Earnings effects that are uniquely attributable to demographic characteristics and to education remain in our most fully specified equations, which include multivariate models of economic structure. Both the organizational and the individual levels of social structure have autonomous direct effects on the earnings process; neither level is entirely reducible to the other. The individual characteristics of workers, such as their education and social group, have a direct effect on their earnings. Industrial structure has both important direct effects on earnings and indirect effects through the matching of categories of the labor force to specific kinds of employment positions.

We can draw certain implications from these findings. Economic structure is important in models of individual earnings, but perhaps it is of most consequence as a net additive effect, rather than as a dimension that alters the effects of individual-level variables. We might, therefore, depict economic structure as important for the study of the creation of other job structures but less important for the study of such processes as economic returns to individual characteristics. That is, economic structure deserves a central place in studies of the success of unionization drives, the creation of class structure, and the creation of economic inequality. However, in the study of such processes as earnings returns to education, economic structure models may be of less central importance. Our findings on the independence of social background and economic structure models of earnings reinforce this interpretation.

In the next chapter we shall pursue these issues further. The roles of demographic characteristics, education, and class in income determination will be analyzed as they vary across industrial and corporate sectors. Much of the literature on labor market segmentation suggests that many of these variables have different effects across economic sectors, and the simple additive models presented in this chapter are not adequate to address the issue fully. We shall also investigate the possibility that the resources provided by corporate economic structure can be utilized with varying degrees of effectiveness by different groups in the labor force.

NOTES TO CHAPTER 7

1. The 45% reduction in the effect of capital intensity when controls are added for demographic and skill characteristics of the labor force indicates that a substantial portion of the effect of this variable on earnings is through the requirements it creates for a more highly trained labor force. However, the larger portion of the effect of capital intensity on earnings is direct, and it is this portion of its effect that we interpret as reflecting the bargaining resources for workers provided by capital intensity.

2. Similarly, the effects of occupation, unionization, and labor demand on earnings are largely unaltered by the inclusion of a model of industrial structure (compare Models 11 and 5 of Table 7.1). In spite of the close theoretical relationships of these dimensions of the workplace, their effects on earnings appear to be largely independent and additive.

3. These sector effects are measured as deviations from the trades sector, which is the left-out category in Table 7.1.

4. These contributions to explained variance are calculated by entering each set of variables last in the fully specified log earnings equation (Model 5 of Table 7.1) and noting the increment to R^2.

5. The explanation for this discrepancy between the findings for education in the CPS industry model and in the Wisconsin company model is as follows. In the CPS sample, where education has a full range of values, education, unionization, and weeks and hours worked have positive correlations. Therefore, when the latter variables are entered as controls, the direct effect of education on earnings is reduced. In the Wisconsin sample, which contains no respondents with less than a high school diploma, education has negative correlations with unionization and with weeks and hours worked. Thus, when these variables are controlled, the apparent effect of education on earnings increases.

6. In Table D.10 in the Appendix we report an evaluation of the fully specified earnings equation, including the industry-level economic structure model, on the Wisconsin and restricted CPS samples. Comparison of these two sets of coefficients offers an important verification of the stability of the effects of economic structure across different samples. Overall, the effects of the industrial structure variables are very similar in both samples (and also highly similar to those for the industry model evaluated on the overall CPS sample, see Table 7.1). Differences across the Wisconsin and restricted CPS sample in the slopes of the three scale measures, size, concentration, and foreign involvement, are not significant at the .05 level. Autonomy has a significantly smaller slope in the Wisconsin sample than in the restricted CPS sample. This pattern may result from the importance of agriculture and other low-wage but "autonomous" industrial sectors in Wisconsin. (See Chapter 6 for a discussion of the interpretation of this scale.) Also, the earnings effects of both the linear and quadratic components of capital intensity are somewhat reduced in the Wisconsin sample. We have no particular explanation for this finding.

The evaluation of the industry-level model with full controls on the restricted CPS and Wisconsin samples shows its parameters to be relatively stable. As a result, differences between the industry- and company-level models cannot be interpreted as resulting from the nonrepresentativeness of the Wisconsin sample, on which the company-level model is evaluated. In addition, the stability of the industry-level model between the total and restricted CPS samples indicates that differences between the industry- and company-level models also cannot be attributed to the restriction of the Wisconsin sample to high school graduates in their mid-30s. As we have argued earlier, such differences must, therefore, be a result of differences between the company- and industry-level models themselves— either substantive differences in the meanings of the concepts when measured at these different levels or differences in the quality of the industry and company data. (See also Note 8.)

7. It should be noted that we have not utilized a path model depicting the indirect as well as the direct effects of the various sets of variables in this model. Such an approach would undoubtedly demonstrate greater total effects for some of the social background and schooling variables. Howev-

er, many of these variables have insignificant effects on earnings even in Model 1 of Table 7.5, which contains only social background variables, schooling variables, and gender.

8. The reduction in the direct effects of the company-level model with the introduction of labor force controls is somewhat greater than in the case of the industry-level model. It seems unlikely that this difference can be explained by greater measurement error in the company data, because it involves the measures of company and plant size, variables that have relatively little missing data. This finding suggests, then, that a greater proportion of the effects of corporate-level economic structure operates through the sorting of categories of workers into employment positions than is the case with industry-level economic structure. Industry-level economic structure appears to function to a greater extent by setting an industrial environment that influences the earnings level of all workers in the industry, regardless of their individual characteristics.

8

Earnings Attainment across Economic Sectors, Classes, and Race and Gender Groups

In previous chapters we have seen that economic structure has a substantial direct impact on individual earnings, even controlling for demographic, human capital, and class variables, and that economic structure also mediates, to some degree, the effects of these other earnings determinants. In this chapter, through an analysis of earnings attainment within economic sectors, classes, and race and gender groups, we shall further investigate the manner in which economic structure interacts with these other determinants of individual earnings.

Much of the literature on economic segmentation suggests that there are different processes of earnings determination operating in the various economic sectors. For example, economic returns to schooling are expected to be larger in the core sectors of the economy because of the use of these returns as a form of social control and because of the drive toward bureaucratic standardization and documentation, which places a premium on the types of skills taught in school, prevalent in the large firms of these sectors. In addition, arguments based on the work of Wright and Perrone (1977) and others assert that the managerial class in core sectors receives the highest educational returns of any segment of the labor force. The segmentation literature also suggests that the pattern of class earnings inequality is more extreme in the core sectors because of the use of income differences as a mechanism of social control in these sectors. The hypothesis of differential returns to education, in particular, is important to the critique of the human-capital model of earnings attainment emerging from the segmentation literature because it implies that not only does the human capital model overestimate the general effects of individual-level characteristics but that these effects are realized to different degrees in the various sectors.

The resource interpretation of economic structure leads to the additional expectation that different groups may be affected in varying ways by the resources and vulnerabilities defined by the dimensions of economic structure. Thus, manual workers and workers who are members of minority groups are expected to be influenced to a greater extent by economic structure than are, respectively, managerial workers and nonminority workers, who are able to rely on personal characteristics legitimated by the social system for the attainment of higher earnings.

EARNINGS RETURNS TO EDUCATION WITHIN ECONOMIC SECTORS

The individual-level earnings attainment model that we developed in Chapter 7 is evaluated within industrial sectors in Table 8.1. Examination of the results in this table allows us to evaluate expectations concerning differential educational returns across sectors and different patterns of class inequality across sectors. Comparing earnings returns to education across sectors, we see that the periphery and trades sectors have higher returns to education than do the core and oligopoly sectors. This is exactly the opposite of the expected pattern. Further, the contrast between the larger educational returns in the periphery and the smaller returns in the core is statistically significant.[1] The highest returns of all are observed for workers in the core utilities sector.[2]

This pattern is repeated when we examine earnings returns to experience. The linear component of experience shows greater returns in the periphery and trades sectors than in the core and oligopoly sectors, exactly replicating the pattern for educational returns. Again, the contrast between the higher returns in the periphery sector and the lower returns in the core sector is statistically significant.

Comparing earnings returns to education across company-level sectors in the Wisconsin sample, we see that the highest returns go to workers in the multiplant sector (see Table 8.2). Although workers in the monopoly sector receive higher returns than do workers in the local sector, this contrast is not statistically significant.[3] Returns to tenure on the job appear to be highest in the local sector and lowest in the monopoly sector, but these contrasts are small in magnitude and are not statistically significant.

These results show a reasonably parallel pattern across samples and measurement levels for both education and experience, which implicitly validates the results for both variables. But the pattern does not strongly support the major hypothesis. At the company level, the contrast between educational returns in the local and monopoly sectors is in the expected direction but is not statistically significant, and the highest returns are received by workers in the multiplant sector. At the industry level, workers in the periphery and the core utilities sector have the highest returns to years of education, whereas returns in the oligopoly and core sectors are relatively low. In addition, the two industry sectors with the highest returns have few structural characteristics in common, and the differences in educational returns across sectors are not large overall.

These findings contrast sharply both with theoretical arguments and with prior empirical findings in the segmentation literature. Osterman (1975), Beck, Horan, and Tolbert (1978), and Tolbert, Horan, and Beck (1980) all report greater earnings returns to education in the core, or primary, sectors. There are several possible explanations for the lack of support for the stated hypothesis. Perhaps a different pattern of returns to education would be observed under a different transformation of employee earnings. Given unequal mean levels of earnings across sectors, equal log earnings returns indicate unequal dollar earnings returns. That is, similar rates of increase at different earnings levels translate into different dollar increments. Accordingly, in spite of the results just reported, it is possible that higher dollar returns to education are received by workers in the core sectors than by workers in the periphery sectors.

We have argued that the natural logarithm transformation of earnings is the appropriate form for the analysis of social processes of earnings attainment because people think of earnings differences in percentage terms, an interpretation well approximated by the log transformation. However, use of a different functional form of earnings might lead to very different conclusions about the role of economic sectors in structuring patterns of earnings returns to education, and the reader should be aware of this possibility. (See Beck *et al.,* 1980; Coleman and Rainwater, 1978; Hauser, 1980; and Jencks, 1979, for further discussion and debate on this topic.)

Alternatively, it is possible that the nature of the sectoral measures utilized in Tables 8.1 and 8.2 is the root cause of these anomalous findings. Whereas our operationalization of sectors is grounded at the level of firms and industries, much of the theory arguing for unequal educational returns is posed in terms of primary and secondary *jobs*. A large portion of the research findings in support of this hypothesis has also been based on measures grounded at the level of occupations rather than at the level of industries or firms (see Osterman, 1975). We have argued that a major fallacy of the dual approach is the refusal to distinguish job or labor market sectors from industrial sectors, and perhaps the hypothesis of higher educational returns in the core sectors is a theoretical legacy of just this fallacy. That is, there may very well be higher educational returns to workers in "primary" job sectors, but this says nothing about the pattern of returns we should expect in different industrial or corporate sectors.

TABLE 8.1

Regression of Log Earnings Model within Industrial Sectors[a]

Variable		Sector						
	Total[b]	Oligopoly	Core	Periphery	Core utilities	Periphery utilities	Trades	Core–periphery contrast t
Female	-.4949	-.3997	-.5251	-.4277	-.3377	-.5881	-.3329	3.58[d]
	(.0122)	(.0490)	(.0182)	(.0202)	(.0334)	(.1243)	(.0400)	
Black	-.1078	[-.0669]	-.1548	[-.0308]	[-.0986]	-.2774	[-.0453]	2.83[d]
	(.0185)	(.0525)	(.0276)	(.0341)	(.0517)	(.1100)	(.0457)	
Education	.0528	.0386	.0430	.0596	.0774	.0422	.0547	3.38[d]
	(.0022)	(.0082)	(.0031)	(.0038)	(.0064)	(.0132)	(.0055)	
Graded[c]	.0448	.0295	.0344	.0437	.0681	[.0246]	.0515	1.44
	(.0032)	(.0112)	(.0038)	(.0052)	(.0101)	(.0152)	(.0071)	
College[c]	.0702	.0510	.0621	.0892	.0856	.1079	.0540	2.82[d]
	(.0047)	(.0132)	(.0060)	(.0075)	(.0094)	(.0317)	(.0114)	
Experience	.0481	.0231	.0355	.0490	.0379	.0616	.0495	5.16[d]
	(.0011)	(.0047)	(.0018)	(.0019)	(.0032)	(.0078)	(.0029)	
(Experience)^2	-.0079	-.0036	-.0055	-.0079	-.0062	-.0101	-.0078	4.24[d]
	(.0002)	(.0010)	(.0004)	(.0004)	(.0007)	(.0015)	(.0006)	
Manager	.4654	.4489	.4268	.3811	.3222	.2792	.5899	0.99
	(.0212)	(.0822)	(.0317)	(.0333)	(.0522)	(.1415)	(.0732)	

	(1)	(2)	(3)	(4)	(5)	(6)	(7)	
Professional	.4112 (.0212)	.2469 (.0638)	.3231 (.0301)	.4196 (.0420)	.2603 (.0609)	.5537 (.2798)	.7424 (.0525)	1.87
White collar	.1614 (.0147) [.0123]	.1196 (.0222) [.0123]	.1196 (.0222)	.1027 (.0297)	.1414 (.0440)	[.1141] (.1790)	.5286 (.0545)	2.87[d]
Union	.2900 (.0138) [.0762]	.1527 (.0182) [.0428]	.1527 (.0182)	.2456 (.0249)	.1414 (.0390)	.3235 (.0710)	.611 (.0429)	3.01[d]
Union power	.0043 (.0003) [.0006]	.0018 (.0004) [.0007]	.0018 (.0004)	.0050 (.0005)	.0027 (.0005)	[.0009] (.0025)	.0141 (.0009)	5.00[d]
Weeks	.0365 (.0004)	.0389 (.0007)	.0389 (.0007)	.0365 (.0007)	.0355 (.0013)	.0391 (.0029)	.0343 (.0011)	2.42[d]
Hours	.0093 (.0003)	.0057 (.0005)	.0057 (.0005)	.0110 (.0005)	.0093 (.0009)	.0055 (.0018)	.0112 (.0009)	7.50[d]
Intercept	0.57	1.66	1.24	0.50	0.53	0.57	0.06	
R^2 (×100)	70.76	71.80	71.02	68.70	66.55	69.01	69.77	
Standard deviation	0.67	0.41	0.52	0.70	0.82	0.95	0.77	
N	20,007	593	5403	7619	1805	383	4181	

[a] Data taken from March–May match 1973 CPS. Sample is private employees with annual earnings of at least $100. Metric regression coefficients are presented with their standard errors reported beneath in parentheses. Except where enclosed in square brackets, all coefficients are significant at the .05 level.

[b] Model includes unreported sector dummy variables (see Model 7 of Table 7.1).

[c] The coefficients for graded and college education are taken from equations in which these two variables replace the single linear education measure.

[d] Significant at the .05 level.

TABLE 8.2

Regression of Log Earnings Model within Company Sectors[a]

			Sector		
Variable	Total[b]	Monopoly	Multiplant	Local	Monopoly–local contrast t
Female	−.6421	−.5478	−.6325	−.6700	2.44[c]
	(.0229)	(.0319)	(.0431)	(.0386)	
Education	.0723	.0809	.0814	.0607	1.93
	(.0049)	(.0066)	(.0101)	(.0081)	
Manager	.2672	.2364	.1407	.3341	1.59
	(.0283)	(.0375)	(.0524)	(.0486)	
Supervisor	.1386	.0946	[.0436]	.1939	2.21[c]
	(.0208)	(.0270)	(.0397)	(.0359)	
Autonomous	[.0021]	.1049	[.0667]	[−.0344]	2.31[c]
	(.0277)	(.0405)	(.0531)	(.0447)	
Union	.1762	.0879	.1829	.2940	3.72[c]
	(.0236)	(.0281)	(.0418)	(.0477)	
Union power	.0017	.0029	[.0005]	[.0010]	2.01[c]
	(.0004)	(.0005)	(.0008)	(.0008)	
Tenure	.0011	.0009	.0012	.0013	1.11
	(.0002)	(.0002)	(.0003)	(.0003)	
Weeks	.0469	.0545	.0472	.0439	5.34[c]
	(.0009)	(.0015)	(.0017)	(.0013)	
Hours	.0172	.0113	.0218	.0186	4.67[c]
	(.0007)	(.0010)	(.0015)	(.0012)	
Intercept	0.44	0.26	0.24	0.65	
R^2 (×100)	77.71	78.62	83.02	74.73	
Standard deviation	0.51	0.39	0.41	0.60	
N	4493	1528	875	2090	

[a] Data taken from 1975 Wisconsin survey. Sample is private employees with annual earnings of at least $100. Metric regression coefficients are presented with their standard errors reported beneath in parentheses. Except where enclosed in square brackets, coefficients are significant at the .05 level.

[b] Model includes unreported sector dummy variables (see Model 5 of Table 7.4).

[c] Significant at the .05 level.

The argument we are making here is that hypotheses about earnings returns to education in different job sectors cannot be extended by analogy to industrial or corporate economic sectors. The hypothesis of differential earnings returns to education has been usefully applied to the study of classes (Wright, 1979) and social groups (Feathermen and Hauser, 1978), but it appears to be less usefully applied to the analysis of earnings processes within economic sectors. The motivation for the hypothesis arose from a critique of the human capital model of earnings and from a concern with issues of equal opportunity and discrimination against blacks and women. But, it may well be that the issue of the unequal rewarding of individual traits is misplaced when applied to the analysis of corporate structure. Corporate structure has, in its own right, important effects that deserve serious consideration. But the concern for patterns of differential educational returns is a carry-over from other theoretical traditions with other leading questions, and the issue has not been adequately theoretically integrated with the analysis of corporate structure.[4]

Class Differences in Earnings Returns to Education

Based on a convergence of class and sectoral arguments about earnings returns to education, the literature on economic segmentation suggests that the highest returns should belong to managers in the core sectors. Although our earlier analysis of returns across economic sectors does not suggest that this pattern will be observed, the hypothesis is still worth investigating. Because this expectation explicitly states that returns should be highest in the core sector managerial class, we shall restrict our evaluation to a consideration of the Wisconsin data, which contains a measure of class based on authority relations at the workplace.

A model of earnings attainment including educational effects, evaluated across classes within company-level sectors, is presented in Table 8.3. Autonomous workers receive the highest earnings returns in each sector, but these are higher in the local sector than in the monopoly sector. For the other three classes—managers, supervisors, and workers—the lowest returns to education are received in the local sector and the highest returns to education are received in the multiplant sector. Although earnings returns to education in the multiplant sector are higher than in the local sector, providing support for the expectation stated previously, the intermediate level of returns in the monopoly sector is contrary to the expectation arising from the literature on economic segmentation. Further, the highest rate of earnings returns to education belongs to autonomous workers in the local sector rather than to managers in the monopoly sector.

In this section few of our expectations about the pattern of earnings returns to education within economic sectors have been supported. Earnings returns to education and experience are observed to be larger in the periphery industrial sector than in the core sector. Results from the company-level analysis are in the expected direction, with monopoly sector workers receiving greater returns than local sector workers, but these results were not statistically significant. Further, the highest returns are received by employees in companies with a regional multiplant structure, not by the employees of either locally based companies or companies of national reputation. The analysis of educational returns to classes within sectors shows that autonomous workers in the local sector, rather than

TABLE 8.3

Regression of Log Earnings Model across the Cells of a Class-by-Sector Classification[a]

	Class			
Variable	Manager	Supervisor	Autonomous	Worker
Monopoly sector[b]				
Female	−.4933	−.6052	−.6572	−.4904
Education	.0701	.0752	.0921	.0751
Union	[−.1577]	[.0421]	[.0685]	[.0713]
Union power	[−.0014]	.0024	[.0029]	.0047
Tenure	[−.0004]	.0006	[.0005]	.0014
Hours	.0102	[.0029]	.0119	.0133
Weeks	.0848	.0626	.0504	.0513
Intercept	−0.58	0.45	0.46	0.26
R^2 ($\times 100$)	65.39	73.68	73.65	79.44
Standard deviation	0.35	0.30	0.42	0.43
N	218	440	129	741
Multiplant sector[c]				
Female	−.4405	−.6281	−.7478	−.5466
Education	.0796	.0761	.0897	.0787
Union	[−.0168]	[.0648]	[.1271]	.2165
Union power	[.0011]	[.0000]	[.0032]	[.0000]
Tenure	[−.0004]	[.0007]	.0025	.0019
Hours	[.0008]	.0180	.0295	.0245
Weeks	.0350	.0577	.0287	.0462
Intercept	2.18	0.08	0.67	0.12
R^2 ($\times 100$)	45.45	79.46	83.71	86.06
Standard deviation	0.31	0.40	0.43	0.42
N	172	270	105	328
Local sector[d]				
Female	−.5521	−.5720	−.7260	−.8194
Education	.0509	.0605	.1077	.0531
Union	[.0924]	.2823	[.0849]	.3057
Union power	[.0011]	[.0014]	[.0025]	[−.0004]
Tenure	[.0002]	.0016	.0027	.0013
Hours	.0056	.0161	.0255	.0199
Weeks	.0443	.0417	.0488	.0418
Intercept	1.82	0.98	−0.47	0.92
R^2 ($\times 100$)	50.77	65.40	74.15	76.00
Standard deviation	0.47	0.59	0.69	0.58
N	346	732	314	695

[a] Data taken from 1975 Wisconsin survey. Sample is private employees with annual earnings of at least $100; $N = 4493$. Except where enclosed in square brackets, regression coefficients are significant at the .05 level.

[b] $N = 1528$.   [c] $N = 875$.   [d] $N = 2087$.

managers in the monopoly sector, receive the very highest earnings returns to education. We argue that these negative findings should be attributed to the lack of theoretical specification of this issue within the segmentation literature. Basically, a hypothesis about earnings determination within job sectors was transferred through analogy to the analysis of earnings determination within industrial and corporate sectors, without allowing for autonomous theoretical development of hypotheses about these processes *at the level of economic sectors*.

CLASS INEQUALITY WITHIN ECONOMIC SECTORS

A second major expectation derived from the segmentation literature suggests that greater class inequality exists in the large-firm core sectors than in the locally based competitive sectors because of the greater reliance in the core sectors on bureaucratic modes of labor control with large and systematic wage differentials. This expectation can be evaluated by examining the earnings returns to occupational and class positions within economic sectors presented in Tables 8.1 and 8.2. (Note that the coefficient for each occupation or class indicates the respective earnings difference between that category and manual workers or working class positions.)

An examination of these results does not lend support to the stated expectation. The greatest occupational earnings differentials are in the trades sector, and managers and supervisors receive the highest wages relative to the working class in the local company sector. These patterns are exactly the opposite of those suggested by the literature. However, lower white-collar workers receive their greatest earnings relative to manual workers in the core industrial sector, and autonomous workers receive their highest wages relative to the working class in the monopoly sector.

One might argue from the theoretical standpoint developed in this book that the finding of greater inequality between managers and workers in the local and trades sectors gives evidence of the lack of structural resources for workers in these sectors. Also, the relatively high wages of white-collar and autonomous workers in the core and monopoly sectors might be interpreted as indicating the workings of a bureaucratic system of labor control that yields large wage premiums for bureaucratic staff and line positions rather than for top management.[5] But whether one accepts these interpretations or not, the findings largely contradict the expectation that the largest class inequalities should be found in the core sectors. These findings undermine the argument that the role of economic structure in wage determination can be understood as primarily operational through its provision of a basis of labor control for management.

ECONOMIC STRUCTURE FOR WHOM?

In the final section of this chapter the effects of corporate structure across social groups will be analyzed. This section is important for understanding the nature of corporate structure as a resource that can be utilized with different degrees of success by various social categories and social classes. With this section we make an important shift in focus from the investigation of the effects of individual resources, such as education and experience, back to our original concern for corporate structure as a structural resource for workers. We shall first investigate the effects of economic structure across occupational and class categories to evaluate the hypothesis that economic structure provides a more important resource for manual and working class positions than for managerial workers, who rely more heavily on individual characteristics such as education. Next, we shall investigate the effects of economic structure across the social categories of race and gender to evaluate the hypothesis that minority-group workers are more strongly influenced by structural characteristics of the workplace than are nonminority workers.

Occupational and Class Categories

In Table 8.4 we analyze earnings across occupational categories, utilizing the industry-level model of economic structure with controls for individual characteristics. For managers, industrial structure is observed to have very little effect on earnings. The signs of the industrial structure variables are consistent between the total sample and the managerial subsample, but the effects are greatly reduced. For manual workers, however, not only are the industrial structure variables significant (with the exception of foreign involvement), but their coefficients are four to eight times larger than they are for the managerial occupations. In particular, manual workers receive especially large earnings benefits from organizational size and from capital intensity. Concerning the effects of foreign involvement, manual workers actually lose earnings whereas managers, professionals, and white collar workers all benefit.[6]

Turning to the company-level economic structure model evaluated on the Wisconsin data (see Table 8.5), we have more difficulty finding interpretable patterns. Few of the company-level measures besides plant size are significant within class subsamples, and no significant variation exists in the magnitude of these effects across classes. Supervisors and autonomous workers appear to receive greater returns to the various components of corporate economic structure than do either workers or managers, but these differences are neither statistically significant nor in the direction of the stated expectation of greater effects for working class positions.

In this section we have analyzed the effects of economic structure on employee

TABLE 8.4

Regression of Industrial Structure Log Earnings Model across Occupational Positions[a]

Variable	Occupation					Manager–manual contrast
	Total[b]	Manager	Professional	White-collar	Manual	
Female	-.4627	-.6249	-.3073	-.3486	-.5106	2.22c
Black	-.1049	[-.2453]	[-.1186]	[.0751]	-.1271	0.83
Education	.0536	.0541	.0687	.0672	.0479	0.77
Experience	.0471	.0380	.0468	.0404	.0514	2.92c
(Experience)^2	-.0077	-.0066	-.0083	-.0068	-.0082	1.87
Size	.1082	[.0192]	[.0435]	.0915	.1606	3.10c
Concentration	-.1103	[-.0144]	-.1567	-.1405	-.0769	1.67
Foreign involvement	.0864	[.0740]	.1345	.1425	[-.0120]	1.91
Autonomy	.0025	[.0004]	[.0015]	[.0018]	.0020	0.73
Capital intensity	.0520	[.0232]	.0748	.0233	.0859	3.24c
Union	.2957	[.0000]	.2178	.1641	.3386	4.90c
Union power	.0034	.0028	.0036	.0020	.0025	0.28
Weeks	.0365	.0387	.0402	.0369	.0352	1.41
Hours	.0094	[.0017]	.0071	.0131	.0092	6.71c
Intercept	0.58	1.62	0.82	0.50	0.80	
R^2 (×100)	71.09	48.82	62.93	67.06	72.00	
Standard deviation	0.66	0.60	0.67	0.66	0.66	
N	20,007	1691	1765	4945	11,606	

[a] Data taken from March–May match 1973 CPS. Sample is private employees with annual earnings of at least $100. Except where enclosed in square brackets, coefficients are significant at the .05 level.

[b] Model includes unreported occupation dummy variables (see Model 6 of Table 7.1).

[c] Significant at the .05 level.

TABLE 8.5

Regression of Corporate Structure Log Earnings Model across Class
Positions[a]

			Class			
Variable	Total[b]	Manager	Supervisor	Autonomous	Worker	Manager–worker contrast t
Female	.6397	−.5170	−.6283	−.7125	−.6505	2.16[c]
Education	.0656	.0562	.0662	.0840	.0620	0.44
Company size	[.0036]	[−.0036]	[.0051]	[.0490]	[−.0050]	0.05
Size dummy	.0666	[.0023]	.1000	[.0623]	[.0726]	1.18
Plant size	.0378	.0295	.0275	.0421	.0324	0.24
Capital intensity	.0254	[.0269]	[.0343]	[.0306]	[.0110]	0.62
Union	.1658	[.0566]	.1098	[.0397]	.1689	1.19
Union power	.0011	[.0004]	[.0011]	[.0016]	.0015	1.03
Tenure	.0008	[−.0003]	.0009	.0017	.0011	3.30[c]
Weeks	.0463	.0505	.0458	.0458	.0452	1.55
Hours	.0173	.0070	.0132	.0244	.0179	5.91[c]
Intercept	0.41	1.32	0.77	−0.02	0.47	
R^2 (×100)	78.27	53.72	70.81	78.42	80.23	
Standard deviation	0.50	0.41	0.49	0.60	0.50	
N	4493	736	1442	548	1764	

[a] Data taken from 1975 Wisconsin survey. Sample is private employees with annual earnings of at least $100. Except where enclosed in square brackets, coefficients are significant at the .05 level.
[b] Model includes unreported class dummy variables (see Model 4 of Table 7.4).
[c] Significant at the .05 level.

earnings within occupational and class positions. Surveying the industry-level model, manual workers appear to receive much higher returns to the various components of industrial structure, especially to size and capital intensity, than do managerial employees. These findings partially replicate those of Rees and Shultz (1970), who found in a case study of an urban labor market that the earnings of manual workers were much more strongly influenced by industrial characteristics than were those of white-collar workers, whereas the earnings of white-collar workers were more strongly influenced by individual characteristics. These findings also support our resource interpretation of economic structure, which operates on the premise that managers and employees are engaged in a struggle over wages in which industrial characteristics may provide important structural resources for employees. The finding of a negative impact of foreign involvement for manual workers and a positive impact for managerial workers also suggests that, to understand the role of economic structure in determining labor force outcomes, we must analyze the potentially variable manner in which it acts as a resource for different actors at the workplace. However, the finding that economic structure measured at the company level does not appear to operate differently across classes indicates that we must remain reserved in our conclusions on this matter and invites further research and theoretical development.

Men and Women, Blacks and Whites

By analyzing the economic structure model of earnings determination across gender and race groups, we can evaluate the hypothesis that the earnings of minority-group members are influenced to a greater extent by the structural resources provided by corporate organization than are the earnings of majority-group members. Table 8.6 presents the industry-level earnings model with controls for individual characteristics, evaluated across gender and race groups. In this comparison, blacks appear to benefit more than whites do from organizational size. In addition, blacks are observed to lose significantly less earnings as a result of being employed in concentrated industries than do whites. This finding contrasts sharply with the dual economy hypothesis that monopoly profits allow prejudiced employers to discriminate against blacks and other minorities (Shepherd, 1970).[7] Finally, blacks are observed to lose earnings, rather than gain as whites do, from foreign involvement by their industry of employment, a finding that parallels the contrast between manual and managerial workers.

Comparing across gender groups we observe that women receive greater returns to size and corporate autonomy than do men but that men benefit more than women do from capital-intensive production. The finding of a greater impact of size for women reinforces our earlier interpretation of size as partially operating through the imposition of bureaucratic procedures, standards whose uniformity may lead to a lessening of implicit wage discrimination against women. Men, however, appear able to secure greater relative advantage from capital-intensive modes of production. Following Bridges's (1980) argument that women are employed primarily in labor-intensive industries, this finding suggests that decisions to replace labor with machinery have been implemented primarily in industries and occupations with heavily male labor forces and that the resulting wage gains have been largely bottled up in these jobs by their male incumbents. For the company-level model, the only significant comparison observed between men and women is that women benefit more from plant size than do men (see Table 8.7). This finding reinforces the relationship between women's earnings and organizational size observed in the industry-level analysis.[8]

The most consistent and significant difference we observe in the analysis of the role of economic structure across race and gender groups is the greater impact of size on the earnings of women than on the earnings of men. This replicates a similar finding by Bibb and Form (1977). Size is also observed to have a greater

TABLE 8.6

Regression of Industrial Structure Log Earnings Model across Race and Gender Groups[a]

Variable	Gender			Race		
	Men	Women	Contrast t	White	Black	Contrast t
Female	—	—	—	−.4703	−.3760	1.93
Black	−.1655	[−.0071]	3.55[b]	—	—	—
Education	.0594	.0448	2.55	.0542	.0342	2.38
Experience	.0595	.0342	9.21[b]	.0483	.0348	3.12[b]
(Experience)^2	−.0095	−.0058	6.35[b]	−.0078	−.0062	2.10
Size	[−.0293]	.2701	10.03[b]	.1021	.1700	1.34
Concentration	−.0833	−.1103	1.02	−.1217	[.0354]	3.50[b]
Foreign involvement	.0988	[.0746]	0.70	.0962	[−.0203]	1.99
Autonomy	[−.0008]	.0043	3.45[b]	.0025	[.0037]	0.52
Capital intensity	.0799	[.0064]	5.54[b]	.0538	[.0369]	0.73
Manager	.3935	.5208	1.94	.4467	[.3892]	0.33
Professional	.3327	.4956	3.00[b]	.4260	.3890	0.34
White collar	[.0504]	.2173	4.55[b]	.1400	[.1686]	0.40
Union	.2333	.3332	2.55	.2923	.3346	0.81
Union power	.0045	[.0011]	4.22[b]	.0035	[.0003]	2.53
Weeks	.0357	.0369	1.20	.0366	.0374	0.51
Hours	.0078	.0110	3.97[b]	.0094	.0085	0.66
Intercept	0.83	0.08		0.57	0.75	
R^2 (×100)	68.38	64.82		71.20	69.20	
Standard deviation	0.63	0.69		0.66	0.64	
N	11,970	8037		18,181	1826	

[a] Data taken from March–May match 1973 CPS. Sample is private employees with annual earnings of at least $100; $N = 20,007$. Except where enclosed in square brackets, coefficients are significant at the .01 level.

[b] Significant at the .01 level.

impact on the earnings of blacks and manual workers than on the respective earnings of whites and managerial workers. These findings on the importance of the key organizational dimension of size for the earnings of minority-group workers and subordinate positions at the workplace strongly support our interpretation of size as providing structural resources that can be utilized by actors at the workplace, particularly by those actors who have limited access to possession and utilization of the type of individual characteristics relied upon by dominant groups (e.g., education).

Foreign involvement also shows a consistent pattern across race, gender, and occupation, although the contrasts are not statistically significant. Minority-group workers and subordinate manual workers appear to benefit less from

TABLE 8.7

Regression of Corporate Structure Log Earnings Model on Male and Female Subsamples[a]

Variable	Men	Women	Contrast t
Education	.0538	.0804	2.18[b]
Company size	.0202	[.0176]	0.11
Size dummy	.0603	[.0560]	0.09
Plant size	.0135	.0578	4.26[b]
Capital intensity	[.0067]	[.0200]	0.60
Manager	.2934	.2585	1.07
Supervisor	.1049	.1645	1.39
Autonomous	.1191	[.0153]	1.91
Union	.0981	.1892	1.51
Union power	[.0005]	[.0012]	0.78
Tenure	[−.0001]	.0021	6.96[b]
Weeks	.0344	.0440	4.80[b]
Hours	.0019	.0297	18.83[b]
Intercept	2.14	−0.84	
R^2 ($\times 100$)	32.42	72.53	
Standard deviation	0.36	0.58	
N	2690	1803	

[a] Data taken from 1975 Wisconsin survey. Sample is private employees with annual earnings of at least $100; $N = 4493$. Except where enclosed in square brackets, coefficients are significant at the .05 level.

[b] Significant at the .05 level.

foreign involvement than do dominant groups, and in the cases of blacks and of manual workers, earnings are actually negatively impacted by foreign involvement. This finding sheds light on earlier ambiguity concerning the pattern of effects for this variable and strongly indicates that the various dimensions of industrial structure may indeed have different effects for different groups at the workplace. Dominant groups appear to benefit from foreign involvement by their employing industry, whereas subordinate groups in these industries are negatively impacted. This alters our earlier intepretation of the role of foreign involvement, which argued that higher earnings are provided for the employees of industries with high levels of foreign involvement to gain their support for imperialist economic and military policies. Instead, as suggested by the divergent theoretical expectations concerning the role of this variable, foreign involvement benefits only dominant actors at the workplace, while lowering the earnings of subordinate groups, presumably through the impact of runaway shops, multiple sourcing, and other tactics utilized to undermine wage structures.

CONCLUSIONS

The expectation of higher earnings returns to education for core sector workers and especially for managerial workers in the core sectors is largely unsupported by the analysis in this chapter. The analysis utilizing the industry-level sectors produces results that are in a pattern opposite to that expected. Utilizing company-level economic sectors, the lowest educational returns are observed in the local sector, but the contrast between these returns and those in the monopoly sector is not statistically significant. Further, sector earnings returns to education are highest in the multiplant sector rather than in the monopoly sector. When earnings returns to education are analyzed within classes, the highest returns are observed for autonomous workers in the local sector rather than for managers in the monopoly sector. Overall, these divergent patterns provide little support for the hypothesis of greater earnings returns to education in core sectors.

The analysis of earnings inequality between classes within economic sectors also produces only insignificant or negative findings. Greater inequality is not observed in the core and large-firm sectors. Indeed, the findings indicate that inequality between the managerial and working classes may be greatest in the local sector. However, the greatest inequality between manual workers and lower white-collar workers is observed in the core sectors. These patterns suggest that our theoretical understanding of the relationship between sectors and classes is seriously underdeveloped if not misspecified. The development of this theoretical understanding may have been seriously retarded by overreliance on the precepts of the dual economy approach, which canonize a parallelism between job segments and industrial sectors.

More interesting results are produced when we examine the different degrees of impact of economic structure across class, race, and gender groups. Manual occupations are influenced to a greater extent by economic structure than are other occupational groups. Also, the key organizational dimension of size has its greatest impact on the earnings of manual workers, women, and blacks. Although the earnings of minority-group workers are more strongly influenced by size than are the earnings of majority-group workers, capital-intensive systems of production appear to have less of an impact on the earnings of minority-group workers. It appears that members of subordinate groups are able to benefit from the large impersonal structures of giant corporations but are still prevented from receiving the full benefit of working with capital-intensive modes of production. An additional finding of perhaps even greater interest is the small but consistent pattern of effects that suggests that subordinate social groups and classes receive an adverse impact from high levels of foreign involvement in their employing industry, whereas dominant groups receive an earnings bonus from such involvement.

The findings relating to differences in the process of income determination across economic sectors were almost uniformly disappointing, even those pertaining to patterns of earnings returns to education. This suggests that our expectations about these patterns were derived from an inadequate theoretical understanding of the role of economic structure in influencing labor force outcomes. Our tentative conclusion from these findings is that, when economic sectors are operationalized on the basis of industrial characteristics rather than on the basis of an implicit good-versus-bad job dimension, consistent patterns of differences in returns to education do not exist (cf. Osterman, 1975; Tolbert *et al.*, 1980). Or, at least our theory of industrial structure, as distinct from our knowledge about the attributes of good and bad jobs, is not sufficiently well developed to guide us in the discovery of these patterns. However, when corporate-level economic sectors tapping mainly a size dimension are utilized, somewhat more interpretable findings emerge (cf. Stolzenberg, 1978). But, even these findings do not form a totally consistent pattern, and again, our theory is insufficiently developed to account for the anomalies.

In sum, the development of expectations concerning earnings determination across sectors may have relied too heavily on prior theoretical developments, which treated economic sectors as if they were job sectors and assumed that similar processes occurred in the good job (core) sector and in the bad job (periphery) sector. The findings in this chapter indicate that our theories of economic segmentation must be liberated from the theoretical constraints of these early approaches.

In attempting to understand these results we offer the following reflections. We believe that the attention given to educational returns in the literature on economic segmentation may be a mistaken focus. Although differential returns to education may be important for understanding inequality across various social groups and categories of jobs, we have much less reason for believing that it is a key dynamic in understanding inequality as it arises from corporate and industrial economic structure. Theoretical reasons for expecting hypothesized patterns of returns across economic sectors are poorly conceived and often contradictory. If jobs in the core sector place more emphasis on credentials than jobs in the periphery sector do, then we should expect greater educational returns in this sector. However, the competitive organization of the periphery sector should lead us to expect a greater association of education and skills with earnings in this sector than in the monopoly sector, which is shielded from competitive processes.

Because both theory and empirical investigations produce only poor results on the issue of earnings returns to education across economic sectors, we suggest that the focus of attention in segmentation studies should be redirected. A concern for educational returns is better addressed utilizing categories of persons (e.g., race or gender) or by a focus on groups of jobs (e.g., occupations or classes). Conversely, the analysis of economic structure can most fruitfully interact with studies of unionization, the generation of inequality, the emergence of "women's jobs," unemployment, underemployment, and so on. It seems that we have too willingly concocted problematics for this field by seizing upon whatever issue is currently popular in the broader areas of labor economics or social stratification rather than by focusing on the difficult work of autonomous theoretical understanding may have been seriously retarded by overreliance on the precepts of the dual economy approach, which canonize a parallelism between job segments and industrial sectors.

The analysis of corporate structure as a differential resource across groups produced results that are more in accord with prior expectations and are very suggestive for future research. The gist of these findings is that corporate sectors should be thought of less as determining different patterns of individual-level processes than as providing resources that can be utilized in their own right by different groups of actors at the workplace. In subsequent theory and research on economic structure we must be careful to specify the occupations, classes, or social groups to which we expect given dynamics to apply. For example, women appear to be affected in a much different way by economic structure than are men. The rapidly growing literature focusing on "women's jobs" might gain important insights from an in-depth study of the economic structure in which these jobs are located. The value of models of economic structure for the study of social stratification will ultimately be realized in studies of attainment processes within groups of persons or groups of jobs, in the analysis of outcomes such as historic or regional differences in earnings inequality or unionization, in studies of the creation of job structures or the rise of job dissatisfaction, or in other such areas.

NOTES TO CHAPTER 8

1. In calcualting tests of significance for the contrasts presented in Chapter 8 we used the following formula for the variance of any contrast: $V(b_1 - b_2) = V(b_1) + V(b_2) - 2 \, \text{Cov} \, (b_1, b_2)$. Because Cov (b_1, b_2) is not readily available from our analysis, we make the simplifying assumption that this covariance term equals zero. The resulting contrast variance is, then, the sum of the variances of the two regression coefficients. This assumption produces a conservative test of statistical significance if the covariance of the regression coefficients is positive. Note that this variance estimate is identical to that for the difference of means in two independent samples, assuming different sample variances (see Blalock, 1972).

2. Also presented in Table 8.1 are the regression coefficients for education, operationalized as a spline function. This transformation allows the estimation of separate effects for graded schooling and for college education. It is possible that differences in returns to graded and advanced education along with different mean levels of education within economic sectors might alter sectoral patterns of earnings returns observed on the basis of a linear education function. However, in the present analysis, the findings using this spline transformation generally reproduce the findings using the linear measure of education (cf. Featherman and Hauser, 1978, Chapter 5).

3. When a variable tapping the interaction of gender and education is added to the earnings equation evaluated within company-level sectors, the contrast across sectors of educational returns

for men increases slightly and becomes statistically significant. However, the contrast of earnings returns to education between the monopoly and local sectors for women is in the opposite direction. Thus, men receive higher educational returns in the monopoly sector and women receive higher educational returns in the local sector. We have no particular interpretation to offer for this anomalous finding. The interactions of education with the company-level continuous-variable measures were also evaluated both for the total sample and for male and female subsamples. Again, these results produced few significant or interpretable findings. (These interactions are reported by Hodson, 1980.)

4. We hinted at the lack of integration of this research issue with the study of economic sectors in Chapter 3, when we discussed alternative theoretical expectations about earnings returns to education across sectors that might be derived from the existing literature. At that point we noted that, although workers supposedly get higher returns in the core sector because of the large firm size in this sector and the use of earnings as a form of social control in these large firms, the periphery sector is where free competition reigns and where the human-capital model of earnings attainment should work best.

5. This interpretation is also supported by the earlier finding that the core sector employs a disproportionate percentage of professional workers (see Chapter 5).

6. The finding that foreign involvement has opposite signs for different occupational subsamples may help explain some of the anomalous patterns observed earlier for the curvilinear specification of foreign involvement, in which its effects approximated a bowl shape. These patterns may have been a result of opposite effects for different classes being forcibly summed together. When the curvilinear specification of the industrial structure model is estimated across occupational categories, the effects parallel those previously reported for the linear specification, with managers having positive returns to foreign involvement and manual workers having negative returns.

7. The finding of a lower rate of earnings loss to concentration for blacks is supported by the earlier observation that blacks are disproportionately represented in the core sectors (see Chapter 5). This earnings pattern may result from core sector employers' historic hiring of blacks to undermine the earnings of whites. Under this argument, a greater negative effect of concentration would be expected for whites than for blacks (see Bonacich, 1976).

8. The across-group analysis for both the industry-level and the company-level measures was repeated without controls for individual-level characteristics, and the results obtained largely replicate those reported in Tables 8.6 and 8.7. The industry-level analysis was also repeated for the model with curvature terms for size, capital intensity, and foreign involvement. These results, too, follow the pattern of those presented in Table 8.6, thus reinforcing the earlier findings.

9

Conclusions

Corporate- and industrial-level economic structure has been shown to be an important determinant of employees' earnings. Organizational, technical, and market factors all contribute to this role. We have interpreted the role of economic structure in terms of the resources it provides to employees for the attainment of improved working conditions, and this approach has produced many new insights into the relationship between economic structure and working conditions.

In this concluding chapter we shall review and highlight the central findings reported in previous chapters. We shall also develop some implications of these findings for theories of economic segmentation and social stratification and for future research in this area. Finally, we shall comment on possible practical implications of these findings and arguments.

SUMMARY OF FINDINGS

Based on a review of the existing literature on economic segmentation, especially as that literature is organized in the dual economy approach, we argued that prior theoretical understandings of the role of economic structure at the workplace provide an inadequate basis for the study of employee earnings and economic structure. In particular, we argued that the concept of a dual economy is primarily descriptive in nature, with few theoretical underpinnings. Further, we argued that this conception is based on the assumptions that the various dimensions of industrial structure are highly correlated and have similar relationships to labor market characteristics and labor force outcomes and that these assumptions are untenable. Finally, we argued that the conspiratorial nature of this approach, which posits labor force outcomes as the result of conscious manipulative acts on the part of the capitalist class, is inadequate for comprehending the actual process of struggle that occurs over these outcomes.

A review of the history of industrial organization demonstrated that various corporate structures have emerged as strategic solutions to the many problems faced by management—problems of labor control, problems of competition with other capitalists, and problems of government support and regulation. These structural solutions represent alternative strategies used to confront historically specific problems. Thus, modern industrial organization is typified by a great diversity of structural forms that cannot be reduced to a dichotomous conception of monopoly and competitive sectors. A review of trade union history also suggested that working class organizations have a great deal of autonomy from the organizational history of capital. Labor history cannot be reduced to a reflection of the growth of specific corporate organizational forms or to concessions granted by the monopoly sector in an effort to stabilize their labor force. Instead, trade union history is a history of working class organizations, which sometimes gain advantage from the organizational structure of capital and sometimes are stymied by that structure.

We suggested that economic structure could usefully be thought of as comprising three sets of factors: organizational, technical, and market factors. Each of these factors defines structural situations faced by labor at the workplace that result in either increased vulnerability or increased opportunity for labor to improve working conditions. Based on this interpretation, we argued that, whereas the type of market factors stressed by previous interpretations may be crucial for the survival and growth of the company, internal organizational factors and technical factors are more imporant for defining resources and vulnerabilities for workers and therefore are more important than market factors are in influencing labor force outcomes.

In Chapter 4, we developed an industry-level sectoral model based on the similarities of pairs of industries across a set of 40 variables measuring the key conceptual dimensions of industrial structure. This sectoral model proved highly interpretable in terms of the major dimensions of industrial structure. In that chapter we also developed a company-level sectoral model based on the local versus regional and national organization of firms, the ownership of subsidiary firms, and appearance on *Fortune* magazine's lists of the largest United States corporations. This scheme is interpretable as delineating qualitatively distinct sectors along the primary corporate dimension of size.

In Chapter 5, we saw that the likelihoods of poverty-level earnings and unionization are sharply differentiated across sectors of the economy, though, of course, in roughly inverse patterns. Similarly, the gender composition of the labor force is strongly patterned across sectors. Women are selected into the peripheral sectors of the economy, and within sectors, women are selected into the bottom rungs of the skill and authority hierarchies. However, we do not find significant racial selection out of core economic sectors. Within economic sectors, blacks are strongly selected into the bottom rungs of the skill and authority hierarchies, but blacks are not selected out of the core economy. We also noted that the core industrial sectors are typified by a divergent class structure containing large numbers of manual and working class positions as well as many professional positions. The peripheral sectors contain the various class and occupational positions in more even proportions, though managers and supervisors are slightly overrepresented. This finding contrasts with the expectation that the core sectors should be typified by a large contingent of managers and supervisors working in the overstaffed supervisory hierarchies thought to be typical of these sectors.

In Chapter 6 we evaluated the industry- and company-level sectoral models developed in Chapter 4 against employee earnings as our primary dependent variable. The results were in the expected pattern, with the employees of the core and monopoly sectors receiving substantially higher average earnings than the employees of the periphery and local sectors.

In Chapter 6 we also selected continuous-variable models of economic structure. The final industry-level model that we selected contains five variables: size, capital intensity, foreign involvement, corporate autonomy, and market concentration. The roles of size and capital intensity in the model indicate that employees receive an earnings benefit from working in industries typified by large firms and capital-intensive systems of production. The positive effect of foreign involvement indicates that at least some employees receive an earnings benefit from the link between U.S. firms and the international market. The positve effect of corporate autonomy indicates that employees in satellite sectors share part of the burden of exploitation of these sectors by core industries. One of the most noteworthy features of the model is that concentration, in contrast to the other major dimensions of industrial structure, has a negative net effect, indicating that the employees of monopoly firms receive lower wages than the employees of other firms that are comparable on the dimensions of size, capital intensity, corporate autonomy, and foreign involvement.

The company-level model that we selected contains a measure of capital intensity and three measures of organizational size. The selection of this model replicates the finding that employees receive an earnings benefit from working in large firms with capital-intensive systems of production. At both the company and industry levels, profits and productivity, the key intervening variables in most economic models of the impact of economic structure on workers' earnings, are not significant and were eliminated from the model.

The important roles of size and capital intensity in the final models suggest that internal organizational and technological factors that are more proximate to the workplace are important determinants of labor force outcomes. This does not indicate that market structure is irrelevant to employees' earnings; indeed, one of the largest effects in the industry-level model is that for foreign involvement. However, we have shown that organizational and technological variables are also important components of economic structure. More importantly, we have shown that certain key variables in the economic interpretation of the role of industrial structure (e.g., profit and productivity) have only a spurious relationship with employee earnings. These findings indicate that there is a considerable gap between what is good for the company and what is good for the worker. The primary factors accounting for workers' earnings concern the internal organization of the workplace and the technology utilized, whereas the viability of the company is largely a market phenomenon and is of less consequence for employee earnings.

The negative effect of concentration and the insignificance of profit in these models seriously undermines the "control" interpretation of the positive earnings effects of size and capital intensity. This interpretation suggests that, under the conditions of large firm size or capital-intensive production, both of which require stable planning horizons, capitalists use their organizational resources to increase wages to create a compliant and reliable work force. Under the control interpretation, size and capital intensity would result in high wages only to the extent that these factors are mediated by the role of high profits or monopoly position, which by implication results in excess profits. But these factors are shown to have insignificant or negative net effects on employee earnings. The finding that plant size has a much larger effect than company size in the company-level model also strongly supports the interpretation that the influence of size on employee earnings is primarily operational through the provision of organizational resources to the labor force.

In Chapter 7, we evaluated more fully specified earnings models containing individual as well as structural characteristics. We found that both the continuous and sectoral models of economic structure have consistent but somewhat reduced effects when evaluated under controls for demographic, training, class, unionization, and labor demand factors. The direct effects range from 43% of the total effects for the industry-level continuous-variable model to 14% of the total effects for the company-level sectoral model. This finding of significant net effects indicates that economic structure impacts employee earnings in an important way that cannot be explained by reference to other labor market or labor force characteristics.

The remaining portion of the total effect of economic structure on employee earnings is realized through the association of economic structure with other variables in the earnings model. Part of the indirect effect of economic structure is realized through the specification of a given volume of labor demand, operationalized in the present study as weeks and hours worked. Class and unionization variables and economic structure are analyzed as jointly determining employee earnings. Because of the shared history of development of these factors, the causal effects involved in their joint relationship with employee earnings cannot be unraveled by cross-sectional analysis. The final component of the total earnings effect of economic structure is realized through the sorting of groups with different labor force characteristics into economic positions with different levels of pay. Thus, part of the effects attributed to these characteristics in earnings models that do not include economic structure are spurious in nature and can be explained by the earnings determination role of economic structure.

The apparent earnings effects of the labor force characteristics of race, gender, and education are reduced by anywhere from 1 to 22% by the inclusion of models of economic structure in earnings equations. Studies that attempt to investigate the effects of these variables on earnings while ignoring the role of economic structure run the risk of being seriously misspecified. However, the reductions in the effects of these variables are not uniformly large, and gender, race, and education retain significant direct effects on earnings. Thus, we see that, although economic structure does mediate the effects of individual-level variables, it does not "explain away" the effects of these variables as the dual economy literature sometimes seems to imply (see Gordon, 1972).

In Chapter 7 we also investigated the relationship of earnings models based on economic structure and those based on social background and schooling characteristics. Rather that representing competing explanations of earnings, we found these models to be highly independent. It follows that each can be pursued and evaluated autonomously without fear of substantive misspecification.

In Chapter 8 we examined the process of earnings attainment within sectors of the economy. We found that earnings returns to education and experience do not conform to the expected pattern across economic sectors. Workers in the periphery industrial sector actually receive higher rates of return to their years of education than do workers in the core industrial sector. The pattern across corporate-level sectors is in the expected direction, but the contrast between educational returns in the local and monopoly sectors is not statistically significant. Our analysis of class by sector patterns of educational returns also produced largely disappointing results. The very highest earnings returns to education are received by autonomous workers in the local sector rather than by monopoly sector managers. Finally, the pattern of class inequality within sectors is also contrary to expectations, with the greatest earnings differentials between workers and managers being observed in the local sector rather than in the monopoly sector.

By also examining in Chapter 8 the effects of economic structure across different classes and social groups, we were able to investigate the manner in which economic structure operates in divergent ways for the various actors at the workplace. Workers in minority groups and subordinate class positions appear to be much more strongly affected by economic structure than are those in dominant groups and class positions, who can rely on individual characteristics legitimated by society for the attainment of higher earnings. Manual workers' earnings are influenced much more strongly by economic structure than are managers' earnings. Workers receive especially large earnings returns from size and capital intensity but lose earnings from foreign involvement. Managers are less affected overall by economic structure but receive an earnings increase from high levels of foreign involvement. Similarly, the earnings of women are more strongly influenced by economic structure than are the earnings of men, and women receive an especially large bonus from organizational size. These findings reinforce earlier research by Bibb and Form (1977) and Rees and Shultz (1970), which indicated that industrial structure has greater effects for women and manual workers than for men and white-collar workers, respectively.

What then is the role of economic structure in relation to other earnings determinants? Considering education, economic structure has a relatively minor role in modifying the effects of this variable (see also Zucker and Rosenstein, 1981). Economic structure is an important factor in models of individual earnings, but it is of most consequence as a direct effect, rather than as a dimension that alters the effects of individual-level variables. That is, to some extent, the market acts in a universalistic, or homogeneous, fashion to reward education. To an important extent the American definition of equality rests on equal rewards given to educational attainment (as well as on equal access to education), and this finding supports the universalistic working of this aspect of equality across sectors of the economy. In the study of such processes as earnings returns to an individual's education and experience, models of economic structure do not appear to be of central importance.

However, equal returns to education across sectors do not indicate that the industrial workplace is homogeneous in the sense that it does not importantly influence the earnings of employees in a manner that cannot be attributed to their individual characteristics. This is aptly demonstrated by the significant direct effects of economic structure on earnings and, perhaps even more importantly, by the finding that economic structure provides differential resources and vulnerabilities across groups. In this sense, the industrial workplace is neither homogeneous in its working nor in its relation to different social groups. We might depict economic structure as being important for the creation of other macro-level structures though less important for the micro-level individual earnings attainment processes. Accordingly, economic structure deserves a central place in the study of the success of unionization drives, in the study of the creation of class structure, and in the study of the creation of economic inequality, particularly gender inequality.

It is also important to review some of the findings that have resulted from the ability of our research design to distinguish between the industry and company levels of analysis. At the company level, measures tapping dimensions that are important for relations of production, such as organizational size and capital intensity, are most central in the determination of employee earnings. At the industry level, these same dimensions plus market relations, such as foreign involvement and conglomerate domination, are important. Thus, the market variables of corporate autonomy and foreign involvement appear to influence employee earnings primarily by setting industry standards for wages and conditions. (Of course, these interpretations must be made with some circumspection because of the possibility of differential measurement error at the industry and company levels and because of the vagaries of regression selection procedures.)

Perhaps the most important benefit of our research design is the ability to substantiate the important roles of organizational size and capital intensity across measurement levels, thus adding reliability to the measurement of these effects and increasing confidence in interpretations focusing on these dimensions. In addition, we have found that plant size is substantially more important for workers' earnings than is company size and that plant and company size are more important than the average company size in the industry. This finding supports the resource interpretation of size and is important in substantiating this interpretation over the alternative control thesis, which argues that managers in large firms seek to control labor through paying above-market wage rates. Our finding that capital intensity operates primarily by setting an industry-average level of technology and capital utilization is also important for understanding the role of capital intensity at the workplace.

Similarly, the replication across company- and industry-level economic sectors of findings on the structural location of poverty and on the distribution of classes and race and gender groups reinforces these findings and adds depth to their interpretation. Company and industry level operationalizations of economic sectors are highly correlated but not ultimately reducible to one another.

A key contribution of this work rests on its attempt to deal seriously with the question of the appropriate level of measurement for economic structure. Our conclusion is that there is no one "correct" level at which economic structure should be measured. The different levels deserve serious consideration, each in its own right. Industry-level measures must be seen as more than just substitutes of questionable quality for economic structure grounded at the level of the firm. Both theoretical argument and empirical findings lead us to the conclusion that different factors are operational at the plant, company, and industrial levels of economic structure. Organizational factors are most important at the plant and company level, whereas technological and market factors appear to operate by setting industry standards for wages and working conditions.

Throughout the analysis we found that the continuous-variable models of economic structure were more interpretable than the sectoral models were, and they provided many more insights useful for the development of theoretical postulates and arguments. In addition, the continuous-variable models produced consistently higher levels of explained variance. When evaluating these competing models of economic structure simultaneously in single earnings equations, we found the industry-level continuous-variable model to have much more stable coefficients than the industry-level sectoral model did. The company-level continuous-variable and sectoral models appear to offer competing explanations for organizational size, whereas the continuous-variable model specifies the additional dimensions of plant size and capital intensity of production.

THE STUDY OF LABOR FORCE OUTCOMES AND CORPORATE STRUCTURE

Economic structure has been demonstrated to strongly influence employee earnings in a unique manner that cannot be attributed to the association of economic structure with occupational, class, human capital, or demographic characteristics of the labor force. In this sense, the industrial workplace cannot be described as a homogeneous market in which workers with given skills exchange these for uniform levels of social rewards.

The effects of corporate economic structure on employee earnings cannot, however, be understood within a dual economy framework. The patterns of association between industrial dimensions observed in our 16-sector model of economic structure are clearly not reducible to a dichotomous pattern of either consistently high or consistently low values for given industries. Similarly, the pattern of employee earnings differentials defined by this model is not reducible to a dualistic contrast of high-versus-low earners. An additional important finding in this regard is the negative net effect of concentration, which indicates that market monopoly position impedes wage increases for workers in monopolistic firms, rather than promoting them as expected. Finally, many of the expectations for labor force outcomes based on the dual economy literature are simply wrong (see also Zucker and Rosenstein, 1981; Hodson and Kaufman, 1982). The inferior jobs held by blacks relative to those held by whites are not a result of the selection of blacks into peripheral sectors of the economy; rather, blacks appear to be selected into core sectors of the economy. The argument for lower returns to education in peripheral sectors, which has received so much attention in the dual economy literature, likewise gains no support from the findings reported here. Indeed, the entire argument that core firms pay higher wages as a technique of labor control is undermined by the findings and interpretations offered here.

What factors, then, should we consider as most important for the study of corporate economic structure and working conditions? The factors specified by economic models as being key to the success of companies do not appear to be the most relevant factors determining the conditions of labor in those companies. What is needed for an understanding of working conditions is less a theory of the enterprise's commodity market structure than a theory of the organization of the productive enterprise itself. These conclusions all point to the importance of the literature of complex organizations in continuing work in this field. This approach allows explanations for labor force outcomes to be grounded in the organization of production rather than solely in market relations. In the task of developing a new theory of the role of economic structure in determining labor force outcomes, sociological and organizational analysis rather than market analysis should play the leading roles.

Employee earnings do not appear to be tied to the level of company profits, and higher wages do not appear to be a result of management strategies to create a stable and compliant labor force where this is allowed by monopoly profits. Rather, we would argue that wage increases are won by employees in certain sectors based partially on the resources provided by the organization of the workplace. Thus, of the many dimensions of economic structure we examined, plant size appears to be the single most important factor in determining higher employee wages. The two dimensions of size and capital intensity consistently demonstrated large and significant effects on earnings across measurement levels and across differing specifications of the earnings model. This finding supports the interpretation that organizational and technical factors of production are more important for wage determination than are the more distant factors of profit and loss on the commodity market for the products or services of a given firm or industry. Organizational and technical factors are crucial aspects of the industrial workplace because they constitute an important part of the resources and vulnerabilities that workers face on the job. This argument is further supported by the finding that the earnings of workers in minority groups and in manual occupations receive a greater influence from economic structure than do, respectively, the earnings of nonminority workers and workers in dominant occupational positions. Indeed, each group of actors appears to be influenced in different ways by the structural resources available at the workplace. For example, whereas minority workers benefit greatly from organizational size and manual workers lose earnings from foreign involvement, managerial employees are relatively uninfluenced by size but receive a wage bonus from foreign involvement.

The primary explanatory variable utilized in the study of social stratification has been social class or some variant of this concept. In the modern world, however, organizations in general, and economic organizations in particular, take on increasing importance. To understand social stratification in advanced society, we need to look not only at the class basis of inequality but also at the organizational structure within which that inequality originates. Thus, a fully developed modern theory of social stratification must include not only a class analysis but also a thorough analysis of the role of economic enterprises.

A theory of social stratification adequate for understanding the dynamics of modern society must focus not only on social classes but also on the economic organizations in which people earn their livelihoods. In this theory, organizational structure would be interpreted as providing resources that can potentially be used by workers to attain improved working conditions and greater social equality. The theoretical argument here is not a corollary of Bell's (1973) thesis that in postindustrial society greater education and skill requirements of production produce heightened equality and order in society. Rather, the argument is that the organizational structure of modern enterprises potentially empowers workers to seek the attainment of improved conditions.

Studies of economic segmentation have an important potential role to play in the development of stratification theory. By analyzing the workplace in terms of structural resources and vulnerabilities, such studies will be in a much better position to fulfill this potential than they have been in the past, when they relied on the dual economy interpretation, which stresses the single factor of management manipulation. The task before us is to develop this theory of economic structure. Based on the research presented here, we feel that we are now in a much better position to proceed with this theoretical task. Clearly, the organizational and technical dimensions of size and capital utilization will play crucial roles in any such theory. But consideration must also be given to such market factors as international linkages, market concentration, and corporate autonomy.

Several research areas seem particularly crucial to the development of a greater understanding of the role of organizational structure in specifying a given system of social stratification. In this book we have indicated that organizational structure potentially plays very different roles for different actors at the workplace. One important area of investigation, then, is the determination of how different groups of actors at the workplace are influenced by organizational structure. In the analysis presented in previous chapters, we suggested that workers in minority groups and subordinate positions at the workplace receive a greater influence from organizational structure than from other variables, whereas workers in dominant groups may be influenced to a greater extent by individual-level human capital characteristics. The role of industrial structure in determining working conditions for women seems particularly key in this regard. The interaction of organizational structure with union viability is a second crucial area of analysis for this field because unionization is an important mechanism in the realization of the potential effects of economic structure. Also, we need to address more systematically the relationship of organizational structure and class structure. Tentative conclusions emergent from the present research indicate that the monopoly sector is the source of both greater divergence and greater equality in class structure. That is, this sector is typified by a very divergent distribution of positions with a great number of working class and manual positions, but this sector is also typified by a lower level of class inequality than are the competitive and small enterprise sectors. In addition, we need to investigate the impact of corporate economic structure on labor force outcomes other than earnings. If we construct our theory and calibrate our measures only in relationship to employees' earnings, we shall develop a very narrow and one-sided specification of the role of economic structure at the workplace, a specification that may not be relevant for broader issues of obvious current importance, such as unemployment, underemployment, and job satisfaction.

Trends in the direction of development of industrial structure and its impact on the workplace constitute a final important area of research. Although industrial structure is a relatively stable feature of the workplace, certain trends do exist. In the post-World War II period these have been primarily secular increases in average firm size and in concentration at the national level. However, new developments have occurred as well. Primary among these are the growth of conglomerates and the rise of the multinational corporation. We have noted that the growth of conglomerates has not made the industry unit of analysis obsolete in the study of economic structure. However, these new forms of workplace organization do represent significant changes, which have broad implications for social stratification at many levels. Future research in the area of economic segmentation must include these new organizational forms as a central focus.

POLICY CONSIDERATIONS

The analysis of the role of organizational structure in social stratification has implications far beyond the halls of academia. This book has been primarily analytic in focus, so these issues remain largely beyond our scope. Potential policy implications arising from this research are also circumscribed by the fact that decisions to alter industrial organization and structure are contingent on forces, politics, and interests far beyond the purview of the present study. Policies directed at labor force outcomes are not independent of broader economic policies. However, this research should heighten our awareness that the creation of social equality depends not only on the manipulation of individual characteristics but also on the manipulation of the system of industrial production. As researchers, citizens, and policymakers concerned with labor issues, we must not confine our attention to individual-level attributes but must continue to struggle with questions arising from the broader interface between the work experience and its industrial setting.

Despite these reservations, let us consider for a moment the possible implications of some of our findings. The erosion of workers' earnings by high levels of market concentration provides another item on the long list of reasons why corporate monopolies should be eliminated or strongly controlled. The positive effects of capital-intensive modes of production speak well of job possibilities in the new and emerging high-technology fields. Jobs in these areas appear to provide at least the potential for highly rewarding and satisfying employment. However, the assumption that high profits lead to high wages, even as this has been incorporated in the radical dual economy perspective, amounts to little more than the argument that what is good for the company is what is good for the worker. Such an analysis accords well with supply-side economic policies, which suggest that the way to improve wages is to minister to the profits of corporations. Our own interpretation leads to radically different policy implications. The way to improve employees' earnings and conditions of employment would be to implement a sectoral policy with different goals for different parts of the economy. Instead of raising the general rate of profit, this policy would focus on aiding employees in specific sectors to improve their situation. Thus, policies that promote greater capitalization of labor-intensive industries and provide greater support for employee benefits in small businesses might be implemented.

Appendix **A**

Industry Variables

The industry-level measures utilized in this study are described in this appendix. The ordering of these measures parallels Table 4.1. Many of these variables were transformed by the natural logarithm function. In some cases a small constant was added or subtracted to the variable before the transformation was made, either to avoid taking the log of zero or to increase the efficacy of the log transformation. Our goal in these transformations was to stretch out parts of the distribution of a variable where observations were grouped and to pull in parts of the distribution where observations were outlying. If the variables were left in their raw form, large numeric differences between average scores and extremely large scores would overshadow smaller but substantively important differences among more average scores. Our consistent motivation in implementing these transformations was a concern for the extent to which the magnitude of numeric relationships between data points mirrors the magnitude of economic relationships between industries. We do not believe either that the dollar metric has greater inherent merit in describing these relationships than the log dollar metric, or vice versa. This implies that we have faith only in the ordinal relationships that the measures represent and not in any particular interval metric. Some evidence of the basic soundness of this procedure is offered by the fact that zero-order correlations between these variables and individual earnings increase when the variables are transformed.

EMPLOYMENT PER COMPANY ("ENTERPRISE STATISTICS," 1977)   The average employment per company is a key measure of the size of companies in an industry. It measures size in terms of the size of the labor force. This variable was transformed by the natural logarithm function to reduce the impact of extremely large positive outliers.

SALES PER COMPANY ("ENTERPRISE STATISTICS," 1977)   An additional measure of corporate size is provided by sales volume. This measure taps the scale of financial activity of average firms in an industry. Sales per company was also transformed by the natural logarithm function.

ASSETS PER COMPANY (INTERNAL REVENUE SERVICE, 1977)   A similar measure of corporate size is provided by the average assets controlled by each company. Assets per company measures size in terms of control of productive resources, that is, plant and materials and financial resources. This variable was also transformed by the natural logarithm function.

NET INCOME PER COMPANY (INTERNAL REVENUE SERVICE, 1977)   The level of net income (profit) results from the volume of financial activity and from the profit rate on that activity. It measures size in terms of level of profit, which represents a pool of resources for the exercise of corporate power. A constant was added to this variable, and it was transformed by the natural logarithm function.

VALUE ADDED PER COMPANY ("INPUT/OUTPUT," 1974; "ENTERPRISE STATISTICS," 1972)   Value added measures the amount and price of activity that occurs at a given stage of production. The addition of a large amount of value (to a product) primarily indicates large corporate size. This variable was transformed by the natural logarithm function.

PERCENTAGE OF COMPANIES THAT ARE CORPORATIONS ("ENTERPRISE STATISTICS," 1977)   Percentage of companies that are corporations measures the extent to which the modal form of productive activity in an industry is the corporation versus the private business or partnership. This measure thus taps an additional dimension of corporate size and structure.

ESTABLISHMENTS PER COMPANY ("ENTERPRISE STATISTICS," 1977)   The average number of plants per company in an industry provides our final measure of corporate size. This variable taps the dimension of single-plant versus multi-plant corporate organization of an industry. A constant was subtracted from this variable, and it was transformed by the natural logarithm function.

VALUE ADDED PER EMPLOYEE ("INPUT/OUTPUT," 1974; "ENTERPRISE STA-TISTICS," 1972)   This measure taps the productivity of labor. It is measured simply as the average value added in production per employee.

VALUE ADDED AS A PERCENTAGE OF TOTAL OUTPUT ("INPUT/OUTPUT," 1974)   This measure taps the extent to which a given industry contributes a large share of the total value of a product. A high value indicates that an industry makes a key contribution to the value of some final product. Thus, key industrial sectors where large amounts of value are created can be located using this measure. The measure is calculated as value added in an industry over total sales of that industry.

NET NATIONAL PRODUCT PER EMPLOYEE ("NATIONAL INCOME AND PRODUCT ACCOUNTS," 1976)   The net national product taps the concept of productivity in a manner identical to "Value added per employee" but relies on a different estimate of the value of production. It is measured as gross national product (the total value of all final goods and services) minus the value of the physical capital consumed in production. In most cases it represents a larger figure than value added.

UNIONIZATION (FREEMAN AND MEDOFF, PERSONAL COMMUNICATION)   We chose percentage of industry employment covered by collective bargaining agreements as our best measure of the extent and power of unionization. Collective bargaining coverage may be greater than union membership because of the coverage of nonunion workers in "right-to-work" states. Alternatively, collective bargaining coverage may be smaller than union membership because of the (sometimes substantial) delay between union certification and successful settlement of a labor contract. In both instances, coverage seems to be the preferable measure of union power.

ASSETS PER EMPLOYEE (INTERNAL REVENUE SERVICE, 1977; "ENTERPRISE STATISTICS," 1977)   Assets per employee measures the average amount of capital utilized per worker in an industry. It provides our most direct measure of capital intensity. A constant was added to the variable and it was transformed by the natural logarithm function.

PAYROLL AS A PERCENTAGE OF SALES (INTERNAL REVENUE SERVICE, 1977; "ENTERPRISE STATISTICS," 1977)   Payroll as a percentage of sales measures payments to labor as a percentage of total expenses. That is, it measures the portion of total expenses (approximated by total sales) paid to labor. A high value indicates a production process that is heavily dependent on labor; a low value indicates a production process employing relatively less labor. This variable was transformed by the natural logarithm function.

CONSTANT CAPITAL AS A PERCENTAGE OF ASSETS (INTERNAL REVENUE SERVICE, 1977)   Constant capital is the cost of repair and maintenance of existing plants and machinery and the cost of replacing worn-out plants and machinery. As a percentage of total corporate assets it shows the proportion of total capital "used up" in the production process and taps an additional dimension of capital intensity.

CONSTANT CAPITAL AS A PERCENTAGE OF CONSTANT-PLUS-VARIABLE CAPITAL ("INPUT/OUTPUT," 1974; INTERNAL REVENUE SERVICE, 1977; "ENTERPRISE STATISTICS," 1977)   Constant capital (plant and machinery) and variable capital (labor) plus surplus value (net income) are the three components of value (Marx, 1887). Constant capital as a percentage of constant-plus-variable capital measures the proportion of these two factors of production that is "used up" as physical capital. Thus, it provides another measure of capital intensity, one similar to constant capital over assets but calculated over a different and more limited base. Because our direct measure of constant capital taken from the Internal Revenue Service reports was highly aggregated (64 categories), we constructed a more detailed but less direct measure of constant capital for use in calculating this measure. Constant capital was estimated by subtracting net income and payroll from value added. Constant capital plus payroll was estimated by subtracting net income from value added. The final measure was then calculated by dividing constant capital by constant capital plus payroll.

PERCENTAGE OF PART-TIME EMPLOYMENT ("NATIONAL INCOME AND PRODUCT ACCOUNTS," 1976; "ENTERPRISE STATISTICS," 1977)   The extent to which an industry employs part-time labor taps a final dimension of labor-intensive production. Industries that rely on labor-intensive production techniques utilize the largest amounts of part-time labor, both because part-time workers can be paid less than full-time workers and because of the greater flexibility in hours allowed. This measure was calculated by subtracting the number of full-time equivalent workers from the actual number of full- and part-time workers and dividing this difference by the number of full-time equivalent workers. A small constant was added to the variable, and it was transformed by the natural logarithm function.

GOVERNMENT REGULATION (SCHERER, 1970)   Formal government regulation of an industry is the major component of what economists call "government intervention in the economy." It has an important impact on such issues as corporate adherence to affirmative action hiring practices. This measure is constructed as a dummy variable that has a value of 1 if the industry is government-regulated and a value of 0 otherwise.

FEDERAL GOVERNMENT PURCHASES AS A PERCENTAGE OF TOTAL OUTPUT ("INPUT/OUTPUT," 1974)   If a large share of the output of an industry is purchased by the federal government, this implies a significant amount of indirect control through such mechanisms as contract negotiations. Our measure of this dimension of government influence is calculated as the percentage of total industry sales purchased by the federal government.

FEDERAL GOVERNMENT PURCHASES PER FIRM (INPUT/OUTPUT, 1974; "ENTERPRISE STATISTICS," 1972)   This measure taps the same concept as the one immediately preceding but it is calculated over a different base. The amount of federal purchasing per firm in an industry provides an additional measure of the degree of control the government may be able to exert on industry labor practices.

STATE AND LOCAL GOVERNMENT PURCHASES AS A PERCENTAGE OF TOTAL OUTPUT ("INPUT/OUTPUT," 1974)   This variable and the one immediately following measure the same concepts as the two preceding variables but for state and local purchases rather than for federal purchases. State and local purchasing is particularly important in construction and in the provision of utility services. It is in these sectors that it probably has the greatest impact on labor relations in the private sector.

STATE AND LOCAL GOVERNMENT PURCHASES PER FIRM ("INPUT/OUTPUT," 1974; "ENTERPRISE STATISTICS," 1972)   This variable measures the potential for state and local government influence on labor relations via government purchases from firms.

EIGHT-FIRM EMPLOYMENT CONCENTRATION ("ENTERPRISE STATISTICS," 1977)   The standard measure of monopoly concentration utilized by economists is based on the employment (or value of shipments) of the top firms in an industry as a percentage of industry total employment (or value of shipments). This measure is typically applied only to the manufacturing sector because, of the various censuses of industries, only the "Census of Manufacturing" publishes statistics directly measuring monopoly power in this way. However, a close approximation to this measure can be calculated from data on the number of companies and employment, by size categories of companies, such as are reported in the "Enterprise Statistics." One simply sums the employment in the top size categories until the employment figures for enough companies have been added (eight in the present case), interpolating within the last-added size category if necessary, and divides this employment figure by total industry employment to calculate the concentration ratio. The eight-firm level was chosen from those levels typically employed (4, 8, 20, and 50) because this is the maximum number of firms that can jointly engage in the full range of oligopolistic behavior—price fixing, restriction of technology, and so on (see Scherer, 1970). However, the 50-firm level of employment, sales, and assets concentration will also be utilized in parts of the analysis because this measure taps elements of oligopolistic behavior across a broader range of industries.

EIGHT-FIRM SALES CONCENTRATION ("ENTERPRISE STATISTICS," 1977) Sales concentration was calculated in an identical fashion to that utilized for employment concentration. Sales taps the volume of financial activity within a firm. Percentage share of sales by the top eight firms in an industry provides our most direct measure of monopoly market control.

EIGHT-FIRM ASSETS CONCENTRATION (INTERNAL REVENUE SERVICE, 1977) Assets concentration was calculated in exactly the same fashion as that utilized for employment and sales concentration, though the data are from a different source. Assets are a measure of financial resources. Monopoly control of assets implies control of technological advances, ability to set the mode for the organization of production in an industry, and so on.

PERCENTAGE OF INDUSTRY SALES BY COMPANIES WITH OVER $250 MILLION IN SALES ("ENTERPRISE STATISTICS," 1977) To provide an alternative operationalization of sales concentration, we calculated the percentage of the value of sales in an industry by firms that can be considered "corporate giants," that is, firms with over $250 million in sales. This variable measures the extent to which such firms dominate a product market. A constant was added to this variable, and it was transformed by the natural logarithm function to reduce its extreme positive skew and to pull in numeric outliers.

PERCENTAGE OF INDUSTRY ASSETS IN COMPANIES WITH OVER $250 MILLION IN ASSETS (INTERNAL REVENUE SERVICE, 1977) This variable was constructed in an identical fashion to the immediately preceding one, though the data were taken from a different source. It provides an alternative operationalization of monopoly control of productive resources. This operationalization is based on the share of the industry assets held by "corporate giants" rather than on the share of the market controlled by the largest firms in the industry.

ADVERTISING PER COMPANY (INTERNAL REVENUE SERVICE, 1977) Corporate spending on advertising has the potential to create demand for products, especially for specific brand-name products, which implies a degree of monopoly control of a market. Thus, large advertising outlays per company provide an additional measure of monopoly organization of an industry, an organization achieved through manipulation of the market rather than through direct monopoly control of production. A constant was subtracted from this variable, and it was transformed by the natural logarithm function to reduce its extreme positive skew and to pull in numeric outliers.

RATIO OF 1972 EMPLOYMENT TO 1967 EMPLOYMENT ("ENTERPRISE STATIS-TICS," 1972, 1977)   Growth in industry employment over the five-year period most recent to the date to which our data apply is a key measure of industry growth and viability. (However, employment changes may have a somewhat ambiguous interpretation as they potentially result from both changes in product demand and from changes in the technology utilized in production.)

RATIO OF 1972 SALES TO 1967 SALES ("ENTERPRISE STATISTICS," 1972, 1977)   The sales ratio measure taps industry growth in a manner similar to employment growth, but it is based on changes in sales. Measures of sales volume changes tap industry viability and market conditions in as direct a manner as possible.

RATIO OF 1970 EMPLOYMENT TO 1960 EMPLOYMENT ("CENSUS OF POPULA-TION," 1962, 1972)   Growth in industry employment from 1960 to 1970 provides an alternative measurement of changes in industry employment to that offered by changes in employment from 1967 to 1972, and it has the same interpretation.

NEW CAPITAL EXPENDITURES PER COMPANY ("ENTERPRISE STATISTICS," 1977)   The size of new capital expenditures (plant and equipment) per company is dependent on company size, but equally importantly, it results from the degree to which the industry is experiencing growth or decline. Companies in industries in decline do not typically purchase new plant and equipment, whereas companies in growth industries expand existing plant and equipment at as quick a rate as possible. A small constant was added to this variable, and it was transformed by the natural logarithm function.

RATIO OF EMPLOYMENT PER FIRM IN 1972 TO EMPLOYMENT PER FIRM IN 1967 ("ENTERPRISE STATISTICS," 1972, 1977)   This measure was calculated by dividing the average employment size of firms in an industry in 1972 by the average employment size in 1967. Change in this measure taps the employment growth of *firms* in an industry. It addresses the question: "Have firms in this industry become any larger over time?'' It indicates potential changes in the nature of the organization of production in an industry.

NET INCOME PER SALES (INTERNAL REVENUE SERVICE, 1977)   Net income per sales is a profit rate based on total revenue or sales. It is a standard, and perhaps the most frequently used, measure of profit. It shows the rate of return on the total volume of financial activity.

NET INCOME PER ASSETS (INTERNAL REVENUE SERVICE, 1977)   Our second measure of profit rate is based on returns to assets. It taps the rate of return to the total capital employed in an industry.

RATIO OF NET INCOME TO CONSTANT-PLUS-VARIABLE CAPITAL (''INPUT/OUT-PUT,'' 1974; INTERNAL REVENUE SERVICE, 1977)   This profit rate is calculated by dividing profit (net income) by the cost of capital expended directly in production. The sum of content-plus-variable capital is estimated by subtracting net income from value added. This variable measures profit rate as a return on the costs of capital and labor expended directly in production.

CORPORATE AUTONOMY (''ENTERPRISE STATISTICS,'' 1977)   We measure corporate autonomy by the degree to which workers in an industry are employed by enterprises whose parent companies' primary operations are in that same industry. This measure taps the dimension of conglomerate domination of an industry by companies based in other industries. A high value on the variable, because it indicates that most of an industry's workers are employed in plants whose parent companies are based in that same industry, shows corporate autonomy. A low value on the variable, because it indicates that many of the workers in that industry work in plants owned by companies whose primary line of production is in some other industry, shows conglomerate domination of the industry. Such an industry is in a subsidiary relationship to some other industry. This measure taps only the degree of corporate autonomy in an industry; it does not indicate whether an industry is itself the source of conglomerate domination.

FOREIGN DIVIDENDS PER COMPANY (INTERNAL REVENUE SERVICE, 1977)   Foreign dividends per company taps the extent to which earnings from foreign holdings are returned to U.S. corporations via direct dividend payments. Earnings from foreign subsidiaries or investments in foreign countries might also be returned to the United States in less direct ways, for example, by internal pricing; however, we believe foreign dividends represent one important dimension of foreign involvement by U.S. corporations. This variable was transformed by the natural logarithm function.

FOREIGN TAX CREDITS PER COMPANY (INTERNAL REVENUE SERVICE, 1977)   United States corporations may subtract from their taxable earnings credits for all taxes paid in foreign nations. The average size of these tax credits in an industry taps another dimension of the foreign involvement of U.S. corporations. A small constant was added to this variable, and it was transformed by the natural logarithm function.

EXPORTS PER COMPANY ("INPUT/OUTPUT," 1974; "ENTERPRISE STATISTICS," 1972)   Exports per company helps to locate the industrial base of the major export firms of the U.S. economy. Many of the firms in industries with high values on this variable operate extensively in foreign as well as domestic markets. A constant was added to this variable, and it was transformed by the natural logarithm function.

EXPORTS AS A PERCENTAGE OF INDUSTRY OUTPUT ("INPUT/OUTPUT," 1974)   This variable measures the same concept as exports per company, but its percentages are calculated over a different base—total industry output. It thus helps to further specify the export sector of the U.S. economy. A constant was added to this variable, and it was transformed by the natural logarithm function.

Appendix **B**

Company Variables

The company-level measures utilized in this study are described here. The ordering of these measures parallels that in Table 4.6. As in the case of the industry variables, several of these measures were transformed by the natural logarithm function to avoid statistical problems caused by large numeric outliers. All of the data except that for subsidiary status refer to the largest owning unit of a reported company.

EMPLOYMENT   The employment variable represents total employment in all the company's operations combined and is an important measure of company size. This variable had an extremely sharp positive skew and was transformed by the natural logarithm function to reduce the problem of numeric outliers.

SALES   The sales measure represents the total volume of financial activity and includes receipts for all goods delivered and for all services rendered. Sales volume is also a measure of company size. This variable was transformed by the natural logarithm function.

NET INCOME   Net income measures the volume of profit and is a measure of corporate size. This variable also serves as the numerator for profit rate (as described later). When used as a measure of size, this variable is transformed by the natural logarithm function because of its large positive skew.

ASSETS   The assets variable measures the total amount of capital that a company controls and is a measure of corporate size. It is perhaps our most direct measure of corporate financial power. Assets was transformed by the natural logarithm function.

NET WORTH   Net worth is the difference between total assets and real liabilities. In publically held corporations, net worth is also known as "stockholder's equity." This variable measures the amount of capital actually owned outright by the company; net worth was transformed by the natural logarithm function.

EXISTENCE OF PLANTS OUTSIDE THE LOCAL AREA   This measure is coded 1 if the company has plants in more than one local area and 0 otherwise. A local area is defined as a city or as a metropolitan area and its suburbs. Thus, if a bank has branch offices in several locations but only within one city, it will be coded 0 on this variable.

FORTUNE LIST   Values of this variable are based on the appearance of the largest owning unit of the company on any of *Fortune* magazine's lists of largest U.S. corporations. This variable contains values denoting appearance on the *Fortune* "500 Largest Industrial Corporations" list, appearance on the *Fortune* "Second 500 Largest Industrial Corporations" list, and appearance on any of the *Fortune* lists of "50 Largest Corporations" in utilities, life insurance, diversified financial, retailing, transportation, and commercial banking. The variable was given a value of 0 if the company appeared on none of these lists.

CAPITAL INTENSITY   Capital intensity is defined as assets per employee and is the company-level measure of capital intensity of production. This measure was transformed by the natural logarithm function.

PROFIT   Profit is defined as net income over sales and is the company-level measure of rate of profit.

SUBSIDIARY STATUS   The subsidiary status variable, coded 1 if the company is the subsidiary of some larger company and 0 otherwise, taps the concept of conglomerate domination.

DOMESTIC SUBSIDIARIES   The domestic subsidiaries measure is the number of all domestic subsidiaries held by the largest owning unit. If the reported company is a subsidiary, it is included in this total. This variable is a measure of the possible magnitude of conglomerate power. Number of domestic subsidiaries was transformed by the natural logarithm function.

TOTAL SUBSIDIARIES   Total subsidiaries is the sum of the number of domestic and foreign subsidiaries (described next); it also measures possible conglomerate power but includes foreign as well as domestic subsidiaries. This variable was transformed by the natural logarithm function.

FOREIGN SUBSIDIARIES   Foreign subsidiaries tallies all foreign subsidiaries held by the largest owning unit. It provides the key corporate level measure of foreign involvement. The number of foreign subsidiaries variable was transformed by the natural logarithm function.

Appendix C

The Operationalization of Class

The operationalization of class utilized throughout this book is based on the exercise of authority at the workplace. Responses to six "yes/no" questions were utilized in constructing the measure. These questions measure both the exercise of authority by the respondent and the authority to which he or she is subject. These six questions were:

1. "I supervise the work of others. That is, what they produce or how much." (*Supervise others*)
2. "I have the authority to hire or fire others." (*Hire/fire*)
3. "I can influence or set the rate of pay received by others." (*Set pay*)
4. "Someone else supervises my work. That is, what I produce or how much." (*Supervised by others*)
5. "Someone else decides what I do, but I decide how to do it." (*Task completion supervised*)
6. "My supervisor exercises little or no control over my work." (*Autonomy*)

The "yes/no" answers to these job descriptions were utilized to allocate respondents into class categories. The allocation procedure is diagrammed in Table C.1. Managers are defined by the ability to exercise the full range of authority over others. Supervisors also exercise authority over others but lack some component of full managerial prerogative. Autonomous workers exercise no authority over others but are themselves either not supervised by others or are only supervised to a minor degree. Workers are at the bottom of the authority ladder. They do not supervise others and are themselves supervised by someone else to more than a trivial extent.

TABLE C.1

Definition of Social Class Categories

Category	Supervise others	Hire/fire	Set pay	Supervised by others		Task completion supervised		Autonomy
Manager	Yes	Yes	Yes					
Supervisor	Yes	(No to either)						
Autonomous worker[a]	No			No	or	(No	and	Yes)
Worker	No			Yes	and not	(No	and	Yes)

[a] Teachers were considered autonomous workers regardless of their answers to any of the questions on workplace authority (see Wright, 1979).

Appendix **D**

Supplementary Tables

The supplementary tables in this appendix present information that is cited in the text but is not sufficiently central, or is too lengthy, to present there. The tables include correlation matrices for the company- and industry-level scale construction and for the company- and industry-level earnings regressions. Also included are regressions of various earnings transformations on the company- and industry-level models, some descriptive statistics used in the validation of the company size index, a cross-classification of occupation by industrial sector, regressions of the industry model with full controls on the Wisconsin and restricted CPS samples, and a regression of earnings simultaneously on the industry-level sectoral and continuous-variable models.

TABLE D.1

Distribution of Persons across Occupational Categories by Industrial Sector[a]

Industrial sector	Occupation				
	Managers	Professionals	White-collar	Manual	Total (100%)
Wisconsin survey					
Oligopoly	11.3	21.4	14.1	53.2	248
Core	11.7	17.6	21.3	49.4	1501
Periphery	14.9	12.1	35.2	37.8	1350
Core utilities	25.0	13.5	42.0	19.6	505
Periphery utilities	17.3	6.1	12.2	64.3	98
Trades	10.3	38.2	13.8	37.8	720
Total	14.0	18.8	26.1	41.1	4422[b]
CPS					
Oligopoly	8.0	25.6	14.3	52.0	130
Core	12.1	17.5	27.0	43.4	784
Periphery	15.4	11.8	30.2	42.6	838
Core utilities	17.2	10.0	48.3	24.5	342
Periphery utilities	12.5	2.3	17.4	67.8	43
Trades	9.6	31.1	13.4	45.9	453
Total	13.2	17.2	27.7	41.9	2590[c]

[a] This table compares the Wisconsin survey ($N = 4493$) with a restricted CPS sample (high school graduates in their thirties; $N = 2603$). Sample is private employees with annual earnings of at least $100.

[b] Seventy-one respondents in the Wisconsin survey have missing values on the industrial sector variable.

[c] Thirteen respondents in the restricted CPS sample have missing values on the industrial sector variable.

TABLE D.2

Intercorrelations of Industry Variables Used in Index Construction[a]

Measure	Correlations				
Size	1	2	3	4	5
1. Sales	—				
2. Assets	.84	—			
3. Value added	.68	.73	—		
4. Employment	.95	.80	.67	—	
5. Percentage corporations	.86	.74	.76	.87	—
Concentration	6	7	8	9	10
6. 50-Firm employment	—				
7. 50-Firm sales	.99	—			
8. 50-Firm assets	.85	.86	—		
9. Sales in large firms (%)	.66	.67	.50	—	
10. Assets in large firms (%)	.83	.84	.81	.46	—
Foreign involvement	11	12	13	14	
11. Foreign dividends	—				
12. Foreign tax credits	.85	—			
13. Exports	.70	.69	—		
14. Production exported (%)	.63	.52	.85	—	

[a] Data taken from March–May match 1973 CPS. Sample is private workers with annual earnings of at least $100; $N = 20,007$.

TABLE D.3

Correlation Matrix for Variables Tested in Selection of Industry Model[a]

Variable					Correlations						
	1	2	3	4	5	6	7	8	9	10	11
1. Log earnings	—										
2. Size	.29	—									
3. Concentration	.24	.82	—								
4. Foreign involvement	.32	.83	.78	—							
5. Profit	.09	.22	.20	.26	—						
6. Growth	.29	.80	.73	.85	.45	—					
7. Productivity	.10	.15	-.01	.16	.25	.33	—				
8. Labor intensity	-.22	-.80	-.72	-.67	-.26	-.66	-.26	—			
9. Capital intensity	.30	.62	.50	.58	.35	.52	.26	-.42	—		
10. Autonomy	-.19	-.58	-.55	-.69	-.35	-.67	-.13	.44	-.34	—	
11. Size scale	.32	.96	.81	.85	.27	.95	.17	-.77	.60	-.66	—

[a] Data taken from March–May match 1973 CPS. Sample is private employees with annual earnings of at least $100; $N = 20,007$.

TABLE D.4

Comparison of Three Functional Forms of Individual Earnings Regressed on Industry Model[a]

Variable	Log earnings		Earnings		Cube root earnings	
	b	beta	b	beta	b	beta
Size scale	.4677	.3683	1097	.1713	1.8972	.3097
	(.0257)		(134)		(.1240)	
Concentration	−.2349	−.1707	−1063	−.1532	−1.1637	−.1756
	(.0193)		(100)		(.0933)	
Foreign involvement	.1147	.0821	1136	.1613	.8544	.1270
	(.0268)		(139)		(.1292)	
Capital intensity	.0364	.0404	294	.0649	.2154	.0497
	(.0127)		(66)		(.0613)	
Autonomy	.0088	.0979	42	.0918	.0443	.1024
	(.0010)		(5)		(.0048)	
(Size scale)^2	−.1171	−.1050	−157	−.0278	−.3941	−.0734
	(.0116)		(60)		(.0558)	
(Foreign involvement)^2	.1210	.0809	483	.0640	.5668	.0786
	(.0152)		(79)		(.0736)	
(Capital intensity)^2	−.0040	−.1640	−159	−.1177	−.2047	−.1586
	(.0039)		(20)		(.0187)	
Intercept	3.21		4185		14.50	
R^2 (×100)	14.57		9.24		14.27	
Standard deviation	1.14		5912		5.49	
Mean of dependent variable	3.67		6670		16.97	

[a] Data taken from March–May match 1973 CPS. Sample is private employees with annual earnings of at least $100; $N = 20{,}007$. Regression coefficients, presented with their standard errors reported beneath in parentheses, are all significant at the .01 level.

TABLE D.5

Intercorrelations of Company Variables Used in Index Construction[a]

	Correlations				
Variable	1	2	3	4	5
1. Employment	—				
2. Sales	.96	—			
3. Income	.73	.75	—		
4. Assets	.88	.94	.77	—	
5. Net worth	.95	.95	.83	.95	—

[a] Data taken from 1975 Wisconsin survey. Sample is private employees with annual earnings of at least $100; $N = 4493$.

TABLE D.6

Means of Key Company Variables by Company Size Index Present or Missing[a]

	Company size index present		Company size index missing	
Variable	Mean	Standard deviation	Mean	Standard deviation
Plant size	1162	4031	109	553
Plants outside local area	0.64	0.48	0.16	0.37
Subsidiary	0.31	0.46	0.86	0.35
Domestic subsidiaries	13.12	46.78	2.33	2.31
Foreign subsidiaries	10.63	22.24	4.67	3.61
Total subsidiaries	21.62	53.03	5.83	2.56
Fortune-list[b]	0.42	0.58	0	0

[a] Data taken from 1975 Wisconsin survey. Sample is private employees with annual earnings of at least $100; $N = 4493$. Missing data not replaced by means or assumed values.

[b] This variable is coded as 1 if the company is on any Fortune list and 0 otherwise.

TABLE D.7

Correlation Matrix for Variables Tested in Selection of Company Model[a]

Variable	Correlations									
	1	2	3	4	5	6	7	8	9	10
1. Log earnings	—									
2. Company size	.19	—								
3. Size dummy	.18	.00	—							
4. Plant size	.33	.41	.38	—						
5. Profit	.06	.15	.00	.02	—					
6. Capital intensity	.06	.01	.00	-.10	.26	—				
7. Domestic subsidiaries	.18	.71	.38	.40	.05	-.05	—			
8. Foreign subsidiaries	.17	.60	.27	.39	-.03	-.13	.67	—		
9. Total subsidiaries	.20	.74	.39	.45	.03	-.08	.96	.81	—	
10. Subsidiary status	.07	.35	.20	.14	-.01	.05	.54	.21	.48	—

[a] Data taken from 1975 Wisconsin survey. Sample is private employees with annual earnings of at least $100; $N = 4493$.

TABLE D.8

Comparison of Three Functional Forms of Individual Earnings Regressed on Company Model[a]

Variable	Log earnings		Earnings[b]		Cube root earnings	
	b	beta	b	beta	b	beta
Company size	.0894	.0842	7.9307	.0826	.1318	.0881
	(.0197)		(1.5525)		(.0236)	
Size dummy	.1891	.0716	[4.0359]	.0191	.1827	.0556
	(.0427)		(3.3679)		(.0511)	
Plant size	.1345	.2806	8.2715	.2243	.1614	.2812
	(.0082)		(0.6488)		(.0098)	
Capital intensity	.1167	.0690	8.4356	.0791	.1475	.0888
	(.0197)		(1.5566)		(.0236)	
Intercept	3.71	—	81.28	—	3.78	—
R^2 (×100)	12.25	—	7.88	—	12.53	—
Standard deviation	1.01	—	79.74	—	1.21	—
Correlation of transformed $\hat{Y}$ with log earnings	.3498		.3500		.3527	
Transformation of $\hat{Y}$	$\hat{Y}$		$\log(\hat{Y})$		$3\log(\hat{Y})$	

[a] Data taken from 1975 Wisconsin survey. Sample is private employees with annual earnings of at least $100; $N = 4493$. Regression coefficients, unless enclosed in square brackets, are significant at the .05 level. Standard errors are reported in parentheses beneath each regression coefficient.

[b] Earnings are reported in hundreds of dollars.

TABLE D.9

Comparison of Industry-Level Sectoral and Continuous-Variable Regression Models of Individual Log Earnings[a]

| | Model | | |
Variable	1	2	3
Industry variable			
Size	.2540	—	.3617
Concentration	−.1773	—	−.1067
Foreign involvement	.3061	—	[.0866]
Capital intensity	.1254	—	.1700
Autonomy	.0061	—	.0105
Industry sector			
Oligopoly	—	1.1671	[−.1172]
Core	—	.8036	.2789
Periphery	—	.1090	[−.0575]
Core utilities	—	.9002	−.2876
Periphery utilities	—	.8408	[.1941]
Trades	—	—	—
Intercept	3.36	3.28	3.05
R^2 (×100)	13.27	10.14	14.22
Standard deviation	1.15	1.17	1.14

[a] Data taken from March–May match 1973 CPS. Sample is private employees with annual earnings of at least $100; $N = 20,007$. Except where enclosed in square brackets, regression coefficients are significant at the .01 level.

TABLE D.10

Comparison of Industry-Level Log Earnings Model with Full Controls on Wisconsin and Restricted CPS Samples[a]

| | Model | | | | t Tests for slope differences | |
| | Wisconsin | | Restricted CPS | | | |
Variable	1	2	3	4	1 vs. 3	2 vs. 4
Female	−.6746	−.6778	−.6276	−.6000	1.03	1.67
	(.0285)	(.0289)	(.0359)	(.0364)		
Education	.0515	.0516	.0405	.0450	1.07	0.64
	(.0062)	(.0062)	(.0082)	(.0083)		
Size	.0549	.0989	[.0285]	.1636	0.69	1.30
	(.0230)	(.0308)	(.0306)	(.0393)		
Concentration	−.1010	−.1059	−.0604	−.0909	1.15	0.41
	(.0218)	(.0230)	(.0279)	(.0286)		
Foreign involvement	.0660	[.0480]	.0800	[.0015]	0.38.	1.01
	(.0226)	(.0287)	(.0286)	(.0359)		
Autonomy	[.0006]	[.0015]	.0038	.0058	2.02[b]	2.62[b]
	(.0009)	(.0010)	(.0013)	(.0013)		
Capital intensity	[.0179]	.0333	.0516	[.0078]	2.17[b]	1.11
	(.0096)	(.0150)	(.0122)	(.0175)		
$(Size)^2$		−.0526		−.0668		0.67
		(.0129)		(.0170)		

(Foreign involvement)²	[.0171] (.0152)		[.0269] (.0195)		0.40
(Capital intensity)²	[.0055] (.0048)		−.0214 (.0058)		3.57ᵇ
Manager	.2683 (.0346)	.3660 (.0454)	.3640 (.0452)	1.71	1.64
Professional	.2576 (.0331)	.3889 (.0447)	.4047 (.0445)	2.36ᵇ	2.70ᵇ
White collar	.0857 (.0287)	.1308 (.0369)	.1210 (.0371)	0.96	0.64
Union	.2141 (.0283)	.2147 (.0360)	.2149 (.0358)	0.01	0.05
Union power	.0020 (.0006)	.0027 (.0007)	.0022 (.0008)	0.76	0.80
Weeks	.0484 (.0010)	.0443 (.0013)	[.0445] (.0012)	2.50ᵇ	2.37ᵇ
Hours	.0182 (.0008)	.0073 (.0009)	.0072 (.0009)	9.05ᵇ	9.05ᵇ
Intercept	0.66	1.05	0.89		
R² (×100)	77.56	74.12	74.57		
Standard deviation	0.51	0.53	0.52		

a Data taken from 1975 Wisconsin survey (*N* = 4493) and March–May match 1973 CPS (subsample restricted to high school graduates in their thirties; *N* = 2603). Sample is private employees with annual earnings of at least $100. Regression coefficients are presented with their standard errors reported beneath in parentheses. The category of manual workers has been left out of these earnings equations to estimate the effects of occupation. Except where enclosed in square parentheses, coefficients are significant at the .05 level.
b Significant at the .05 level.

References

Aldrich, Howard E.
   1972   Technology and organizational structure: a reexamination of the findings of the Aston group. *Administrative Science Quarterly* 17:26–43.
Althauser, Robert P., and Kalleberg, Arne L.
   1981   Firms, occupations, and the structure of labor markets. *In* "Sociological Perspectives on Labor Markets" (Ivar Berg, ed.), pp. 119–149. New York: Academic Press.
Amin, Samir
   1976   "Unequal Development" (Brian Pearce, tran.). New York: Monthly Review Press.
Averitt, Robert T.
   1968   "The Dual Economy." New York: McGraw Hill.
Azumi, Koya, and Hage, Jerald
   1972   "Organizational Systems." Lexington, Massachusetts: Heath.
Bailey, William R., and Schwenk, Albert E.
   1980   Wage rate variation by size of establishment. *Industrial Relations* 19:192–198.
Bain, J. S.
   1964   The impact of industrial organization. *American Economic Review* 54:28–54.
Baran, Paul A., and Sweezy, Paul M.
   1966   "Monopoly Capital." New York: Monthly Review Press.
Barnet, R. J., and Muller, R. E.
   1974   "Global Reach." New York: Simon and Schuster.
Baron, Harold M., and Hymer, Bennett
   1968   The Negro worker in the Chicago labor market. *In* "The Negro and the American Labor Movement" (Julius Jacobson, ed.), pp. 232–285. New York: Doubleday.

227

Baron, James, N., and Bielby, William T.
1980   Bringing the firms back in: stratification, segmentation, and the organization of work. *American Sociological Review* 45:737–765.
Beck, E. M., Horan, Patrick M., and Tolbert, Charles M., II
1978   Stratification in a dual economy: a sectoral model of earnings determination. *American Sociological Review* 43:704–720.
1980   Social stratification in industrial society: further evidence for a structural alternative, a reply to Hauser. *American Sociological Review* 45:712–719.
Becker, Gary S.
1957   "The Economics of Discrimination." Chicago: University of Chicago Press.
1964   "Human Capital." New York: National Bureau of Economic Research.
Bell, Daniel
1973   "The Coming of Post-Industrial Society." New York: Basic Books.
Berg, Ivar
1970   "Education and Jobs: The Great Training Robbery." New York: Praeger.
Bibb, Robert, and Form, William
1977   The effects of industrial, occupational and sex stratification on wages in blue-collar markets. *Social Forces* 55:974–996.
Blalock, Hubert M., Jr.
1972   "Social Statistics, 2nd Edition." New York: McGraw Hill.
Blau, Peter M., and Duncan, Otis Dudley
1967   "The American Occupational Structure." New York: Wiley.
Blau, Peter M., and Meyer, Marshall W.
1971   "Bureaucracy in Modern Society," 2nd ed. New York: Random House.
Blau, Peter M., and Schoenherr, Richard
1971   "The Structure of Organizations." New York: Basic Books.
Blauner, Robert
1964   "Alienation and Freedom." Chicago: University of Chicago Press.
Bloom, G. F., Fletcher, F. M., and Perry, C. R.
1972   "Negro Employment in Retail Trade." Philadelphia, Pennsylvania: University of Pennsylvania Press.
Bluestone, Barry
1970   The tripartite economy: labor markets and the working poor. *Poverty and Human Resources* 5:15–35.
1971   The characteristics of marginal industries. *In* "Problems in Political Economy: An Urban Perspective"(David M.Gordon,ed.),pp.102–107.Lexington,Massachusetts:Heath.
Bluestone, Barry, and Harrison, Bennett
1980   "Corporate Flight: The Causes and Consequences of Economic Dislocation." Washington, D.C.: Institute for Policy Studies.
1982   "The Deindustrialization of America." New York: Basic Books.
Bluestone, Barry, Murphy, William M., and Stevenson, Mary
1973   "Low Wages and the Working Poor." Ann Arbor: Institute of Labor and Industrial Relations.
Bonacich, Edna
1976   Advanced capitalism and black/white race relations in the United States: a split labor market interpretation. *American Sociological Review* 41:34–51.
Boudon, Raymond
1974   "Education, Opportunity, and Social Inequality." New York: Wiley.
Boyer, Richard O., and Morais, Herbert M.
1955   "Labor's Untold Story." New York: United Electrical, Radio, and Machine Workers of America.

Braverman, Harry
  1974 "Labor and Monopoly Capital." New York: Monthly Review Press.
Brecher, Jeremy
  1972 "Strike!" San Francisco: Straight Arrow Books.
Bridges, William P.
  1980 Industrial marginality and female employment: a new appraisal. *American Sociological Review* 45:58–75.
Bright, James R.
  1958 "Automation and Management." Boston: Harvard Business School.
Brooks, G. W.
  1960 "The Sources of Vitality in the American Labor Movement." Ithaca, New York: Cornell University Press.
Cain, Glen G.
  1976 The challenge of segmented labor market theories to orthodox theory: a survey. *Journal of Economic Literature* 14:1215–1257.
Caplow, Theodore
  1954 "The Sociology of Work." New York: McGraw-Hill.
Chandler, Alfred DuPont, Jr.
  1962 "Strategy and Structure: Chapters in the History of the Industrial Enterprise." Cambridge, Massachusetts: MIT Press.
  1969 The structure of American industry in the twentieth century: a historical overview. *Business History Review* 63:255–298.
  1977 "The Visible Hand: The Managerial Revolution in American Business." Cambridge, Massachusetts: Belknap Press.
Child, John
  1973 Predicting and understanding organizational structure. *Administrative Science Quarterly* 18:168–185.
Cohen, Jacob
  1968 Multiple regression as a general data-analytic system. *Psychological Bulletin* 70:426–443.
Coleman, Richard P., and Rainwater, Lee
  1978 "Social Standing in America." New York: Basic Books.
Comanor, W. S.
  1973 Racial discrimination in American industry. *Economica* 40:363–378.
Commons, John R.
  1951 "The History of Labor in the United States." New York: Macmillan.
Dalton, James A., and Ford, E. J., Jr.
  1977 Concentration and labor earnings in manufacturing and utilities. *Industrial and Labor Relations Review* 31:45–60.
Daymont, Thomas N., and Kaufman, Robert L.
  1979 Measuring industrial variation in racial discrimination using log linear models. *Social Science Research* 8:41–62.
Doeringer, Peter, and Piore, Michael J.
  1971 "Internal Labor Markets and Manpower Analysis." Lexington, Massachusetts: Heath Lexington.
Duncan, Otis Dudley
  1961 A socioeconomic index for all occupations. *In* "Occupations and Social Status" (A. J. Reiss, Jr., ed.), pp. 109–138. New York: Free Press.
Dunlop, John
  1944 "Wage Determination Under Trade Unions." New York: Macmillan.

Dunlop, John, and Chamberlain, Neil W. (eds.)
   1967   "Frontiers of Collective Bargaining." New York: Harper and Row.
Edwards, Richard C.
   1979   "Contested Terrain." New York: Basic Books.
Featherman, David L., and Hauser, Robert M.
   1978   "Opportunity and Change." New York: Academic Press.
Feinberg, Robert M.
   1979   Market structure and employment instability. *Review of Economics and Statistics*
          61:497–505.
Freedman, Marcia K.
   1976   "Labor Markets: Segments and Shelters." Montclair, New Jersey: Allanheld, Osmun.
Freeman, John Henry
   1973   Environments, technology, and the administrative intensity of manufacturing organiza-
          tions. *American Sociological Review* 38:750–763.
Friedman, Samuel R., and Friedman, Judith J.
   1979   Class conflict in a dual economy: a critique of some current theories. Paper presented at
          the Society for the Study of Social Problems Annual Meeting, August 26–30, Boston.
Galbraith, John Kenneth
   1967   "The New Industrial State." Boston: Houghton Mifflin.
   1973   "Economics and the Public Purpose." Boston: Houghton Mifflin.
Garbarino, Joseph W.
   1950   A theory of inter-industry wage variation. *Quarterly Journal of Economics* 64:282–305.
Giddens, Anthony
   1973   "The Class Structure of Advanced Societies." New York: Harper and Row.
Gordon, David M. (ed.)
   1971   "Problems in Political Economy: An Urban Perspective." Lexington, Massachusetts:
          Heath.
   1972   "Theories of Poverty and Underemployment." Lexington, Massachusetts: Heath.
Granovetter, Mark
   1979   Toward a sociological theory of income differences. Paper presented at the American
          Sociological Association Annual Meetings, August 30–September 3, Boston.
Hage, Jerry, and Aiken, Michael
   1970   "Social Change in Complex Organizations." New York: Random House.
Hall, Richard T.
   1975   "Occupations and the Social Structure," 2nd ed. New York: McGraw-Hill.
Hauser, Robert M.
   1980   On 'Stratification in a dual economy' (A comment on Beck, Horan, and Tolbert, 1978).
          American Sociological Review 45:702–712.
Hauser, Robert, M., and Hodson, Randy
   1977   Labor market sectors and the occupational mobility of U.S. men. Paper presented at the
          American Sociological Association Annual Meetings, September 5–9, Chicago.
Hendricks, Wallace
   1975   Labor market structure and union wage levels. *Economic Inquiry* 13:401–416.
Hickson, D. J., Pugh, D. S., and Pheysey, D.
   1969   Operations technology and organization structure: an empirical reappraisal. *Administra-
          tive Science Quarterly* 14:378–397.
Hodson, Randy
   1978   Labor in the monopoly, competitive, and state sectors of production. *Politics and Society*
          8:429–480.
   1980   The social impact of industrial structure on working conditions. Ph.D. Dissertation,
          Department of Sociology, University of Wisconsin, Madison.

1981 Industrial structure as a worker resource under corporate capitalism. Paper presented at the Society for the Study of Social Problems Annual Meetings, August 26–30, Toronto.

Hodson, Randy, and England, Paula

1982 How industrial placement affects the sex gap in wages. Paper presented at the American Sociological Association Annual Meetings, September 6–10, San Francisco.

Hodson, Randy, and Kaufman, Robert L.

1981 Circularity in the dual economy (A comment on Tolbert, Horan, and Beck, 1980). *American Journal of Sociology* 86:881–887.

1982 Economic dualism: a critical review. *American Sociological Review* 47:727–739.

Hogan, Dennis

1975 The situs and status dimensions of social mobility in the labor force: an exploration of industry and occupation. University of Wisconsin Center for Demography and Ecology, Working Paper No. 75–13, Madison.

Holliday, Fred

1978 Iran: trade unions and the working class opposition. *Middle East Research and Information Project Reports* 8:7–13.

Horan, Patrick M., Tolbert, Charles M., II., and Beck, E. M.

1981 The circle has no close (A reply to Hodson and Kaufman). *American Journal of Sociology* 86:887–894.

Jencks, Christopher

1979 "Who Gets Ahead?" New York: Basic Books.

Johnson, G. E.

1975 Economic analysis of trade unionism. *American Economics Review* 65:23–28.

Kalleberg, Arne L., and Sorenson, Aage

1979 The sociology of labor markets. *Annual Review of Sociology* 5:351–379.

Kalleberg, Arne L., Wallace, Michael, and Althauser, Robert P.

1981 Economic segmentation, worker power, and income inequality. *American Journal of Sociology* 87:651–683.

Kaufman, Robert L.

1981 Racial discrimination and labor market segmentation. Ph.D. Dissertation, Department of Sociology, University of Wisconsin, Madison.

Kaufman, Robert L. and Daymont, Thomas N.

1981 Racial discrimination and the social organization of industries. *Social Science Research* 10:225–255.

Kaufman, Robert L., Hodson, Randy, and Fligstein, Neil D.

1981 Defrocking dualism: a new approach to defining industrial sectors. *Social Science Research* 10:1–31.

Kerr, Clark

1954 The bulkanization of labor markets. *In* "Labor Mobility and Economic Opportunity" (Paul Webbink, ed.), pp. 92–110. New York: Wiley.

Kimberly, John R.

1976 Organizational size and the structuralist perspective: a review, critique, and proposal. *Administrative Science Quarterly* 21:571–597.

Leibowitz, Arleen

1977 Family background and economic success: a review of the evidence. *In* "Determinants of Socioeconomic Success Within and Between Families" (Paul Taubman, ed.), pp. 9–33. New York: North-Holland.

Leigh, Duane E.

1976 The occupational mobility of young men, 1965–1970. *Industrial and Labor Relations Review* 30:68–72.

Lenin, V. I.
    1939 "Imperalism: The Highest Stage of Capitalism." New York: International Publishers.
Levinson, Harold
    1967 Unionism, concentration, and wage changes: toward a unified theory. *Industrial and Labor Relations Review* 20:198–205.
Litwack, Leon
    1962 "The American Labor Movement." Englewood Cliffs, New Jersey: Prentice-Hall.
Maddala, G. S.
    1977 "Econometrics." New York: McGraw-Hill.
Mandel, Ernest
    1968 "Marxist Economic Theory" (Brian Pearce, tran.). New York: Monthly Review Press.
    1975 "Late Capitalism" (Joris De Bres, tran.). London: New Left Books.
Marsh, Robert M., and Mannari, Hiroshi
    1981 Technology and size as determinants of the organizational structure of Japanese factories. *Administrative Science Quarterly* 26:33–57.
Marshall, R.
    1974 The economics of racial discrimination: a survey. *Journal of Economic Literature* 12:849–871.
Marx, Karl
    1887 "Capital" Vol. 1. New York: International Publishers.
Masters, Stanley M.
    1969 An inter-industry analysis of wages and plant size. *Review of Economics and Statistics* 51:34–45.
Mileti, Dennis S., Gillespie, David F., and Haas, J. Eugene
    1977 Size and structure in complex organizations. *Social Forces* 56:208–217.
Mohr, Lawrence B.
    1971 Organizational technology and organizational structure. *Administrative Science Quarterly* 16:444–459.
Montagna, Paul D.
    1977 "Occupations and Society." New York: Wiley.
Mueller, Willard F.
    1970 "A Primer on Monopoly and Competition." New York: Random House.
Nore, Peter, and Turner, Terisa (eds.)
    1980 "Oil and Class Struggle." Westport, Connecticut: Zed Press.
O'Connor, James
    1973 "The Fiscal Crisis of the State." New York: St. Martin's Press.
Oppenheimer, Valerie
    1970 "The Female Labor Force in the United States: Demographic and Economic Factors Governing its Growth and Changing Composition." Population Monograph Series, No. 5. Berkeley: University of California Press.
Oster, Gerry
    1979 A factor analytic test of the theory of the dual economy. *Review of Economics and Statistics*. 61:33–39.
Osterman, Paul
    1975 An empirical study of labor market segmentation. *Industrial and Labor Relations Review* 28:508–523.
Perlman, Selig
    1932 "A History of Trade Unionism in the United States." New York: Macmillan.
Piore, Michael J.
    1969 On-the-job training the dual labor market. *In* "Public-Private Manpower Policies"

(Arnold R. Weber, Frank H. Cassell, and Woodrow L. Ginsburg, eds.), pp. 101–132. Madison: University of Wisconsin Industrial Relations Research Association.

Porter, Lyman, W., and Lawler, Edward E., III
  1965 Properties of organizational structure in relation to job attitudes and job behavior. *Psychological Bulletin* 64:23–51.

Poulantzas, Nicos
  1975 "Classes in Contemporary Capitalism." London: New Left Review.

Pugh, D. S., Hickson, D. J., Hinings, C. R., and Turner C.
  1968 Dimensions of organizational structure. *Administrative Science Quarterly* 13:65–105.

Rainwater, Lee
  1974 "What Money Buys." New York: Basic Books.

Rees, Albert
  1962 "The Economics of Trade Unions." Chicago: University of Chicago Press.

Rees, Albert, and Shultz, George
  1970 "Workers and Wages in an Urban Labor Market." Chicago: University of Chicago Press.

Reich, Michael
  1971 The economics of racism. In "Problems in Political Economy: An Urban Perspective" (David M. Gordon, ed.), pp. 107–113. Lexington, Massachusetts. Heath.

Reich, Michael, Gordon, David M., and Edwards, Richard C.
  1973 A theory of labor market segmentation. *American Economic Review* 63:359–365.

Ritzer, George
  1977 "Working: Conflict and Change," 2nd ed. Englewood Cliffs, New Jersey: Prentice–Hall.

Rosenberg, Samuel
  1975 The Dual Labor Market: Its Existence and Consequences. Ph.D. Dissertation, Department of Economics, University of California, Berkeley.
  1980 Male occupational standing and the dual labor market. *Industrial Relations* 19:34–49.

Ross, Arthur M.
  1957 The external wage structure. In "New Concepts in Wage Determination" (G. Taylor and F. Pierson, eds.), pp. 173–205. New York: McGraw-Hill.

Ross, Arthur M., and Goldner, William
  1950 Forces affecting the inter-industry wage structure. *Quarterly Journal of Economics* 64:254–81.

Scherer, F. M.
  1970 "Industrial Market Structure and Economic Performance." Chicago: McNally.

Schervish, Paul G.
  1981 The structure of employment and unemployment. In "Sociological Perspectives on Labor Markets (Ivar Berg, ed.), pp. 153–86. New York: Academic Press.
  1983 "Vulnerability and Power in Market Relations: The Structural Determinants of Unemployment." New York: Academic Press.

Segal, Martin
  1964 The relation between union wage impact and market structure. *Quarterly Journal of Economics* 78:96–114.

Sewell, William H., and Hauser, Robert M.
  1975 "Education, Occupation, and Earnings." New York: Academic Press.

Shepherd, William G.
  1970 "Market Power and Economic Welfare." New York: Random House.
  1979 "The Economics of Industrial Organization." Englewood Cliffs, New Jersey: Prentice–Hall.

Spilerman, Seymour
   1977   Careers, labor market structure, and socioeconomic achievement. *American Journal of Sociology* 83:551–593.
Spilerman, Seymour, and Miller, Richard E.
   1976   Community and industry determinants of the occupational status of black males. University of Wisconsin Institute for Research on Poverty, Discussion Paper No. 330–76. Madison.
Stolzenberg, Ross M.
   1978   Bringing the boss back in: employer size, employee schooling, and socioeconomic achievement. *American Sociological Review* 43:813–828.
Stone, Katherine
   1974   The origins of job structures in the steel industry. *The Review of Radical Political Economy* 6:113–173.
Sweezy, Paul M.
   1942   "The Theory of Capitalist Development." New York: Monthly Review Press.
Sweezy, Paul, M., and Magdoff, Harry
   1979   Iran: new crisis of American hegemony. *Monthly Review* 30:1–24.
Szymanski, Albert
   1976   Racial discrimination and white gain. *American Sociological Review* 41:403–414.
Thieblot, A. J., and Fletcher, L. P.
   1970   "Negro Employment in Finance: A Study of Racial Policies in Banking and Insurance." Philadelphia: University of Pennsylvania Press.
Thurow, Lester C.
   1975   "Generating Inequality." New York: Basic Books.
Tolbert, Charles M., II, Horan, Patrick, and Beck, E. M.
   1980   The structure of economic segmentation: a dual economy approach. *American Journal of Sociology* 85:1095–1116.
Treiman, Donald J.
   1977   "Occupational Prestige in Comparative Perspective." New York: Academic Press.
Vietorisz, Thomas, and Harrison, Bennet
   1970   "The Economic Development of Harlem." New York: Praeger.
Wachtel, Howard M.
   1970   The impact of labor market conditions on hard-core unemployment. *Poverty and Human Resources* 5:5–13.
Wachter, Michael L.
   1974   Primary and secondary labor markets: a critique of the dual approach. Brookings Papers on Economic Activity No. 3:637–680.
Wallace, Michael, and Kalleberg, Arne L.
   1981   Economic organization of firms and labor force consequences: toward a specification of dual economy theory. *In* "Sociological Perspectives on Labor Markets" (Ivar Berg, ed.), pp. 77–117. New York: Academic Press.
Ward, J. H.
   1963   Hierarchical grouping to optimize an objective function. *Journal of the American Statistical Association* 58:236–244.
Weiss, Leonard W.
   1966   Concentration and labor earnings. *American Economic Review* 56:96–117.
   1971   "Case Studies in American Industry." New York: Wiley.
   1974   The concentration-profits relationship and antitrust. *In* "Industrial Concentration: The New Learning" (Harvey J. Goldschmid, H. Michael Mann, and John F. Weston, eds.), pp. 184–245. Boston: Little Brown.

Wishart, D.
   1968   "A Fortran II Program for Numeric Classification." Fife, Scotland: St. Andrew's
          University.
Woodward, Joan
   1964   "Industrial Organizations: Theory and Practice." London: Oxford University Press.
"World Alamanac"
   1975   New York: Newspaper Enterprise Association.
Wright, Erik Olin
   1979   "Class Structure and Income Determination." New York: Academic Press.
Wright, Erik Olin, and Perrone, Luca
   1977   Marxist class categories and income inequality. *American Sociological Review*
          42:35–55.
Zucker, Lynne G., and Rosenstein, Carolyn
   1981   Taxonomies of institutional structure: dual economy reconsidered. *American Sociologi-
          cal Review* 46:869–884.

INDUSTRY DATA
U.S. Bureau of Economics Analysis
   1976   "The National Income and Product Accounts of the United States, 1929–74. Statistical
          Tables." Washington, D.C.: U.S. Government Printing Office.
U.S. Bureau of Labor Statistics
   1975   "Handbook of Labor Statistics." Washington, D.C.: U.S. Government Printing Office.
U.S. Bureau of the Census
   1962   "Census of Population, 1960. Subject Reports: Occupation by Industry." Washington,
          D.C.: U.S. Government Printing Office.
   1972a "Census of Population, 1970. Subject Reports: Occupation by Industry." Washington,
          D.C.: U.S. Government Printing Office.
   1972b "Enterprise Statistics, 1967. General Report on Industrial Organization" Vol. 1. Wash-
          ington, D.C.: U.S. Government Printing Office.
   1972c "Public Use Samples of Basic Records From the 1970 Census: Descriptive and Techni-
          cal Documentation." Washington, D.C.: U.S. Government Printing Office.
   1976   "Census of Manufacturers, 1972. Subject and Special Statistics" (Vol. 1). Washington,
          D.C.: U.S. Government Printing Office.
   1977   "Enterprise Statistics, 1972. General Report on Industrial Organization" Vol. 1. Wash-
          ington, D.C.: U.S. Government Printing Office.
U.S. Department of Commerce, Interindustry Economics Division
   1974   "Input-Output Study, 1967: Inter-industry Transactions and Trade and Transportation
          Costs" (machine readable data file). Washington, D.C.: U.S. Department of Commerce
          (producer). Madison, Wisconsin: Data and Program Library Service (distributor).
U.S. Executive Office of the President, Office of Management and Budget, Statistical Policy
   Division
   1972   "Standard Industrial Classification Manual." Washington, D.C.: U.S. Government
          Printing Office.
U.S. Internal Revenue Service
   1977   "Statistics of Income, 1972. Corporation Income Tax Returns" Vol. 1. Washington,
          D.C.: U.S. Government Printing Office.

ENTERPRISE DATA
"American Bank Directory"
   1977   Norcross, Georgia: McFadden Business Publications.

American Hospital Association
 1975 "Guide to the Health Care Field." Chicago: American Hospital Association.
"Directory of Corporate Affiliates: 'Who Owns Whom'"
 1977 Skokie, Illinois: National Register Publishing Company.
"Directory of Inter-Corporate Ownership"
 1972 New York: Simon and Schuster.
Dun and Bradstreet
 1975a "Middle Market Directory." New York: Dun and Bradstreet.
 1975b "Million Dollar Directory." New York: Dun and Bradstreet.
 1975c "Reference Book (May)." New York: Dun and Bradstreet.
"Financial Briefs of Wisconsin Corporations"
 1978 Milwaukee, Wisconsin: Robert W. Baird and Company.
Fortune
 1975a The Fortune 500 largest industrial corporations. *Fortune* **91**:210–235.
 1975b The Fortune second 500 largest industrial corporations. *Fortune* **91**:122–148.
 1975c The Fortune fifty largest corporations in utilities, life insurance, diversified financial, retailing, transportation, and commercial banking. *Fortune* **92**:116–129.
Moody's Investors Service
 1975a "Bank and Finance Manual." New York: Moody's Investors Service.
 1975b "Industrial Manual." New York: Moody's Investors Service.
 1975c "Over the Counter Industrial Manual." New York: Moody's Investors Service.
 1975d "Public Utility Manual." New York: Moody's Investors Service.
 1975e "Transportation Manual." New York: Moody's Investors Service.
Standard and Poor
 1978 "Register of Corporations, Directors, and Executives" Vol. 1. New York: Standard and Poor.
"Wisconsin Business Directory"
 1975 Menasha, Wisconsin: George Banta Company.
Wisconsin Department of Industry, Labor, and Human Relations
 1975 "Wisconsin Companies and Employment" (machine-readable data file). Madison, Wisconsin: Department of Industry, Labor, and Human Relations.
Wisconsin Manufacturers' Association
 1975 "Classified Directory of Wisconsin Manufacturers." Racine, Wisconsin: Western Publishing Company.

Index

A

Administrative ratio, 106
Advertising expenditures, 116
Agriculture sector, 81
Aircraft manufacturing, 83
American Federation of Labor, 45
Autonomous workers
  earnings effects across sectors, 178
  economic returns to education, 175

B

Blacks, *see also* Race
  earnings expectations, 59
  importance of organizational size for
    earnings, 184
Brand names, 87
Broken home, 95
Brokerage sector, 81
Bureaucratic
  labor control, 177
  standards, 169

C

Capitalist class
  action to fragment working class
    consciousness, 32
  power, 14
Capital intensity, 14, 16
  as key variable across models, 139
  as resource, 56
    for workers, 48–49, 60, 167
  correlation of company and industry
    measures, 142
  decreasing rate of return, 124
  earnings effect, 135
    interpretation, 123, 136–137
  importance of industrywide workplace
    environment, 144
  nonlinear effects, 122
Categorical measures of industrial structure, 64
Census Industry Classification, 65
Centralization, 12, 42, *see also* Concentration
Class, 2, 151, 161
  as earnings determinant, 58
  as mediator of industrial structure effects, 51

contradictory class locations, 2, 13
definition, 94
earnings effects of economic structure, 178
earnings inequality, 169, 184
operationalization, 212–214
relation to occupational categories, 101, 111
within economic sectors, 105
Class consciousness
discrimination, 28
Cluster analysis, 70–72
anomalies, 82–83
fusion of clusters, 71
six-sector solution, 84
16-sector solution, 72
College aspirations, 96
Companies
as employers of Wisconsin Survey respondents, 63
coding of company data, 88
coding of company names, 86–87
ultimate ownership, 87
Company data, 87–92
missing data, 90–92
Company sectors
correspondence to labor characteristics, 168
definition, 92
earnings effects, 130
direct, 160
Company size, 16, see also Size
as resource, 55
for capitalists, 49
for workers, 49
earnings effect, 136
Company size index, 148
earnings effect, 136
Company strategies of growth, 44
dimensions, 44

Company variables, 89
direct earnings effects, 159
missing data, 140
model selection, 132–136
Concentration, 12, 21, 32, see also Centralization
as resource, 48, 56
earnings effect, 33, 119, 140
interpretation, 124–125
heightened corporate power, 125

Conglomerate domination, see also Corporate autonomy, Monopoly
earnings effect, 140
Conglomerate organization, 14, 49
Congress on Industrial Organization, 45
Continuous measures of industrial structure, 64
Control perspective, 145
Core sector, 79
earnings effect, 114
in six-sector cluster solution, 84–85
Core transport sector, 80
Core utilities and finance sector, 80
Core utilities sector, 85
Corporate autonomy, see also Conglomerate domination
as earnings predictor, 137
as resource, 57
correlation with log earnings, 118
earnings effect
interpretation, 125
CPS, see Current Population Survey
Cube root transformation of earnings, 146, 148
Current Population Survey, 7, 62, 93
restricted sample, 127
continuous-variable industry model, 129
industrial sector earnings, 128
Curvature
in industry variables, 122
increase in explained variance, 122

D

Demographic characteristics
earnings effects, 151
as mediated by industrial structure, 51
Deskilling, 34, 42
Discrimination, 28
Diversification, 42
examples, 43–45
Division of labor, 42
Dual economy, 4–5, 18–37, see also Dual labor markets
as critique of neoclassical model, 30, 37
critique, 29–36
circularity, 33
correspondence to dual labor markets, 34–35
descriptive nature, 29
empirical inconsistencies, 29

parallelism, 37
  of dimensions, 31
  of effects, 33
  unspecified model, 29
empirical support, 32
full-time employment, 35
labor discipline, 27
monopoly sector, 21
origins, 21
periphery sector, 20
Dual labor markets, 22–25, *see also* Dual
    economy
  class consciousness, 24
  employment stability, 23
  labor control
    bureaucratic, 25
    direct, 24
    technical, 25
  on-the-job training, 24
  origins, 24–25
  poverty, 26
  skill specificity, 24

E

Earnings, 93, *see also* Log transformation
  determination, 4
Economic structure
  as resource for workers, 178
Economics
  institutional, 13–14
  labor economics, 14–16
  neoclassical, 11–12
Education, 93
  as earnings determinant, 58
  direct earnings effect, 158
  economic returns, 17, 19, 27, 35
    across sectors, 170–175, 184
    alternative expectations, 35
    critique of human capital model, 169
    direct effects, 161
    in large firms, 61
      managers, 59
    mediation of effects by industrial
        structure, 157
  spline function, 186
Education and nonprofit sector, 81
Experience, 94
  as earnings determinant, 58

contribution to explained earnings variance,
    158
  curvilinear component, 94
  earnings effect, 157
    mediation of effect by industrial structure,
        157
Exploitation by monopoly sector, 21

F

Factor analysis, 69
Family background, 58, 61
Farm background, 94
Father's occupational status, 95
Foreign involvement, *see also* Multinational
    corporations
  as earnings predictor, 137
  as resource, 57
  earnings effect
    across occupations, 187
    interpretation, 124
  nonlinear effects, 122
  summary of effects, 140
Fortune companies, 91
  earnings effect, 131
Full-time employment, 51
  as effect of industrial structure, 52

G

Gender, 28, 93, *see also* Women
  earnings effect, 157
    direct, 158, 160–161
    mediation of effect by industrial structure,
        157
  economic returns to education
    across sectors, 186
  social division of labor, 36
Government
  market segmentation, 22
  regulation, 118, 146
    as resource, 56
  workers, 88
Growth, 121
  as resource, 56

H

High school experience, 162
High school rank, 95, 162

Hours, 93
Human capital, 2
  economic returns to education, 187

I

Imperialism, 12
Individual characteristics, 93–96
  as mediated by industrial structure, 58
  as selected by industrial structure, 52
Industrial structure, 3
  contribution to explained earnings variance, 159
  differentiation, 45
  earnings effect
    direct, 54, 152–153, 161
  history, 41–46
  stages of development, 42–43
Industry data, 7, 68
  missing values, 68
  comparison to company sectors, 139
    as earnings determinants, 143
  cross-classified with company sectors, 141
  definition, 68
  earnings effects, 114
    direct, 153
  factor scores, 70
Intelligence, 95, 162
Interaction
  of economic structure with individual characteristics, 169
Interindustry distances, 70

K

Knights of Labor, 45

L

Labor control
  class inequality, 177
Labor demand, 151
Labor markets, 14–15
  expected characteristics, 57–58
  external, 23–24
  homogeneity, 3
  internal, 23–24
  job ladders, 23
  ports of entry, 23, 26
  segments and shelters, 17
  social mobility, 26

Labor supply, 161
Local monopoly sector, 81
Local sector
  earnings effect, 131
Log transformation
  of company variables, 209
  of earnings, 101, 148, 171
  of industry variables, 200

M

McCarthy Era, 45
  union retrenchment, 46
Managers
  earnings effects across sectors, 178
Manual labor, 2, 170
  earnings effect
    across sectors, 178
    of foreign involvement, 178, 182
  earnings expectation, 59
  importance of size, 184
Marginal jobs, 111
Market factors of production, 138, 141, 189
  importance of industrywide workplace environment, 144
Marxism, 12–13
Mergers, 42
Middle class, 13
  administrative ratio, 111
  within economic sectors, 105
Minimum wage, 103
Minority workers, 170
  earnings effects of foreign involvement, 182
Missing and low earners, 98
Model selection method, 8
Monopoly
  capitalism, 12
  conglomerate organization, 12
  of labor, 11
  of product market, 12
  product differentiation, 12
  profits, 25
  stable planning horizons, 25
  wages, 15–16
Monopoly sector
  earnings effect, 131
Multicolinearity, 113
  in industry data, 119
Multinational corporations, 49, *see also* Foreign involvement
Multiplant sector
  earnings effect, 132

N

Nonmanual labor, 2

O

Occupational aspirations, 95, 162
Occupations, 94, 151
  earnings effects of economic structure, 178
Oligopoly sector, 77
  in six-sector cluster solution, 84
Ordnance sector, 81
  earnings effect, 114
Organic composition of capital, 12
Organizational
  analysis, 41
  characteristics, 99
  environments, 41
  factors of production, 137, 141, 189
  history, 41–43
  structure, 3
  theory, 18
Orthogonal variable space, 69

P

Parental income, 95, 162
Periphery sector, 79
  earnings effect, 114
  in six-sector cluster solution, 85
Periphery transport sector, 80
Periphery utilities sector, 80, 85
Place of origin, 94
Plant size, 94, *see also* Company size, Size
  as worker resource, 136, 138
  earnings effect, 136
  economies of scale, 13
Plants outside local area, 91
Poverty, 102–104
  measures, 103
  vicious circle, 28
  within company sectors, 104
  within industrial sectors, 104
Prestige, 2
Primary jobs, 171
Product market, 14–15
Productivity, 13
  as resource, 55–56
  earnings effect, 125–126
  institutional economic theory, 126
  neoclassical economic theory, 125
Professional services, 83

Profit
  as resource, 56
  as variable rejected from earnings model, 139
  earnings effect, 119, 125, 135
  social control, 42
  technology, 41–42

Q

Quality-of-data measures, 91, 133
  as statistical controls, 134

R

Race, 28, 93, *see also* Blacks
  earnings effects, 156
    direct, 158
    mediation of effects by industrial structure, 156–157
    of market concentration, 182, 187
    of size, 182
  employment discrimination, 107
    across economic sectors, 108
    across occupational hierarchy, 108
  social division of labor, 36
Real estate sector, 81
Regression
  selection of variables, 113
    company data, 132
    industry data, 119–122
    test for difference between coefficients, 119
Research design, 63, 141
Resources, *see also* specific factors; Workers, power
  internal factors, 47, 51, 55–56
  market factors, 47, 51
  technical factors, 47, 51
  theoretical perspective, 5–6, 145
Rubber products manufacturing, 83

S

Sample selection, 96–98
Scale construction
  company size index, 133–134
  industry variables, 116–117
  industry–level size index, 121
Secondary jobs, 171
Self-employment, 88
Ship and boat manufacturing, 83
SIC, *see* Standard Industry Classification

Size, *see also* Company size, Plant size
  as key variable across models, 139
  as resource
    for workers, 126, 196
  correlation of company and industry
    measures, 142
  decreasing rate of return, 124
  earnings effect
    interpretation, 123
  importance of company and plant levels of
    analysis, 144
  nonlinear effects, 122
  union viability, 153
Size index
  quality-of-data measure, 147
Small-shop sector, 79
Social background, 162
  contribution to explained earnings variance,
    164
  relation to economic structure, 164
Social division of labor, 28
Social mobility, 35
Sociology
  of labor markets, 16–18
Spillover effect, 158
Standard Industry Classification, 65
Status, 2
Subsidiaries, 89, 91
Subsidiary status, 132
  earnings effect, 134
Supervisors
  earnings effect across sectors, 178

T

Technical factors of production, 137, 141, 189
Tenure, 94
  earnings effect, 161
    within sectors, 170
Textile industries, 83
Tobacco sector, 81
  earnings effect, 115
Trades sector, 85
  earnings effect, 114

U

Unions, 45–46, 151, 161
  as mediator of industrial structure effects, 51
  as resource, 56

  autonomy from organizational strategies of
    capital, 46
  earnings effect, 116
  in large companies, 105
  membership, 94, 158
  organizing economies of scale, 16
  power, 15, 158
  trade union movement, 40
Unit of analysis, 6–7, 52–54, 64
  company-level, 7, 90
  comparison of industry and company levels,
    139–144
  effects on findings, 141

V

Vocational school aspirations, 95
Vulnerability of labor, 50, 189

W

Weeks, 93
Wholesale sector, 79
  earnings effect, 114
Wisconsin Survey, 7, 62–63, 93
  continuous-variable industry model, 129
  industrial sector earnings, 128
Women, *see also* Gender
  earnings effects
    of capital intensity, 182
    of corporate autonomy, 182
    of organizational size, 182
  earnings expectation, 59
  importance of organizational size for
    earnings, 184
  labor-intensive employment, 112, 182
  marginality, 112
Workers
  as active subjects, 6, 50
  power, 14, 189
    through industrial structure, 6
Working class
  consciousness, 27–28
  earnings effects across sectors, 178
  fragmentation, 19, 27–28, 32

STUDIES IN POPULATION

Under the Editorship of: H. H. WINSBOROUGH

Department of Sociology
University of Wisconsin
Madison, Wisconsin

Samuel H. Preston, Nathan Keyfitz, and Robert Schoen. Causes of Death: *Life Tables for National Populations.*

Otis Dudley Duncan, David L. Featherman, and Beverly Duncan. Socioeconomic Background and Achievement.

James A. Sweet. Women in the Labor Force.

Tertius Chandler and Gerald Fox. 3000 Years of Urban Growth.

William H. Sewell and Robert M. Hauser. Education, Occupation, and Earnings: *Achievement in the Early Career.*

Otis Dudley Duncan. Introduction to Structural Equation Models.

William H. Sewell, Robert M. Hauser, and David L. Featherman (Eds.). Schooling and Achievement in American Society.

Henry Shryock, Jacob S. Siegel, and Associates. The Methods and Materials of Demography. *Condensed Edition by Edward Stockwell.*

Samuel H. Preston. Mortality Patterns in National Populations: *With Special Reference to Recorded Causes of Death.*

Robert M. Hauser and David L. Featherman. The Process of Stratification: *Trends and Analyses.*

Ronald R. Rindfuss and James A. Sweet. Postwar Fertility Trends and Differentials in the United States.

David L. Featherman and Robert M. Hauser. Opportunity and Change.

Karl E. Taeuber, Larry L. Bumpass, and James A. Sweet (Eds.). Social Demography.

Thomas J. Espenshade and William J. Serow (Eds.). The Economic Consequences of Slowing Population Growth.

Frank D. Bean and W. Parker Frisbie (Eds.). The Demography of Racial and Ethnic Groups.

Joseph A. McFalls, Jr. Psychopathology and Subfecundity.

Franklin D. Wilson. Residential Consumption, Economic Opportunity, and Race.

Maris A. Vinovskis (Ed.). Studies in American Historical Demography.

Clifford C. Clogg. Measuring Underemployment: Demographic Indicators for the United States.

Doreen S. Goyer. International Population Census Bibliography: *Revision and Update,* 1945-1977.

David L. Brown and John M. Wardwell (Eds.). New Directions in Urban–Rural Migration: *The Population Turnaround in Rural America.*

A. J. Jaffe, Ruth M. Cullen, and Thomas D. Boswell. The Changing Demography of Spanish Americans.

Robert Alan Johnson. Religious Assortative Marriage in the United States.

Hilary J. Page and Ron Lesthaeghe. Child-Spacing in Tropical Africa.

Dennis P. Hogan. Transitions and Social Change: *The Early Lives of American Men.*

F. Thomas Juster and Kenneth C. Land (Eds.). Social Accounting Systems: *Essays on the State of the Art.*

M. Sivamurthy. Growth and Structure of Human Population in the Presence of Migration.

Robert M. Hauser, David Mechanic, Archibald O. Haller, and Taissa O. Hauser (Eds.). Social Structure and Behavior: *Essays in Honor of William Hamilton Sewell.*

Valerie Kincade Oppenheimer. Work and the Family: *A Study in Social Demography.*

Kenneth C. Land and Andrei Rogers (Eds.). Multidimensional Mathematical Demography.

John Bongaarts and Robert G. Potter. Fertility, Biology, and Behavior: *An Analysis of the Proximate Determinants.*

Randy Hodson. Workers' Earnings and Corporate Economic Structure.

In preparation

Mary B. Breckenridge. Age, Time, and Fertility: *Applications of Exploratory Data Analysis.*

Neil G. Bennett (Ed.). Sex Selection of Children.